Seven Years in France

François Mitterrand and the
Unintended Revolution, 1981–1988

Seven Years in France

François Mitterrand and the Unintended Revolution, 1981–1988

Julius W. Friend

Westview Press
BOULDER, SAN FRANCISCO, & LONDON

Copyright © 1989 by Westview Press, Inc.

Published in 1989 in the United States of America by Westview Press, Inc., 5500 Central Avenue, Boulder, Colorado 80301, and in the United Kingdom by Westview Press, Inc., 13 Brunswick Centre, London WC1N 1AF, England

Library of Congress Cataloging-in-Publication Data
Friend, Julius Weis.
  Seven Years in France.
  1. France — Politics and government — 1981– .
  2. Socialism — France — History — 20th century.
  3. Mitterrand, François, 1916– . I. Title.
DC423.F75 1989   320.944   88-5485
ISBN 0-8133-0610-8

Printed and bound in the United States of America

 The paper used in this publication meets the requirements of the American National Standard for Permanence of Paper for Printed Library Materials Z39.48-1984.

10   9   8   7   6   5   4   3   2

TO LOUISE

Contents

Contents   *ix*

Acronyms

CDS	Centre des Démocrates Sociaux
CERES	Centre d'Etudes, de Recherches, et d'Education Socialiste
CFDT	Confédération Française et Démocratique du Travail
CGT	Confédération Générale du Travail
CGT-FO	Confédération Générale du Travail-Force Ouvrière
CGTU	Confédération Générale du Travail Unifié
CIR	Convention des Institutions Républicaines
CNAL	Centre National d'Action Laïque
CNCL	Conseil National des Communications et des Libertés
CNPF	Conseil National du Patronat Français
DGSE	Direction Générale de Sécurité Extérieure
EEC	European Economic Community
EMS	European Monetary System
ENA	Ecole Nationale d'Administration
FEN	Fédération de l'Education Nationale
FGDS	Fédération de la Gauche Démocratique et Socialiste
FNLKS	Front National de Libération Kanak Socialiste
FNSEA	Fédération Nationale des Syndicats d'Exploitants Agricoles
FO	See CGT-FO
INSEE	Institut National de la Statistique et des Etudes Economiques
MRG	Mouvement des Radicaux de Gauche
MRP	Mouvement Républicain Populaire
OAU	Organization for African Unity
OECD	Organization for European Cooperation and Development
PCF	Parti Communiste Français
PR	Parti Républicain
PS	Parti Socialiste
PSU	Parti Socialiste Unifié
RCPR	Rassemblement Calédonien Pour la République
RPR	Rassemblement Pour la République
SFIO	Section Française de l'Internationale Ouvrière
SMIC	Salaire Minimum Interindustriel de Croissance

UDC   Union Démocratique du Centre
UDF   Union Pour la Démocratie Française
UDSR   Union Démocratique et Socialiste de la Résistance
URC   Union du Rassemblement et du Centre

Acknowledgments

To attempt what purports to be the history of a period which has only just ended is both ambitious and rash. The first part of the material I discuss has been written about extensively by political scientists and economists in America, France, and Great Britain, often in great detail. My ambition as a historian therefore cannot be to re-do better what so many have done well, but to bring a historian's approach to a recent and very important period of French history. The chronological technique has its defects, but it is a good way to examine why intelligent men often do foolish things, why politicians are not always entirely insincere when in the heat of a campaign or the intoxication of ideology they promise the impossible, and even why success can sometimes be born out of failure. Politics in action is such a confused battleground that political analysis runs the risk of over-clarification. Confusion was not lacking in French politics between 1981 and 1988, and I have thought it useful to describe the manner in which events happened before attempting to sort out their meaning.

Much that has been written about France under Mitterrand ends in 1986, when the Socialists lost their majority. I lay stress here on what the Socialists deliberately did, but even more on the chain of events set in motion by Mitterrand's victory in 1981. An account of reactions to Mitterrand on the Right, its march toward a brief victory, and its conduct in office belongs in my history.

My project is rash, because the meaning of very recent events is frequently hard to discern. I have nevertheless taken the risk of bringing my narrative (and analysis) up through the end of Mitterrand's first term, his re-election, and the equivocal success of the 1988 legislative elections. My excuse is that since historians very properly never tire of reassessing the meaning of events, whether they are as distant from us as the Peloponnesian wars or as close as those described in the last chapters of this book, one may as well start a process which is certain to continue.

This book is in part the result of nearly two hundred interviews conducted between 1983 and 1988. I regret that I have no space to thank by name all those who have helped me; some, but by no means all, are mentioned in the footnotes. I must, however, record my particular gratitude to those who have given me a great deal of their time and aided my research in many ways. To Jean-Claude Casanova, Lyne Cohen-Solal, Thierry Pfister, Jacques Huntzinger, and Pierre-André Wiltzer go my special thanks. I also wish to thank Serge Hurtig, secretary-general of the Institut d'Etudes Politiques, for giving me permission to use the invaluable facilities of the *Sciences Po* library, and Madame Françoise de Bellemare of the Centre d'Accueil des Professeurs Etrangers for help in Parisian housing.

Anton DePorte and Ronald Tiersky, who read drafts of several chapters of this book, are not responsible for my errors, but are responsible for much improvement. My thanks go to them also.

My family has been not merely forbearing but cooperative in this enterprise. Alex, Julia, and Michael Friend were copy-readers and editors. My greatest debt is to Louise Friend: gentle but severe critic, editor, all-around assistant. This book is dedicated to her.

Julius W. Friend
Chevy Chase, Maryland

Introduction

The story of François Mitterrand's first seven-year term narrated in this book tells of rapid reversals of fortune. After the unexpected defeat of conservative president Valéry Giscard d'Estaing by the Socialist Mitterrand there followed the election of a Socialist parliamentary majority, and a brief honeymoon spent in intoxicated self-assurance. Then came economic difficulties which forced a retreat from original Socialist principles. Unacknowledged at first, then admitted, retreat undermined popular confidence in the president and the government, engendering confusion about their real policy and doubts of their competence.

In 1986, the Right won back a parliamentary majority. A conservative prime minister ruled France while the president reigned — above the melee but still the guarantor of the constitution. Two years later, the president had won the game of cohabitation and renewed his popularity. He easily won a second term, dissolved the National Assembly as he had done in 1981 — and failed to win a stable majority.

Some writers have seen the years 1981-1986 as a botched effort by the Socialists to assert their ideas and principles, in which failure under Prime Minister Pierre Mauroy was followed by retrenchment, normalization under his successor Laurent Fabius, and defeat in 1986. The elections of 1988 oblige us to review the meaning of the earlier years. Their significance is clearest on the institutional level, where they marked an end to the exclusively conservative legitimism of the Fifth Republic. Mitterrand's victory in 1981, his party's defeat in 1986, and his re-election confirm the legitimation of the Socialists as a governing party. The cohabitation of a Socialist president and a conservative prime minister demonstrated the strength and flexibility of the constitution of the Fifth Republic, a document that also turns out to have been expressly designed to cope with the problems presented by the lack of any National Assembly majority in 1988.

Rapid shifts in electoral fortune must not obscure the many lasting changes of these seven years. Both deliberate and unintended, they have affected many aspects of French life. The Socialist government and parliamentary majority produced a flood of legislation. Laws on nationalization, decentralization, labor relations, legal reform, restructuring of both radio and television, educational reform, and much else tumbled from the National Assembly.

Did the years 1981-1986 then really see the defeat of socialism? Mitterrand's re-election seems to contradict that notion, but the signals are mixed. Socialist failures in 1981-1986 were those of the inflated hopes and ill-adapted policies that carried them into office. The rhetoric of *rupture* — a break with capitalism—vanished with the collapse of their neo-Keynesian policy of reflation and hopes of stemming unemployment. Nationalization of industry and of the banking system provided no medicines for a rapid cure of the ailing economy. Substantive Socialist legislative reforms failed to sway voters more concerned with unemployment and other economic worries. Amid a general impression of administrative muddle, Socialist ratings in polls and interim elections slipped badly. The change in policies and leaders in 1983-1984 permitted a slow recovery in late 1985 and early 1986, but not enough; the election of 1986 was lost because of the mistakes of 1981-1983.

That defeat was expected, even discounted in advance. Still, by winning thirty-one percent of the vote, the Socialist party confirmed to itself that the Left electorate had accepted the sober notion that the desirable is not always the possible.

Socialist retrenchment might have benefited a Communist party which had not hesitated to criticize the Socialist shift when it was still in office, and left the government to resume embittered opposition in 1984. Throughout the 1960s and 1970s the Communist vote had remained at a level slightly above twenty percent of the electorate. From 1981 through the presidential elections of 1988 it went down at every election, recovering in the legislative elections of 1988 to a point roughly half its level of the 1970s. As the Communist vote sank, the Socialists concluded that Left voters had rejected the PCF as a valid critic of Mitterrand's performance. A high Communist vote would have encouraged fissile tendencies within the Socialist party. A low one allowed the Socialists to establish near unanimity on a gradualist course that abandoned the leftist rhetoric of a few years earlier. Mitterrand cannot take the entire credit for the demolition of the Communist party; it has largely self-destructed. One may however fairly ask whether the damage would have been as great if Mitterrand had not in 1971 adopted the dangerous but effective tactic of alliance with the PCF.

The Socialist victory of 1981 thus unintentionally created a new kind of French Left. It discredited one kind of socialism — and gave birth to another. After French Socialists had discussed for years whether they could or should have a Bad Godesberg congress to confirm their reformist social democracy (like the West German SPD in 1959), they have lately discovered that their own Bad Godesberg took place in 1985, at the Congress of Toulouse. There the party which had entered office under the illusion that a generous spirit and vigorous policy could vanquish all obstacles, which had found mean-spirited and shortsighted capitalists responsible for almost all the faults of the French economy, saw all its factions agreeing that the equitable distribution desired by socialism can take place only where imaginative enterprise has created profitable production.

Since 1945 the French Right had taken almost as an axiom that the state should have the leading role in the economy. After 1981 it found itself in opposition to a more thoroughgoing Socialist version of this same doctrine. The Right's response was to look westward to Ronald Reagan's America for a new-found belief in free-enterprise capitalism. Jacques Chirac and his RPR and UDF ministers returned to power after March 1986 singing the praises of less government, more free enterprise — and full cooperation with the United States. Whether or not Charles de Gaulle would have approved of them (they claim he would have) the tune was new.

Gaullist foreign policy was both amended and adhered to by Mitterrand. Amended, in that France abandoned a now mythical "special relation" with the Soviet Union for a closer tie to the United States, at least in North Atlantic affairs. France followed Gaullist traditions in seeking both to improve her nuclear deterrent and move closer to West Germany. Outside Europe, Socialist policies on Central America first challenged the United States, then retreated. The tyranny of the real that the Socialists faced in domestic affairs was reflected also in the frustration of early attempts to change traditional Gaullist policies on Africa. Mitterrand's policies there, despite early Socialist declarations, became largely consonant with the Gaullist tradition. The years of cohabitation saw no real disagreement on foreign policy between president and prime minister.

The conservative interpretation of 1981-1986 argued that after twenty-three years of Gaullist and post-Gaullist rule the voters, having become bored or dissatisfied, had foolishly elected a Socialist-Communist coalition which proceeded to make all manner of doctrinaire and dangerous mistakes. Rapidly understanding their error, the voters then tilted right again, and in 1986 returned a conservative majority. However, the neo-Gaullists of Jacques Chirac's Rassemblement pour la République bitterly criticize the Giscard years, and their neo-liberal allies in what was once Giscard's own Union pour la Démocratie Française preach a free-enterprise doctrine not conspicuously applied in 1974-1981. The policies followed by the Chirac government in 1986-1988 claimed to assert this free-enterprise idea. Yet something evidently was missing — and voters ended by choosing to re-elect Mitterrand, and even to give the advantage (though not a clear majority) to the Socialists in new National Assembly elections.

Did they vote for Mitterrand, or against Chirac? The elections of 1981-1988 can all be read in a negative key, that is that the French did not want Giscard in 1981, or in their majority want socialism either. When they had more of the Socialists than they desired they turned again to the Right, only to accord a precarious tenure and withdraw it again.

Post-1981 politics have been de-ideologized on both sides. The two years of cohabitation by a Socialist president and a conservative prime minister have finished the job. The Right can no longer claim to offer the only possible non-collectivist and democratic government for France. Neither side can warn, or promise, that a change of governments means a change of worlds. In a supreme paradox, the *décrispation* (relaxation) in political manners and society that Valéry Giscard d'Estaing thought to introduce through moderate economic liberalism with a social democratic topping has instead emerged from the peculiar dialectic of a Socialist-Communist alliance, the terminal decline of French Communism, and the social-democratization of French Socialism. In a country where the them/us division has persisted since 1789, seven years have seen a fundamental change.

This account of the years 1981-1988 does not seek to compete with specialist essays describing in detail particular aspects of Socialist rule — decentralization, unions, education, etc. References to several excellent books containing such essays will be found in my footnotes and bibliography. My first concern is to set forth how, to inquire why things happened during these seven years in France, in the interaction of political ideas and needs with economic stresses. I aim first to interrelate the origins, strengths, handicaps, achievements, and failures of the Socialists, scrutinizing François Mitterrand, his two prime ministers, and their governments from 1981 to March 1986. Mitterrand's *septennat* (seven-year term) is then examined as a whole, including the fortunes of the parties of the Right and the period of cohabitation from March 1986 to early May 1988. Final chapters look at foreign policy in the *septennat*, and at the signposts which point toward the future.

I have also tried here to give a succinct and coherent account of the major Socialist projects and their results, positive and negative, and of the ways in which the returning conservatives accepted or undid them. My principal concern is to accomplish what scholarly compendia cannot easily do — give a single, balanced, and coherent description of an important moment in very recent history.

I have felt a need to set the scene for my story, to explain how François Mitterrand, who formally became a Socialist only on the day he took over the ailing Socialist party in 1971, was able to rebuild his party and simultaneously to form an alliance with the stronger Communist party that avoided all the obvious dangers of shipwreck. Mitterrand's success had a price, as I will explain. Competition with the Communists kept the Socialists further left than they might otherwise have been, and hindered their understanding of the changes in the French economy taking place in the 1970s.

The Socialists elected in 1981 had been talking of a break with capitalism; some have said they broke with socialism instead. It is never easy to fix boundaries and tell where socialism begins and where it ends, and I do not propose to enter into this theological argument. I address myself here to the processes of change which the Socialists began, or occasioned, or underwent. In their totality, socialist or not, they make up an unintended revolution.

1

Genesis

PROLOGUE: *"ON A GAGNÉ!"*

In the morning of May 10, 1981 Valéry Giscard d'Estaing cast his ballot in an election he hoped would give him seven more years as president of the French republic. A hard rain fell as Giscard emerged from the city hall of the Auvergne village of Chanonat, entered his car and regained his nearby chateau.

Giscard's antagonist François Mitterrand voted in another small country town, Château-Chinon in the high Morvan country of western Burgundy. The Socialist party candidate for the presidency had been mayor of the town for twenty-two years and was deputy for the local department, the Nièvre. He had just ended his third presidential campaign, first against Charles de Gaulle in 1965, then against Giscard in 1974.

In this third race Mitterrand was optimistic. Two weeks earlier he had won 7,500,000 votes in the first round of the two-stage elections — 700,000 fewer than Giscard, but enough to place him well for the second round. There he could hope to draw heavily from candidates knocked out of the race in the first round.

Much the most important of these was Georges Marchais, secretary general of the powerful French Communist party (PCF), and Mitterrand's quarrelsome ally throughout most of the 1970s. Marchais had hoped to equal or surpass the twenty percent vote the PCF had received in recent elections. Instead, a quarter of the Communist vote had deserted to Mitterrand on the first round. Mitterrand expected to gain most of the Communist vote on the second round, but with the PCF thus weakened he hoped also to win uncertain voters worried about voting for a Socialist who owed too much to a Communist alliance.

Giscard still had reasons for hope on election morning. When his own experts had begun to warn him in December that polls both public and private indicated potential trouble, he was not at first alarmed. Scandals and con-

7

stantly mounting unemployment had undermined his popularity, but he was sure the French would never elect Mitterrand.

In 1977, when opposed by a seemingly solid Socialist-Communist Union of the Left, Giscard had expected to lose the 1978 parliamentary elections. When in September 1977 the Communists backed away from a victory they feared would leave them junior partners, the Left alliance collapsed. Polls continued to predict a Left victory, and the vote for all parties of a now disunited Left in the first round of the 1978 elections was 50.2 percent. In the second round a week later, French voters fell back in seeming revulsion from what they had almost done, and produced a solid majority for the Center-Right.

Thereafter the Socialists and Communists had continued to quarrel. Giscard knew that Georges Marchais' scarcely hidden aim in 1981 was to ensure Mitterrand's defeat in the second round. Marchais' Soviet friends, with whom the French Communists had recently patched up their Eurocommunist quarrel, had endorsed Giscard in *Pravda* in mid-March, praising him as "a consequent and prudent political personality."[1]

Washington and Bonn expected and welcomed Giscard's re-election. In November 1980, sixty percent of poll respondents expected to vote for him; even after the gap between the candidates narrowed few believed at first in Mitterrand's victory.[2] After the first round, Giscard may have been reassured to learn that the total left-wing vote in the first round was smaller than it had been in 1978.[3] Conservative winds were blowing in the world: witness the elections of Margaret Thatcher in 1979 and of Ronald Reagan in 1980. If the French Left had crested in 1978, why should it — how could it — win in 1981?

The candidates remained in the country to await the count; Giscard in his chateau, Mitterrand in the Hotel du Vieux Morvan, his local headquarters over the years. The polls closed at six except in the big cities, where voting continued until eight. Computer extrapolations based on results from sample districts rapidly indicated a swing toward Mitterrand. At 6:28 an excited journalist approached the Socialist candidate, who was phlegmatically expounding the reasons for the Morvan's bad weather to the group around him. "Monsieur Mitterrand, you have won; you have between fifty-two and fifty-three percent!" Ostentatiously calm, Mitterrand continued his meteorological conversation. "What will you do tomorrow morning?" demanded a journalist. "I will get up."

At eight, exactly as the voting ended, the evening television news announced the computer projections made by all polling organizations. They were unanimous. The excited crowd at the Vieux Morvan began to sing the *Marseillaise,* while Mitterrand slipped off to his room to draft the victory statement he had postponed till this moment. The journalists at the gates of

Valéry Giscard d'Estaing's chateau found them locked. Giscard too had heard the projections; he knew that his presidency had ended. At eight--fifteen, the television announced his concession and congratulations to the victor.

In Paris, the Socialists had optimistically organized a victory celebration in the vast and evocative Place de la Bastille. Quickly, the word spread. Thousands of excited Socialists and Communists, political militants and ordinary citizens streamed toward the Bastille to share in a common intoxication. Still half-incredulous of the long hoped-for, forever-deferred victory, they cried *"on a gagné, on a gagné"* — we won, we won!

Socialist (and opportunistic Communist) speakers harangued the crowd. Mitterrand was still on his way to Paris. As his automobile arrived at the tollgate entrance to the super-highway leading to Paris, it was met by a motorcycle escort of security police. Power, which had slipped from Valéry Giscard d'Estaing that day, was descending upon François Mitterrand.[4]

HISTORY AND MYTHOLOGY

In 1981 France had been governed by conservatives for twenty-three years — a whole political generation, as long as the uninterrupted Republican party ascendancy in the United States from Abraham Lincoln to Grover Cleveland. Divided and dispirited even before de Gaulle's return in 1958, the Socialists had had more than enough time to meditate on their complex party history. Some of it had passed into mythology, a series of latter-day *chansons de geste* telling, like most such legends, largely of glorious defeats.

Mitterrand's Parti Socialiste (PS) descended from French socialist parties founded as early as 1882. In 1905 they had merged into the Section Française de l'Internationale Ouvrière (French Section of the Workers' International), or SFIO. Forged into painful unity under two very different leaders, the bureaucratic Marxist Jules Guesde and the great humanist tribune Jean Jaurès, the SFIO split in 1920. A majority followed left-wing leaders who wished to affiliate French socialism with Lenin's new revolutionary workers' international, creating the new French Communist Party.

Under the leadership of the brilliant journalist Léon Blum, the defeated rump SFIO was speedily rebuilt. In the 1920s and 1930s it consistently won more votes than the PCF. Mutual hostility was magnified by PCF obedience to Stalin's anti-Socialist policy of 1928, which changed only when the Soviet dictator began to see a special menace in Nazi Germany. In 1935 the two parties formed a "Popular Front against war and fascism."

The Popular Front alliance (including the then-powerful Radical Socialists) won the 1936 elections. The SFIO emerged as the strongest coalition party, and Léon Blum became prime minister. Except for the World War I years, Socialists had never before participated in a government, much less led one. The Communists supported the government in parliament, but chose to remain outside.

Blum took office in a profoundly disunited France, sundered by class hatred, battered by depression, fearful for the future. The failures and the successes of Blum's government entered the mythology of the French Left. For some leftists, Blum was a symbol of lost revolutionary opportunity and betrayal to the forces of capitalism. For the Socialists of the 1970s the Popular Front was a symbol of important milestones — the forty-hour week and paid vacations for workers.

Blum's ministry lasted only thirteen months. His rapid loss of momentum, his defeat in a key Senate vote and resignation in June 1937 also became part of Socialist mythology. He had battered in vain against "the wall of money." Though Blum became vice-premier in the next government and again briefly headed a government in March-April 1938, the Chamber of Deputies that had ushered in the Popular Front slid rapidly to the right.

In July 1940, after the defeat of the French armies, this same chamber voted overwhelmingly to give full powers to Marshal Philippe Pétain, thereby dissolving the republic. Of the eighty deputies and senators who voted no (out of 569), thirty-six were SFIO, thirteen Radicals, and the others from the Center and Right. Ninety SFIO senators and deputies voted for Pétain's authoritarian rule. A few leading personalities of the SFIO sided with Pétain, notably long-time secretary general Paul Faure.

The Communists submitted to Moscow's orders in late September 1939 to condemn a war of no interest to the working class as a struggle between rival imperialisms. They survived their shameful compliance to Moscow by taking the lead in a resistance which was still in its earliest phases when they joined it after Hitler's attack on the Soviet Union. When the Allies landed in June 1944 the PCF had become a major force to be reckoned with in postwar France. Its new weight became apparent in the first postwar elections in October 1945, when the PCF took 26.2 percent of the vote, the SFIO only 23.4 percent. In two national elections the next year the gap between the two parties widened rapidly. In elections for a second constituent assembly the PCF had 25.9l percent, the SFIO only 21.1. In the November 1946 voting for the first National Assembly of the Fourth Republic the PCF rose to 28.3 percent (its all-time high); the SFIO sank to 17.8 percent.

Popular Front enthusiasm had led to reunification in 1936 of the major French union, the Confédération Générale du Travail (CGT). After the 1920 split it had been fairly close to the SFIO, but was by no means its labor wing. The Communists had founded a "Unified CGT" (CGTU), their Leninist transmission belt to the workers. In the unification period the Communists were able to organize a sudden influx of new unionists, especially among metal and chemical workers, railroadmen, and in the building trades. After World War II Communists dominated the major organization of French labor.

The Communists vaunted their Resistance record (forgetting September 1939-June 1941). The SFIO had its individual Resistance heroes, but the party itself had not played a distinctive role in the anti-Hitler struggle. While the Communist party incited in its young adepts the notion that Communism and the Resistance were one large generous movement, the Socialists evoked a kind of party patriotism tainted with a musty smell of bureaucracy.

Léon Blum had miraculously returned safe from Nazi captivity. But he and the new first secretary Daniel Mayer, a leading SFIO Resistance figure, were disavowed in August 1946 by a leftist majority which thought Blum's postwar views too far right and believed that only vociferous leftism would allow the SFIO to compete with the Communists for the votes of post- Resistance France. The new first secretary was the young deputy and mayor of Arras, Guy Mollet.

Mollet's catastrophic reign over the SFIO lasted for twenty-three years. The leftist and anticlerical rhetoric which brought him to power could not have been worse timed. The anticlerical SFIO was a coalition partner with the Catholic Mouvement Républicain Populaire (MRP) in most of the postwar governments. The party which talked proletarian internationalism furnished leading ministers to governments which integrated France into the Atlantic Alliance. Antimilitarist and anticolonialist, the SFIO backed repression in Madagascar, Vietnam, and then in Algeria. Government after 1947 meant the Third Force—denying power both to the Communists and the Gaullists. Corseted in these Third Force governments, the SFIO found its hot rhetoric flagrantly at odds with its daily conduct. Small wonder that its vote steadily diminished, dropping to 14.6 percent in the parliamentary elections of 1951. In the last elections of the Fourth Republic in 1956, the SFIO's 15.2 percent of the votes made it the strongest single governmental party in a badly fractionized Assembly. Mollet became prime minister (François Mitterrand was his justice minister) in the government which sent draftees to fight in Algeria and conspired with Great Britain and Israel in the disastrous Suez expedition.

Mollet backed de Gaulle in May 1958, and did not break with him until 1962. The result of this long record of ideological incoherence was to disgust many within the party and repel the young people who regarded the SFIO as a party of opportunist bureaucrats. The SFIO had always had leftist factions, but from 1956 on fissile tendencies increased. The most important was a movement calling itself the Parti Socialiste Autonome which later merged into the Parti Socialiste Unifié (PSU). One of its leaders was a young technocrat named Michel Rocard, who had been the secretary general of the SFIO student organization.

The Fifth Republic posed new problems for an SFIO which had grown fiercely anti-Communist during the years of the Fourth Republic; General de Gaulle's new regime was more anti-Communist still, and intent on leaving no viable forces between itself and the Communist party. Faced with the prospect of heavy losses in the 1962 parliamentary elections, Mollet mitigated his anti-Communism to negotiate a partial alliance with the PCF leaders. SFIO candidates would withdraw in favor of better placed Communists in the second round, and vice-versa.

The presidential election of 1965 was the first held under universal suffrage. A group of young publicists and intellectuals, most of them admirers of Fourth Republic prime minister Pierre Mendès France, were seeking the ideal candidate to oppose de Gaulle. Mendès, who rejected the institutions of the Fifth Republic, was not available. They opted instead for Gaston Defferre, the moderate Socialist mayor of Marseilles, whom they built up in a press campaign as the "Monsieur X" who could beat de Gaulle. Guy Mollet was not enthusiastic. Defferre's plan was to re-federate the French Center-Left and non-Communist Left, in other words to regroup the battered and divided troops of the old Third Force of the Fourth Republic. To win, however, he needed a Communist vote he was unwilling to bargain for. If the PCF followed him, very well. But he was not going to negotiate with it. He did not have to. Defferre's candidacy collapsed under the blandly malevolent eye of Guy Mollet by trying to reach too far right and not far enough left.

After Defferre's failure, no one in France supposed that any candidate could defeat Charles de Gaulle. The only question seemed to be what symbolic candidacies would be advanced, how many, and how poor their scores would be. In this unpromising situation one far-sighted and adventurous politician glimpsed real opportunity. His name was François Mitterrand.[5]

THE NEW LEADER OF THE LEFT

The Mitterrand who ran for president in 1965 was very far from being the Socialist leader of 1981. At forty-nine, he was a veteran of eleven coalition cabinets of the Fourth Republic, in which he represented the small, mildly left Union Démocratique et Socialiste de la Résistance. Leftists knew that he came from the well-to-do middle class, that his background was Catholic and that his education until university level was entirely in Catholic schools. To many Frenchmen on the Left he was an improbable standard bearer. They wanted to know whether Mitterrand really belonged to the Left or was merely an opportunist. If he was now genuinely on their side, how had he arrived there?

François Mitterrand was born on October 26, 1916, in the small town of Jarnac in south-western France. His father, Joseph Mitterrand, was a stationmaster who later took over his father-in-law's vinegar distillery. The Mitterrands were intensely Catholic, but not intolerant. In the great turn of the century crisis they had not been anti-Dreyfus (nor *Dreyfusards* either). Comfortably well-off but not rich, they were overshadowed by the patrician and Protestant brandy makers of Cognac, six miles distant. The thrusting world of money was repugnant to them. "My family," wrote Mitterrand many years later, "was revolted by [the idea that] money could be more important than the values they held important: country, religion, liberty, dignity. It was the enemy, the corrupter. . . . "[6] This suspicion of capitalism was born of medieval Catholicism and owed nothing to the ideas of the Left. In the mid-twentieth century, however, they met and married.

There were eight Mitterrand children, four of them boys. One went to the prestigious Ecole Polytechnique and became a successful industrialist, another to St. Cyr (the French West Point) and became a general. François, the most meditative, the most withdrawn, was good at literature, poor in math (economics would never be his strong point). Foreign languages did not appeal either. The Mitterrand boys were regularly sent off across the Channel in summer to polish up their language lessons, but François took positive pleasure in not learning English.

Arriving in Paris at eighteen, Mitterrand lived in a Catholic *pensionnat* run by Marist fathers while attending classes at the Sorbonne and the Ecole des Sciences Politiques. These were the years leading up to and including the Popular Front, but the young Catholic student was not much interested in politics. Called up for army service in 1938, he was a sergeant in a regiment of colonial infantry when war broke out.

Wounded by mortar fire near Verdun in May 1940, Mitterrand was hospitalized, then made prisoner of war in June. The eighteen months he spent as a POW altered Mitterrand's life. This introverted, bookish child of a devout and devoted family had been partly sheltered from the world of army service by being stationed in Paris. The months of the "phony war" do not seem to have much affected him.

In the prisoner of war camps, despair over the collapse of the world he had known compounded with physical hardship — degrading hunger and the impossibility of personal privacy. Mitterrand had already encountered the crudity of army life. Now for the first time he discovered the mixed ugliness and exhilaration of shared privation. Men were capable not only of quarreling over the nauseating rutabaga soup the Germans gave them and of stealing one another's ration of bread, but also of organizing themselves to share food, the packages they received, and all their small belongings. The comrades he discovered in POW camp were not only the fortunate youth of the middle classes he had always known, but also workers and Communists. He learned that the moral qualities men show in misfortune do not necessarily follow from their educational advantages or their social position.

However instructive the university of prison camp may have been, Mitterrand had no desire to stay there. As soon as he had recovered from his wound, he began to plot escape. In March 1941 he and another prisoner succeeded in breaking away from a camp near Weimar and walked six hundred kilometers before being caught near the Swiss border. In November he escaped again, walking as far as Metz in German-annexed Lorraine. There he incautiously took a hotel room and was betrayed by the hotel keeper. This time he would have been sent to a camp for recidivist escapees in Poland, but on December 10 he seized the chance to escape again from the temporary camp where he was held, and with the aid of helpful cafe proprietors was confided to an escape net led by a courageous nun. He was home in Jarnac for Christmas. But Jarnac was in occupied France, where he could not stay without false papers that the frightened mayor refused to give him. Escaped POW's were however welcome in unoccupied France and even given a tiny escapee's bonus. Family friends helped him find a job in the Commission for War Prisoners in Vichy.

Vichy in early 1942 had still not plunged into the lower depths of collaboration. To be anti-collaboration and anti-German was not yet automatically to be anti-Pétain. Mitterrand found himself working in an office trying to aid POW's, where some of his fellow employees were deeply involved in making false papers and organizing escape nets for prisoners. When his chief at the Prisoners' Commission was replaced in early 1943 by a man thought close to Pierre Laval, Mitterrand and his friends decided to use their organization as a resistance net.

Rapidly ex-sergeant Mitterrand showed himself to be a leader. Bits of intelligence coming from escaped prisoners were forwarded to General de Gaulle's headquarters in London. While working against the Germans, Mitterrand tried to appear a loyal Vichy official. He allowed friends with credit on Marshal Pétain's staff to propose him for a Vichyite decoration, the *francisque*. Later in his career enemies both among the Gaullists and the Communists used his receipt of it to imply that Mitterrand had played an opportunist role in Vichy.

Mitterrand was awarded the *francisque* in the fall of 1943 — when he was in London. He had gone underground when his double life as Vichy official and member of the Resistance became too dangerous. The prisoner of war movement needed a contact with de Gaulle's National Liberation Committee, now headquartered in Algiers, and Mitterrand proposed himself. A

British Lysander picked him up at a clandestine airfield and flew him to London.

From there the twenty-seven year old emissary, now "Captain Morland" of the Resistance, flew to Algiers for another of the formative events of his life, a meeting with de Gaulle. As Catherine Nay remarks in her biography of Mitterrand, *The Black and the Red,* every ingredient for instant understanding was present in the two men's background: the same literary temperament, a deep Catholicism, a sense of the nation. Instead, there was instant antipathy. As another Mitterrand biographer reconstructs it, the conversation began badly. They were introduced by the Resistance leader Henri Frenay. De Gaulle's first words were: "It seems that you arrived here on a British airplane." To which young Mitterrand allegedly retorted: "I didn't look at the make before going aboard."[7] There were no airplanes other than British ones shuttling between London and Algiers, of course. De Gaulle seems to have meant that the plane did not belong to those assigned to his own intelligence service; Mitterrand was already suspect of sympathizing with his rival General Henri Giraud. Worse, he refused to merge his network with one led by de Gaulle's nephew and place himself under the latter's orders. As a result, he found himself a near prisoner in Algiers, in danger of being sent off to fight in Italy instead of returning to the Resistance in France.

Nevertheless, the disagreements were smoothed over, and Mitterrand returned to London, where he met not only with Colonel Passy, de Gaulle's chief of intelligence, but also with the Communist party representative in the London Resistance office, Waldeck Rochet — who as PCF secretary general would back him in 1965 as the candidate of the Left against de Gaulle.

Returning to France in February 1944, Mitterrand merged his organization with the network organized by de Gaulle's nephew and with another led by the Communists. He emerged as the leader of the new organization, active in aiding prisoners, gleaning intelligence from them and re-forming them into resistance units.

After the liberation of Paris Mitterrand hoped to become minister for war prisoners (a million and a half young Frenchmen were still in German camps). He was passed over by de Gaulle, but remained the leader of the war prisoners movement. His backing of their demands on de Gaulle's provisional government brought another showdown with de Gaulle, and perhaps their final rupture.

The young Resistance leader now moved another step away from his Catholic background. In the spring of 1944 he had met Danielle Gouze, the sister of a Resistance friend. Her family could not have differed more from the Mitterrands: atheist schoolteachers and freemasons, the very stereotype of everything passionately distrusted by conservative Catholic France. Six months after they met, Danielle married François Mitterrand — in church. If the young bride compromised her own principles (and probably shocked her family) by acceding to a religious marriage, Mitterrand must have raised eyebrows among his relatives. A good Catholic boy . . . married to a militant atheist?

Sometime during the war, Mitterrand's religious faith, or more precisely his belief in the beneficent role of the Catholic church, had slipped its moorings. He did not cease at once to practice his religion — witness the church marriage — and a political associate recalls seeing him kneel in prayer during a visit to Cologne cathedral as late as 1956. But gradually, in a development in which the influence of his wife cannot be overlooked, he moved toward a deism strongly marked by suspicion of the social role of the Catholic church. In 1973 he told an interviewer: "I was born a Catholic and will doubtless die as one. But in the meantime, well . . . the Christian explanation of the world is richly resonant. But I also have an irreconcilable argument with a certain attitude of the Church, as the accomplice across the centuries of an established order that I abhor."[8]

His doubts on the social role of the Church helped to keep young Mitterrand from joining the new Catholic party, the MRP. His preference lay with the forces emerging from the Resistance (though former Resistance leaders like Georges Bidault were prominent in the MRP). Finding the SFIO too bureaucratic and (like the PCF) altogether too desirous of swallowing them up, some Resistance elements ended by founding their own party, the Union Démocratique et Socialiste de la Résistance. It combined left-wing Gaullists, socialists, and moderates. Mitterrand in 1945 belonged to the last category.

Mitterrand had played a significant role in the Resistance and discovered that he could be a leader of men. He had no taste for a purely administrative career. To fill a political role he needed to be a deputy, and a small party where he could shine suited him well enough. His first attempt at election to the Constituent Assembly failed in June 1946. In October of the same year that brief assembly finally produced a constitution for the Fourth Republic that was a near carbon copy of the constitution of the Third, and called for new elections. Mitterrand was offered a difficult constituency in the department of the Nièvre and won.

Thirty years old, the new deputy became in 1947 the youngest minister in France, in charge of veterans' affairs in Paul Ramadier's cabinet. He would be one of the most frequent office holders of the Fourth Republic, named to eleven of its twenty-four brief and sometimes stillborn governments. No one would have called him a leftist. His wife wore dresses from the fashionable couturiers; he took up golf and frequented the beau monde. He attended the wedding of Grace and Rainier of Monaco; he was a guest in the Florentine salon of Violet Trefusis,[9] an Englishwoman whose mother had been Edward VII's mistress.

Mitterrand in the Fourth Republic was a centrist moving toward the left under the whips of his enemies. He made a number of them in 1951 as minister for Overseas France when he negotiated with African leaders who were near rebellion and satisfied their immediate grievances. Several of them were deputies, and their small group sat in parliament with the Communist party. Mitterrand's dealings with them and his success in bringing them over from the PCF alliance to one with his own UDSR outraged diehard defenders of colonialism who thought he was opening the gates of respectability to a pack of African Reds. The African deputies included Felix Houphouet-Boigny, later president of the Ivory Coast, and Sekou Touré of Guinea.

Mitterrand's next crisis was the notorious *affaire des fuites* (leaks) in 1954, a McCarthy-style provocation mounted against the government of Pierre Mendès France and Mitterrand, his interior minister. Mitterrand had fired the very anti-Communist Paris prefect of police Jean Baylot, whose intelligence service wanted to move against the PCF using evidence fabricated by the police themselves. Baylot's chief expert on the PCF, Jean Dides, responded with a plot against Mitterrand which branded him as a PCF informant for material leaking from the National Defense Council.[10]

The initial investigations were sabotaged by the police, but the real leakers were eventually discovered. In the meantime Mitterrand had been suspected of being a traitor, his name dragged in the mud by gossip and the denunciations of right-wing deputies. If the mud did not stick, the memory that there had been mud was not entirely effaced.

Mitterrand went on to be minister of justice in the disastrous Mollet government of 1956 which sent draftees to Algeria and covered up for torture. He disapproved, but he went along. Apparently he hoped that soon he would become prime minister, and able to do better. Instead, the Fourth Republic collapsed amid military disobedience that frightened the politicians into supporting the providential return of Charles de Gaulle. This time Mitterrand did not go along.

This star of the Fourth Republic thought that at forty he should already have been prime minister; he had hoped to attain that office in the crisis year of 1958. Was the fact that he disliked de Gaulle and had little credit with him solely responsible for his decision to join a handful of Fourth Republic notables in rejecting the general? Or did de Gaulle's return force Mitterrand to make the move to the left which he had always desired but had postponed in the interests of routine ambition?

There is no way to determine the weight of old quarrels with the general and his men in Mitterrand's decision. His hatred for some of the Gaullists was certainly a factor. Among them were men who had attacked his honor in the *affaire des fuites*. Leaders who had rallied to de Gaulle during the war, like Pierre Mendès France, now opposed the general. Some men of the Left, notably Guy Mollet, now backed him. Mitterrand had friends among the Gaullists — but not many. He could expect nothing from them, and his small party was hopelessly split by the general's return. But to refuse to support de Gaulle in 1958 meant a move to the left and a long political exile.

By 1958 Mitterrand clearly wanted to be seen as a man of the Left. The collapse of the Fourth Republic meant the defeat of his hopes to lead France, but it also provided the chance finally to break with the compromises his ambition had urged him to accept. We know at least that his wife had often reproached him for his association with coalitions oriented toward the right.[11]

Mitterrand's rejection of the Gaullist regime was amplified by a provocation mounted against him in 1959, usually called the Observatory affair, in which he was accused of arranging a false assassination attempt against himself in order to appear a hero. When a suspicious character claiming to be an unwilling conspirator against his life suggested they collude in a fake shooting, Mitterrand foolishly did not inform the police. After his experiences with the Fourth Republic's police in 1954 when he was their boss, he presumably had little confidence in de Gaulle's police. Mitterrand cooperated, and what seemed an assassination attempt (staged at the Place de l'Observatoire) at first won him sympathy. Then his "co-conspirator" denounced him as the instigator of the plot.

Mitterrand was faced by the sneers of his enemies and the doubts of many he had thought his friends. Worse, the government demanded the lifting of his parliamentary immunity to face a charge that he had not informed the police. Mitterrand defended himself well, but his immunity was lifted; the charge was then dropped. After this attempt to frame him Mitterrand had every reason to dislike the Gaullist regime.

By 1965, however, Mitterrand had emerged from the obloquy that had threatened to destroy him, from a period when "his fingers sufficed to count his friends."[12] He had become one of the strongest opponents of Gaullism among the old politicians of the Fourth Republic, had won back his seat in the National Assembly, and published a much-discussed attack on Gaullist rule, *Le Coup d'état permanent*. Consistent opposition to a Gaullist regime inconsistently opposed by the SFIO gave him new credentials as a man of the Left.

Mitterrand had always been anti-Communist. But in 1962, when a referendum changed the constitution to allow direct election of the president, he won two cardinal insights into the new politics. First, an elected president would be the most important man in France. Second, de Gaulle's hold on the centrist vote was too strong and the non-Communist Left too weak for any anti-Gaullist leftist to succeed without the active support of the Communist party.

In the 1965 presidential elections, after the collapse of Defferre's candidacy, this support was available even (perhaps especially) for so newly fledged a leftist as Mitterrand. Under its new secretary general Waldeck Rochet the PCF was trying cautiously to move away from its public role as Moscow's agent in France. Also, Moscow briefly flirted in the early 1960s with a revival of the Popular Front tactic; Rochet may have thought the Soviets would give him no trouble if he contested de Gaulle by backing a candidate of the entire Left (instead of a PCF candidate) if a suitable person could be found.

Maneuvering rapidly, Mitterrand won support for his candidacy from both the SFIO and the Communists. No one believed he would achieve even relative success. Jean-Jacques Servan-Schreiber, editor of the weekly *l'Express* which had tried to launch Defferre, wrote disparagingly that Mitterrand could not hope for more than twenty to twenty-five percent of the vote, even counting the Communists — the worst score the Left had ever had "since the Second Empire."[13] The disparate forces of the Left in splinter parties and unions backed Mitterrand, but without enthusiasm. Another candidate, the MRP leader Jean Lecanuet, competed for centrist votes. Mitterrand had no illusions of victory. At the least he wanted political rehabilitation, but his real goal was the leadership of the Left.

The campaign was remarkable for its vagueness of program, but many French voters were weary of de Gaulle and still more of the arrogant and all-powerful Gaullists. In the first round the general fell short of a decisive majority. He had only 44.6 percent of the votes against Mitterrand's 31.7 percent and Lecanuet's 15.6 percent. Forced into a second round by his pygmy opponents, the great man lost something of his prestige. He was decisively re-elected in the second round with 55 percent, but Mitterrand with 44.8 percent had, in this "brilliant defeat," made himself the most prominent leader of the opposition.

Mitterrand proceeded to craft an electoral coalition called the Fédération de la Gauche Démocratique et Socialiste (FGDS) which included the SFIO, the Radicals, and his own miniscule organization, the Convention des Institutions Républicaines (CIR). Mitterrand was president. The FGDS approved good, though not warm relations with the PCF for mutual aid in the second round of elections. In the 1967 elections, even though the FGDS garnered fewer votes than the Radicals and SFIO together had won in 1962, it was able — thanks to Communist aid — to elect a larger number of deputies.

The turmoil of May 1968 smashed the FGDS and Mitterrand's prospects. The Federation was as much surprised by student unrest as was the government (or the Communists). Like the other politicians, Mitterrand was booed and spat at by the excited young people in the streets. After twenty-five days of street fighting, de Gaulle tried and failed to calm the situation with his old device of a referendum. Mitterrand suggested a declaration to the leaders of the FGDS: "The state no longer exists, and what replaces it does not even have the appearance of power." De Gaulle's departure seemed inevitable, and Mitterrand proposed a provisional government, to be headed by Mendès France, and declared his candidacy in the presidential election which would be called immediately thereafter.

The canny tactician had blundered. Two days later de Gaulle disappeared from Paris to seek the support of the army, and after a day of panic for the Gaullists reappeared with the assurance that it would back him in the event of more street violence. But to avoid violence he dissolved the National Assembly and called new elections.

The wave of leftism was followed by a strong backlash. The conservatives were returned in force; the FGDS lost sixty-one of its 118 deputies, the Communists forty of their seventy-three. Mitterrand appeared to the man in the street as an adventurer, a clumsy opportunist who had grabbed for power that was not for the seizing. The FGDS speedily collapsed. When in August the Soviets marched into Prague, Mitterrand was quick to condemn Soviet actions. The PCF first "reproved," then in an overnight amendment only "disapproved" the invasion. The next year de Gaulle resigned after a lost referendum, and Mitterrand wondered whether he should be a candidate. The PCF was ready to back him, but Guy Mollet coldly let it be known that he would not back him.[14] Mitterrand was again branded as an opportunist and the man of the Communist alliance.

THE MAKING OF A NEW SOCIALIST PARTY

The year 1969 marked the nadir of the Left. A Mitterrand candidacy in that year might have ended his political career. The Gaullists found an immediate replacement for the general in his former prime minister Georges Pompidou; the anti-Gaullist Right and Center were attracted to the suddenly plausible candidacy of Alain Poher, president of the Senate and interim president after the general's resignation. Guy Mollet favored a symbolic leftist candidacy for the first round and a switch to Poher on the second. But

Defferre succeeded in 1969 where he had failed in 1965, declaring himself a candidate and winning SFIO backing. The PSU nominated Michel Rocard; the Trotskyites put up Alain Krivine, one of the central figures of May 1968; and the PCF decided to run its own candidate.

The Communist choice fell on a party veteran of nearly fifty years standing, the Resistance hero and confirmed Stalinist Jacques Duclos. In a campaign marked by oratorical brilliance and down to earth bonhomie, Duclos succeeded in making himself the most plausible campaigner of a divided Left. When the votes of the first round were counted Pompidou was far ahead with forty-four percent, and Duclos with 21.27 percent had very nearly beaten out Poher for the second round. Defferre, the SFIO candidate had 5.01 percent, only a percent and a half more than the young PSU candidate Rocard.

The results of the 1969 elections conditioned the political behavior of the French Left for another decade. Defferre's humiliation, following the collapse of his 1965 candidacy, demonstrated again that the politics of an anti-Communist Third Force were condemned to fail. If a Stalinist candidate (whatever his meridional charm on the television) could do four times as well as a Socialist so soon after the Czech events of 1968-1969, while the moderate electorate preferred a conservative centrist, then French Socialists had no choice. They must pursue some sort of alliance with the Communists, whatever the risks. Otherwise the Socialist party would disappear – to the profit of the Communists. The Communists meanwhile interpreted Duclos' success to mean that their core electorate would always rally to them no matter what party policy might be. They concluded that alliances with a weak Socialist party posed no danger and much prospective profit.

Defferre's defeat strengthened the strategy that Mitterrand had stood for since 1965, though he gained no immediate benefit. The election had interrupted a congress intended to reunify and renew the disparate groups composing French socialism, including Mitterrand's small group. A conglomerate of the political clubs that had sprung up after 1958, his Convention des Institutions Républicaines could as easily have been entitled "the Friends of François Mitterrand." Of the sixty-one members of the directing group of the CIR in 1969, two would serve President Mitterrand as presidential counselors, one was to be president of the National Assembly in 1981, another president of the Socialist parliamentary group, seven were ministers, and ten others deputies.[15] Mitterrand and his followers were always a close-knit unit, in good times as in bad. In the 1960s the CIR had been Mitterrand's safety raft. Now he needed to grapple his craft to something larger.

There were difficulties. A discredited Guy Mollet did not try to remain first secretary of the renamed Parti Socialiste that was to emerge from the congress, but he intended to continue to influence it by placing his men in directing positions. Two small splinter groups, led respectively by Jean Poperen and Alain Savary, went together with the SFIO into the new party. Mitterrand sniffed some sort of trap by Mollet and announced that the CIR would not join the new PS.

Mollet then decided to let Savary be the new secretary general, surrounding him with his own men but excluding his former dauphin Pierre Mauroy. The new PS was supposed to seek an alliance with the Communists. But Mollet braked and Savary moved too slowly. By mid-1970 Mitterrand, working with Mauroy and Defferre, was calling for a new congress of real unification that would actively seek a Communist alliance.

The congress finally met in June 1971 in the distant Paris suburb of Epinay-sur-Seine. The PS had agreed to take in the CIR as a bloc, with a guaranteed place in the directing bodies. Mitterrand and his friends had solidified their alliance with Mauroy, but needed more support to win a majority at the congress. They turned to the CERES (Centre d'Etudes, de Recherches et d'Education Socialistes), which had been the farthest left faction in the SFIO. Guy Mollet had initially encouraged the young CERES leader Jean-Pierre Chevènement and his friends, but Savary was finding them obstreperous – the CERES was a party within the party – and threatening to discipline them. Alliance with Mitterrand offered them immunity, and a more important role.

The intrigues at Epinay were not all spun by Mitterrand. Mollet and Savary, though not fully cognizant of the forces gathering against them, had decided to replace the old system of majority voting for the *Comité directeur* (steering committee) with proportional voting for party factions weighted in favor of the larger groups. After complex maneuvering, the congress opted for simple proportionality. Mitterrand's heterogeneous alliance could now win if all its factions could be brought to vote for a common motion. The delegates only realized what was going on when Mitterrand stood up and proposed a synthesis between the Mauroy-Mitterrand motion and one proposed by CERES. Not all of the CERES delegates were happy to be pushed into bed with "that right-winger," until their leaders explained that the victory was really theirs. The final vote was narrow: 48.4 percent of the delegates for Mitterrand's alliance, forty-six for Mollet and Savary, the rest abstaining or absent. But it was enough. The new Parti Socialiste had supposedly been founded in 1969. It really dated from the June day in 1971 when François Mitterrand, who had never been a member of the SFIO, became its first secretary.

Mitterrand and his allies had won the leadership of the PS by backroom maneuver in order to conduct a bold new policy. Savary and Mollet had wanted an ideological debate with the Communists to clarify the terms of an alliance. Mitterrand said: "The dialogue with the Communist party should not proceed on the basis of the imprecise themes of ideological debate. It will concern the concrete problems of a government with the mission of beginning the socialist transformation of society."[16] Mitterrand wanted the alliance with the Communists as soon as the PS was ready. He called, however, for a clear understanding on democracy and national sovereignty.

THE DANGEROUS ALLY

In 1971-1972 the French Communist party, with almost 400,000 members, was the largest party in France and by far the best organized.[17] The PCF's behavior in May 1968 had hurt its image in the upper intelligentsia, and its parliamentary representation had also plummeted in the 1968 elections. But many thousands of young workers and members of the lower intelligentsia awakened to politics by the events of 1968 had concluded that the organized power of the PCF and not spontaneous agitation was the way to change society. The party exerted complete control over the Confédération Général du Travail, with over two million members the country's largest trade union organization. After the 1971 municipal elections, Communist mayors administered cities with a total population of some five million, including forty-five of the 193 cities with a population above 30,000. Socialists controlled only thirty of the largest cities.[18]

Much of the Socialist party's municipal base was composed of fiercely anti-Communist small town mayors and city officials, intensely uneasy at the idea of any alliance with a Communist party, which they feared would "eat them up."[19] The Communist party was monolithic and centrally governed, and internal dissent was impossible. The new PS, a freshly united coalition of factions, was still imperfectly controlled by a newcomer and outsider who had yet to prove his leadership qualities and assert complete authority.

The PCF was considered by most Frenchmen to be fundamentally undemocratic. In 1968, only twenty percent of polling responses directly disagreed with the proposition that the PCF was "a foreign national party . . . giving too much weight to Soviet interests in its decisions."[20] Many people thought that in advocating a close alliance and common governmental program with the PCF Mitterrand was acting the part of a desperate and ruined gambler playing a roulette wheel he knows to be crooked. His PS had at most 80,000 members, few of them real militants, and those concentrated in the north and the Marseilles area. Mitterrand would certainly lose some of the more anti-Communist municipal elites of the old SFIO. If he replaced these forces with the new leftists represented by Jean-Pierre Chevènement's CERES (soon to compose a quarter of party militants), how could he stay in office without swinging wildly to the left? It seemed probable that the alliance would merely help the Communist party to appear more respectable, thereby reassuring voters worried about the weight of Soviet views in PCF councils and strengthening the PCF.

Other questions concerned the balance of a Communist-Socialist alliance if it should attain power, how many Communist ministers would sit in the government, what portfolios they might have. Even if the most sensitive posts were not given to Communists, could the PCF be prevented from seeding the civil service, nationalized industry, and radio-television with its servants?

Mitterrand was undeterred by these questions. After his takeover of the PS in June 1971 he moved rapidly forward to sign a political agreement with the Communists. In early October 1971 the PCF published a complete program for an "advanced democracy." On December 19 the PS Executive Committee proposed its program, which was amended and adopted in March 1972 by the PS Suresnes Congress.[21]

After two months of intensive negotiation, a Common Program of Government was announced on June 26, 1972 and signed on July 12 by the PCF, the PS, and a junior partner, the Movement of Left Radicals. The Left Radicals were a faction of the once-great Radical party, inclined to the left but not uninfluenced by the need to protect constituencies — mostly southern — where Socialist and Communist support was essential in second-round contests.

The Common Program was the product of great hopes — and of mutual bad faith. Mitterrand was quite frank about it. Two days after the final agreement of June 26 he flew off to Vienna, where he told a meeting of the overwhelmingly social-democratic Socialist International (deeply disturbed by his infringement of the Cold War injunction against alliances with Communists) that three out of five million voters for the French Communist party were potential Socialist voters, and that he intended to win them. Next day PCF secretary general Georges Marchais told his Central Committee that he fully recognized that the PS was an untrustworthy partner and admitted that the PCF had made compromises to reach an agreement. But he added that "the development of independent party activity in the masses" would parallel the parliamentary path to power. (Marchais' speech was not made public until the PCF-PS quarrel of 1974-1975.)[22]

The PCF in 1972 was an undemocratic party with vestiges of revolutionary rhetoric but no firm revolutionary intent. Its strategy aimed at a reprise of the Popular Front of 1936. After the Liberation this strategy had brought the PCF into de Gaulle's government of national unity. Providing important ministers and filling civil service ranks with its devotees, the PCF had hoped to expand its hold on the social bases of French industrial society and make itself an indispensable and ever more powerful component of French government.

After its dismissal from the government in 1947, the PCF had been commanded by Stalin to counter the American offensive embodied in the Marshall Plan. From 1947 until well after Stalin's death in 1953 the PCF had isolated itself in bitter opposition to the governments and governors of France, and was accordingly isolated by them.

By 1962 the SFIO had broken with de Gaulle and needed a PCF electoral alliance to maintain itself in legislative and local elections. Under Khrushchev, Moscow favored Communist Popular Front style alliances with Socialist parties — if they were sufficiently weak. PCF leader Maurice Thorez consequently suggested a "common program of government." Mollet wanted no such close ties. The Communist strategy had not changed over the years, only some of its language. Its immediate aim was "advanced democracy," which meant a larger measure of Communist power in a system that would still be nominally pluralist and democratic.[23]

Mitterrand had since 1965 been a consistent advocate of a Communist alliance, but he had few illusions about the PCF. He wrote in 1969, when his chances for a leadership role seemed poor:

> I observe simply that the unification of the Left involves the Communist party. . . . And from this stems the importance which I attach to the formation of a political movement able first to equalize and then to dominate the Communist party, and finally, to obtain by itself and of itself a majority role. . . . One may doubt the sincerity of Communist intentions, but to found a political strategy on the intentions one imputes to others makes no sense. What is important is to create the conditions which makes these others act as if they were sincere.[24]

This statement expressed Mitterrand's long range strategy. Though Communist leaders could not be compelled to act as Mitterrand desired, their voters might desert them if they reacted evasively and insincerely to his policy. Post-war Europe's experience in Socialist alliances with Communist parties suggested that the better-organized Communists always won out. Mitterrand's task was to prove that France could be an exception to the rule.

MITTERRAND'S SOCIALIST PARTY

The PS in 1971 was weak, still discouraged, split into several factions. By changing party rules to elect officials by proportional representation the PS had in fact raised factionalism to a principle of government. Mitterrand, who owed his election to this change of rules, would show how skillfully he could manipulate them. His first task, however, was to assert his leadership and overcome the doubts of older Socialists about this upstart leader, who in the scornful phrase of Guy Mollet had had to learn to "speak Socialist."[25]

Mitterrand's success in uniting the PS behind him and leading it to victory in 1981 was achieved by his idiosyncratic methods of rule, which even as they succeeded prepared new problems for the future. Always before a leader of small groups — the UDSR and later the CIR — he depended on an inner clan of close associates even when he became the leader of a large party. In order to control the factionalized PS he allied himself with first one faction, then another. The CERES, the most leftist group, was part of his coalition until 1975, then banished from it until he needed it to face a challenge from Michel Rocard and Pierre Mauroy in 1979. But the CERES was not the only left faction in the party. Among Mitterrand's new partisans were the followers of Jean Poperen, an ex-Communist and independent socialist more anti-Communist than the CERES, and anti-clerical in the old SFIO manner. (Thirty to forty percent of CERES members came from the new Catholic left.) Another left-oriented Mitterrandist was Pierre Joxe, son of a Gaullist father who had been de Gaulle's ambassador to Moscow.

Wary old militants at first nicknamed their new first secretary "the foreign prince," but Mitterrand charmed opposition even as he outmaneuvered it. In 1972, before signing the Common Program, Mitterrand had to fight leftists at the PS Suresnes congress who demanded a policy of neutralism with complete departure from the Atlantic Alliance. In 1973 at the party's Bagnolet congress still another formal debate was needed to determine PS policy on Europe and France's membership in the European Community. Mitterrand needed simultaneously to speak to the more leftist militants and those sickened by years of compromise, call out to Communist voters over the heads of their leaders and hold old SFIO members who wanted a pro-European policy.

The title of the new alliance, l'Union de la Gauche, expressed in the incantatory phrase *la gauche* at once a reality, an aspiration, and an illusion. Reality, in that the Left included all those Frenchmen whose historical reference points were Voltaire, the French Revolution, the 1848 revolution (but not that of 1830), the Paris Commune, the fight to rehabilitate Dreyfus, and Jaurès the martyr (though not necessarily Jaurès the non-dogmatic politician). There were few common historical references after the Socialist-Communist split of the 1920 Tours Congress.

A generalized aspiration for social justice united Socialist and Communist voters and militants, convinced that the government and economy of France had been monopolized and dominated by a narrow class of big capitalists whom they thought intellectually no better than the common people and morally much worse. Where conservative governments had introduced social measures (and France by the 1970s was a thoroughgoing welfare state), they got little credit for them from the Left. Moreover, the Left found such measures both approximate and incomplete, sops to the working class to keep it quiet.

This leftist mentality was profoundly and voluntarily ignorant of economic reality. When an economist or politician spoke of the fragility of the French economy, the Left immediately recognized the language of the enemy. Leftists were possessed by an intense and moralistic voluntarism, the notion that ill will had created intolerable conditions which good will would suffice to change, what the French call the "all you have to do is . . . " spirit—all you have to do is raise minimum wages, nationalize industry, introduce equalized salaries, soak the rich, forbid capital flight, etc. etc.

Illusion entered on the scene with the hope that all who joined in the mutual aspirations of the Left could work harmoniously together. This had not been possible in the Fourth Republic after the demise of the left-oriented coalition of late 1944-early 1947. (That period saw enactment of some of the most radical social measures of the twentieth century, but as it was largely presided over by de Gaulle, it did not enter into the mythology of the Left.) During the Cold War, Guy Mollet had said that the Communists were not on the Left, but on the East. The new hope was that the Cold War had ended. A Communist party no longer commanded by Stalin, which dared to express intermittent criticism of Moscow, had to be an acceptable and even honorable ally.

The expression *la gauche* could also be read in two ways. When it was synonymous with what Mitterrand likes to call *"le peuple de gauche"* it easily included the voters of the Communist party. If it meant the parties of the Left, then there was an irreconcilable difference between them, and a common ambition: each wished to eat the other up. Some members of the PS might not formulate the Socialist design this way; Mitterrand did. But he had realized by the mid-1960s that the only way to reach and then seduce Communist voters was by entering into an extended alliance with their leaders; appeals from without were useless.

Mitterrand's problem was that the language needed both to appeal to the Communist voter and to tell the Socialist voter that the PS was not the old SFIO possessed a leftist vocabulary ringing with echoes of Marxism. In 1972 Mitterrand told an interviewer:

I have acquired the conviction that the economic structure of capitalism is a dictatorship and in my eyes it represents a danger for that taste for liberty which is at the depths of my being. . . . My reflex was not ideological but one of sensibility and then a political one. . . .

In my upbringing there was the susceptibility of a *petit-bourgeois* who does not like to have his feet stepped on, who belongs to a very liberal and proud family living on the edges of the [upper] bourgeoisie.[26]

This comment probably represents the real Mitterrand better than some of his borrowings from the old revolutionary language. There, Mitterrand talked of "breaking with capitalism," and denounced multinational corporations as the quintessence of evil. Here is a sample of Mitterrand, vintage 1976:

The Socialists think that . . . the supreme law of profit has the natural consequence of eliminating the individual or collective aspiration toward values like beauty, celebration, love, dialogue, that the will of the ruling class continues to flatten down imagination, diversity, knowledge, and even more the demand for responsibility, that diamond tip of a civilized society.[27]

Reminiscing on the Mitterrand of those years, the veteran Socialist Gilles Martinet remarks, "When he happened in the 1970s to talk about 'the exploitation of man by man,' I used to look fixedly at the tips of my shoes."[28]

At the same time, Mitterrand did not discard his strong belief in increasing European unity, although the European idea was currently embodied in a European Economic Community that was an expression of the successes of late twentieth century capitalism. When more consistent radicals in his own ranks like the CERES leaders, Jean Poperen, or his follower Pierre Joxe argued for a break with the EC he opposed and defeated them.

It would be an exaggeration to say that Mitterrand never believed in his own highfalutin leftist language. Rather, he did not take it at the letter. One of his critics in the PS remarks that in internal PS discussions on economic matters Mitterrand always approved of the riskiest proposals if they seemed politically attractive. "The time for serious decisions seemed far off, and in the euphoria of the debate Chevènement's dialectics amused him more than realistic talk in Mendès' style." And this same critic adds: "He does not think that a text, whatever it may be, can block his projects; he is so profoundly pragmatic that he thinks of a program as a symbol rather than a contract."[29]

By adopting a leftist language which was not his native speech Mitterrand encouraged emulation. The young followers of the CERES naturally welcomed the marxophonic mode. It excited many other new PS members, or those reawakened to politics by 1968 and formerly discouraged by the bureaucratic politics and seedy compromises of the old SFIO. The SFIO standard bearers who had rallied to Mitterrand, such as Gaston Defferre in Marseilles and Pierre Mauroy in the north, had a horror of being identified as the right wing of their party and also fell in with the fashion. Jacques Julliard, a careful and critical historian and journalist of the Left, wrote in 1977: "The old Marxism of our childhood, which still constitutes the primary school of all social science, for which we must preserve the veneration given to our first teacher . . . the Marxism which all the same, let's admit it, is leaking at every seam . . . this Marxism — or is it the same? — is in the process of becoming the official ideology of the Socialist party."[30]

The spread of leftist language only confirmed the apprehensions of those on the Right and Center (and some on the Left) who saw with dramatic clarity all the dangers of a Communist alliance, while discounting Mitterrand's ability to keep control of it.

The evidence of the succeeding decade is that Mitterrand knew well what he was doing in the area he best understood — the political and institutional one — but made grave mistakes in the economic area, where he was not only ignorant but insouciant. Thus in the negotiations over the Common Program he held out against a Communist demand for automatic dissolution of the legislature when either party deemed that its "contract" had been broken, which would have given the PCF great power of blackmail. The Common Program reflected Mitterrand's views on yielding power if the Left lost an election, adherence to the European Community and remaining (provisorily, at least) in the Atlantic alliance. France's nuclear deterrent on the other hand was to be abandoned (the pacifist and even neutralist current in the PS was still strong). In the economic negotiations, however, Mitterrand settled for a vaguely worded call for nationalizations, set in a framework of anticapitalist language that could only discourage or frighten medium and small entrepreneurs, whose cooperation was necessary for the Program's economic success.

The rise of the Socialist party from 1972 until the victories of 1981 stemmed from its growing acceptance by both believers and skeptics: some voters desired to believe in it, and others wanted to vote against the Right but hoped that most Socialist promises would not be kept. Communist voters became more reconciled to voting for Socialists (and especially for Mitterrand); leftist Socialists supported a leader they had regarded with deep suspicion a few years earlier; less leftist Socialists comforted themselves with the idea that strong leadership more than made up for deficiencies in economic perception; uncertain voters tested out the idea that Mitterrand's PS could control the Communists and without overly radical measures improve a system exclusively directed since 1958 by the Gaullists and their allies.

Mitterrand's prestige grew from election to election, strengthening his position within the PS and his leadership in the country at large. In the legislative elections of 1973 nine months after the signature of the Common

Program, the PS won 19.3 percent of the vote, the PCF 21.4 percent. Both parties could draw comfort from results better than those of the disastrous post-May elections of 1968. But the Socialist vote was higher than it had ever been since erosion began in 1946. Mitterrand's objective, however, was the presidency. President Pompidou's term would run out in 1976. In 1973 it was already clear that the president's health was failing. However, the presidential staff, aided by a press that does not inquire into the state of a chief executive's bowels, contrived to hide the gravity of Pompidou's state from the public at large.

The PS hoped the election would not come until 1975 or 1976; Mitterrand did not think his party ready yet. When Pompidou died in early April 1974, however, Mitterrand waited for the call from the PCF, the PS and the Left Radicals which he knew would come. Then he moved from the dilapidated PS headquarters in a private street near Pigalle to a suite in the Tour Montparnasse, the ugly new skyscraper dominating Paris. He chose a campaign staff that included some members from outside the PS, and he did not run on the Common Program.

Socialist unreadiness for a presidential campaign was largely compensated by a split on the Right. The Gaullist candidate, former prime minister Jacques Chaban-Delmas, was suspect to many in his party as too social-democratic. The other conservative candidate was Valéry Giscard d'-Estaing, perennial economics minister under de Gaulle and Pompidou and leader of his own party, the Independent Republicans. A faction of Pompidou loyalists in the Gaullist party led by the late president's protege Jacques Chirac refused to support Chaban. Hampered by rumors about his private life and his (technically legal) non-payment of income taxes, wretchedly poor on television, Chaban was easily eliminated in the first round. In the second, Mitterrand faced in Giscard a younger opponent whose immense self-assurance, especially on economic topics, left the Socialist leader at frequent disadvantage. Giscard campaigned on the slogan "change without risk."

In the second round of voting Mitterrand was outpointed by an able adversary. The French electorate was uneasy at the potential weight of the Communists in a future government, but he nevertheless won 49.3 percent of the vote to Giscard's 50.7. The loser was momentarily discouraged, but the Left in general took this narrow defeat as a presage of victory on the next occasion. Later in 1974 the ranks of the PS were swelled by the adherence of the former PSU leader Michel Rocard and some of his associates, as well as leaders from the formerly Catholic and democratic-leftist French Democratic Labor Confederation (CFDT). These new recruits from the former leftists of 1968 were soon to show themselves the modernists of the

PS (or as the CERES said, meaning it of course as an insult, the "American Left.")

The rallying of Rocard and his friends was rapidly followed by PS victories in by-elections. These triggered a sudden and ferocious PCF attack on the PS. The Communists had suddenly realized during the summer of 1974 that the enormous prestige accruing to Mitterrand was benefiting the Socialists and not themselves. Their calculation of 1972 was proving false. They sought to energize their ranks with a torrent of abuse against the PS, and accused it of having taken a sudden turn to the right.

Mitterrand's reaction to this storm was essentially to stand on the defensive. He was still aiming at the Communist voter over the heads of his party chiefs, and he saw that the Politburo's tactic was to provoke him into angry reply and then invoke party loyalty against an accuser. But he was annoyed at his own leftists, who in their desire to pull him further to the left accepted part of the PCF criticisms. Mitterrand responded by dropping the CERES from the party majority at the Pau congress in 1975.

By late 1975 the PCF leaders decided to call a halt to their criticism of the PS. Almost simultaneously, the party underwent what seemed almost a camp meeting conversion to the milder Italian style of Communism. Marchais flew to Rome and signed a programmatic agreement with Italian Communist leader Enrico Berlinguer, which with an earlier Italian-Spanish Communist agreement occasioned an enormous outpouring of comment on the new "Eurocommunism," the conversion of major parties to a pro-democratic stance and a critical view of the Soviet Union.

Eurocommunism in the PCF turned out to be a false face assumed in part to imitate the consistent electoral successes of the Italian party, a quick fix sold to Marchais by his foreign policy adviser Jean Kanapa. Other senior members of the party remained skeptical, and Eurocommunism was never meshed into a long range party strategy exploiting the Union of the Left. It fit well however with the needs of 1976-1977, which saw the preparation of nationwide municipal elections for which renewed good relations with the PS were essential, and from which the PCF expected and received large gains.

Municipal offices confer no great power in the nation. They were and are, however, the bread-and-butter of the PCF, providing numerous jobs for full-time party militants and extensive opportunities for lucrative graft.[31] The parliamentary elections of 1978 were more crucial. They could open the door to power on a national level, with Communists receiving important ministries. In Washington, where the danger of Eurocommunism was much discussed, former U.S. Secretary of State Henry Kissinger told a conference on Eurocommunism in June 1977 that one should not imagine "that a Communist electoral victory [in France or Italy] would be an accidental, transitory, or inconsequential phenomenon."[32]

The French Communists were not gloating over a victory which advance polls depicted as almost certain. They were asking themselves whether it would indeed be a Communist victory in any meaningful sense, or instead make them the electoral prop for a more powerful Socialist party over which they would have only limited control. Exactly when they decided to break with the Socialists is still unclear. Some ex-Communists who were highly placed but not in the innermost councils of the party ask themselves in retrospect whether there was any real end to the anti-Socialist campaign of 1974-1975, or only a long truce broken by the final rupture over a renegotiated Common Program in September 1977.[33] If so, French Eurocommunism was even more a charade than it seemed at the time. In any event, the PCF leaders had decided by early 1977 that they must try to extract maximum concessions from the PS, renegotiate the Common Program to permit more nationalizations, and fashion machinery that would give the PCF and the CGT control of powerful administrative councils in nationalized industry.

The Socialists had seen the Communists move away from their Soviet allegiance under the banner of Eurocommunism. They concluded from this that the PCF was interested in fighting loyally at their side in the elections — though they expected a power struggle once victory was won. It followed that too many concessions before the elections risked strengthening the PCF hand by frightening hesitant voters, and would endanger their own future hegemony in government. Therefore they held firm — and the Communists broke off negotiations. In March 1978, despite polls that showed a strong possibility of victory for the no longer united Left, second round results returned a conservative majority to the National Assembly. The PS, which had hoped to be the largest party in an Assembly numbering 477 seats, had only 104. France had looked at the possibility of a government of the Left (or a government shared by two quarreling parties of the Left) and flinched. Mitterrand's strategy seemed to have failed.

AGAINST ALL HOPE

When they sabotaged what had once seemed certain victory, the Communists told themselves they had foregone an illusory triumph in order to prepare a more solid future. They hoped that in its disappointment the Socialist party would fall to quarreling, that Mitterrand would leave the scene, and that they could rebuild a powerful and hegemonic Communist party on the ruins of the PS.

Socialist infighting began promptly on schedule. Mitterrand's response to the quarrel sought by the Communists had always been to turn the other cheek and remain "unitary for two." Michel Rocard and his friends had always been skeptical of this "unity," which was responsible for a constantly leftist rhetoric. Worse, it enforced the pursuit of an economic policy increasingly out of line with the new economic realities of the late 1970s. Now that the disappointing results of the election were in, the Rocardians (and others) doubted that Mitterrand could or would lead the PS in 1981 in a campaign which would be his third try for the presidency.

Defeat in March 1978 convinced Rocard of the necessity of a new strategy and a new economic line. Immediately after the election he told a television audience that although the Left had lost its eighth election since the beginning of the Fifth Republic, future defeat was not inevitable. He went on to criticize the PS campaign — and implicitly its strategy. "Loyalty to the Common Program led us to reduce it to a list of demands," he charged. And the next week he told a journalist, "The faculties of imagination and invention of the PS must not be indefinitely sterilized by a detailed programmatic document."[34] Rocard was in fact declaring his bid to take over the party and become its 1981 presidential candidate.

Here was a direct challenge to the master strategist of the PS. But Mitterrand did not mean to cede the leadership. Whatever his moments of discouragement, it seems that throughout the troubles of 1977 and thereafter he maintained his intent to recoup in the presidential elections of 1981. One of his associates who had followed him from the days of the CIR tells of consulting Mitterrand in mid-1977 on a detail in the PS-PCF negotiations on reworking the Common Program. Should he be conciliatory or hold firm? "Make no concessions," was Mitterrand's reply. "But if they threaten to break off the talks?" "They are going to break off." "But that would mean that we will lose the elections?" "Yes," said Mitterrand, "but we will win in 1981."[35]

Mitterrand may or may not have had the goal of 1981 in such clear focus after the discouragement of 1978. However, no one in the "Mitterrand clan" that had followed him from the CIR to the PS or among his younger disciples had much love for Rocard. Among the younger leaders were men like Lionel Jospin, whom he chose to succeed him as first secretary of the PS in 1981, Laurent Fabius, his second prime minister in 1984, and Paul Quilès, his second defense minister. For them, Mitterrand *was* the PS, and any attack on him or the line he had followed since the Epinay congress of 1971 was lèse-majesté — and a threat to their own positions in the party. Rocard had his own following, some of them men who had followed him from the PSU, some from the CFDT, the ex-Catholic trade union, others new adherents who deeply distrusted the Communists and found Rocard's views on economics more realistic than the Common Program. Mitterrand had been suspicious of Rocard and his people since they were brought into the PS in 1974. He remembered too well how he and his own small group had taken over the PS from outside, and feared a reprise. Gilles Martinet, one of Rocard's friends, recalls Mitterrand's sharp remark to him in the mid-1970s: "Remember, Martinet, this party is not for the taking — it has been taken."[36]

The Mitterrand clan did not intend to let Rocard and his friends evict them from their positions. In mid-June 1978 thirty friends of the first secretary signed a text called "a contribution to the strengthening of the Socialist party and the victory of socialism in France." It rejected "any search for a professedly technical and modernist solution which would place our party in mortal peril." An unintended effect was to push Pierre Mauroy into Rocard's arms. The number two man in the PS had not been informed of this demarche, which was signed by several national secretaries of the party. He was both furious at the slight to his authority and suspicious of a total takeover by Mitterrand henchmen.

Amid great press and television publicity Rocard moved toward inevitable confrontation at the PS congress, held in Metz in April 1979. Mauroy had wanted only to move Mitterrand toward a new line, but ended as Rocard's ally. Skillful as always at inner-party maneuver, the first secretary outflanked Mauroy and again allied himself with the leftist CERES to gain a majority at the congress. A defeated but still determined Rocard announced that if Mitterrand were to run for the presidency in 1981 he would withdraw — an odd way of declaring his continuing candidacy. Mitterrand delayed declaring himself until early November 1980. Rocard, maneuvered into believing that the first secretary would not run, had declared formally in October and was then forced into a humiliating withdrawal.

These maneuvers were not merely incidents in the biography of Michel Rocard, but had an effect on the PS as a whole. From spring 1978 to late 1980 the PS was caught up in an internal power struggle that left little time for more important affairs. Because Rocard carried the banner of economic modernism against the first secretary's "archaism," the Mitterrandists took up the chant "we are all archaic." As the economic crisis worsened and unemployment rose, the PS shut its collective mind against any rethinking of its economic program, much of which had been questionable in 1972 and was now eight more years out of date.

In the faction-ridden party which Mitterrand had fostered new ideas could not simply bubble up from below — they had to be carried by a faction. If this faction was not in the majority its ideas would be rejected. Because the Mitterrandists were uncertain whether they could hold the party in 1979-1980, the party apparatus simply sat on its dossiers and refused to consider new economic problems. It was easier instead to follow its leftist bent: when

Mitterrand brought the leftist CERES back into the party majority, he gave its leader Jean-Pierre Chevènement the job of drawing up the 1980 "Socialist project." The result was a pompous, dogmatic, and thoroughly unrealistic manifesto.

By 1981, when Mitterrand became president, PS economic ideas were wilfully retrograde. The journalist Roger Priouret wrote presciently in June 1980 that any Socialist president would find himself burdened with demands legitimated by the PS as well as the PCF, facing an electorate which had been instructed by both parties that the economic crisis had been "manufactured" by the government and the bosses.[37] When Rocard's friend Jacques Julliard, editorialist of *Le Nouvel Observateur*, the principal newsweekly favoring the PS, told a Mitterrandist that the crisis was real, not something created by the bad policies of Prime Minister Raymond Barre, the other asked, "Are you a Socialist?"[38]

In setting forth its positions in late 1978 the Rocard-Mauroy group wrote: "The problems facing the world from now to the end of the century are only linked in part to the capitalist mode of production. We are witnesses to the crisis of the model of development of the industrial society, whatever its specific forms of property." This was a controversial and even daring statement in the PS of 1978.[39]

The political need to appeal to Communist and left-Socialist voters thus clashed with economic realism. Mitterrand, the brilliant political tactician, won out over Rocard, a mediocre one. In so doing, Mitterrand ensured difficult days for the PS once it achieved power. But by not changing his old economic program and by refusing to quarrel with the PCF (though he criticized its leaders), Mitterrand won over a million Communist voters in 1981 who voted for him on the first round.

In 1981 the French Left was still intensely ideological. Too few Socialist militants and voters (and very few Communists) were ready to believe in Rocard's economic realism. If Mitterrand had been less vague on economics and less opportunist, the Socialists might have thought more deeply about the economic problems of 1981. But if Mitterrand had behaved differently, would the Socialists have won in 1981? Questions like this are of course impossible to settle. One can analyze the opportunistic and demagogic tactics Mitterrand employed in refounding the Socialist party and winning the confidence of a large majority of the generic Left, but no one can say what might have happened, if. . . . The only alternative presenting itself was the Rocardian model. Rocard told his biographer, after much water had flowed under the Seine bridges, that the PS would not have accepted the compromises of 1982-1984 had he made them, and not Mitterrand.[40] The Communist-controlled CGT would not have accepted them either.

In retrospect, Mitterrand's success in 1981 was almost inevitably purchased at the expense of professing the ideas of 1972. Without doubt, many mistakes in detail made in 1981-1982 could have been avoided by a more economically alert president and party. But the larger frame of reference was an ideologized Socialist party still wet from the backwash of May 1968, and a *peuple de gauche* with long memories.

The 1968 movement had accredited the old idea that French capitalism was both strong and unjust (with the added notion that French capitalist society was boring). When the crisis years began after the oil shock of 1973-1974 and French conservatives began saying that the economy was weak, neither the old Left nor the young postgraduates of May believed them.

The PS could also not overlook the constant Communist charge that the Socialists were the party of social treason — those who talked a plausible leftist line but did not mean it, who always betrayed the aspirations of the Left — in World War I, in the 1920s, under Blum, under Mollet. Communist leaders were ex-workers, heading a party proudly proclaiming itself the party of the working class. The leaders and the militants of the PS came overwhelmingly from the middle class (though many had working-class parents or grandparents whose memory influenced them). Many were vulnerable to the insidious charge that they should feel guilty because they were not real workers. The burden of past Socialist errors hung upon Mitterrand. So did the whole mythology of the Left. The late comer to Socialism assumed the mythology, tradition and nonsense together. It was a heavy burden, but it is hard to see how he could have escaped it.

NOTES

1. *Pravda*, March 13, 1981.

2. *Le Monde*, January 13, 1981, comparing the poll data of the recent months.

3. Alain and Marie-Thérèse Lancelot, "The Evolution of the French Electorate," in *The Mitterrand Experiment*, eds. George Ross, Stanley Hoffmann and Sylvia Malzacher, p. 77.

4. Description drawn from *Paris-Match*, May 22, 1981, and Albert du Roy and Robert Schneider, *Le Roman de la rose*, pp. 9-12.

5. For the SFIO, see Yves Roucaute, *Le Parti socialiste*; Jacques Kergoat, *Le Parti socialiste*; Neill Nugent and David Lowe, *The Left in France*; R.W. Johnson, *The Long March of the French Left*; and Jean Touchard, *La Gauche en France depuis 1900*.

6. Quoted in Franz-Olivier Giesbert, *François Mitterrand ou la tentation de l'histoire*, pp. 21-22.

7. Catherine Nay, *Le Noir et le rouge*, pp. 116-117; Giesbert, *Mitterrand*, pp. 59-61.

8. Giesbert, *Mitterrand*, p. 23.

9. Nay, *Noir et rouge*, pp. 143-144. Violet Trefusis' portrait has come down to us in Nigel Nicholson's *Portrait of a Marriage*, and also as the supremely selfish Lady Mountdore in Nancy Mitford's *Love in a Cold Climate*. How odd to find a link between the worlds of François Mitterrand and Nancy Mitford!

10. Cf. Giesbert, *Mitterrand*, p. 146.

11. Cf. Giesbert, *Mitterrand*, p. 73.

12. Giesbert, *Mitterrand*, p. 191.

13. Quoted in Nay, *Noir et Rouge*, p. 281.

14. Giesbert, *Mitterrand*, pp. 239-252.

15. Cf. du Roy and Schneider, *Roman de la rose*, p. 31.

16. Du Roy and Schneider, *Roman de la rose*, p. 80.

17. Cf. Philippe Buton, "Les Effectifs du p.c.f. 1920-1984," *Communisme* 7 (1985), p. 8.

18. Cf. Ronald Tiersky, *French Communism 1920-1972*, p. 350.

19. Denis Lacorne, "Left-Wing Unity: Picardy and Languedoc," in *Communism in Italy and France*, eds. Donald L. M. Blackmer and Sidney Tarrow pp. 328-329.

20. Georges Lavau, "The PCF, the State, and the Revolution," in *Communism in Italy and France*, eds. Blackmer and Tarrow, p. 95.

21. *Programme pour un gouvernement démocratique d'union populaire* (Paris: Editions Sociales, 1971); *Programme de gouvernement du Parti socialiste* (1972).

22. Giesbert, *Mitterrand*, p. 267; for Marchais' 1972 speech see Etienne Fajon, *L'Union est un combat* (Paris: Editions Sociales, 1975) pp. 109-110.

23. Cf. Julius W. Friend, "Soviet Behavior and National Responses: the Puzzling Case of the French Communist Party," *Studies in Comparative Communism* 15 (Autumn 1982) pp. 212-235.

24. François Mitterrand, *Ma part de vérité*, pp. 78-79; 71-72.

25. Quoted in Nay, *Noir et Rouge*, p. 314.

26. Ibid., p. 342.

27. Ibid., p. 343.

28. Gilles Martinet, *Cassandre et les tueurs*, pp. 171-172.

29. André Salomon, *PS — La mise à nu*, p. 32ff.

30. *Esprit*, February 1977, pp. 187-188, quoted in Branko Lazitch, *L'Echec permanent*, pp. 200-201.

31. Cf. Jean Montaldo, *Les Finances du p.c.f.* (Paris: Albin Michel, 1977), pp. 85-132.

32. Henry Kissinger, "Communist Parties in Western Europe: Challenge to the West," in *Eurocommunism: the Italian Case*, eds. Austin Ranney and Giovanni Sartori (Washington, D.C.: The American Enterprise Institute for Public Policy Research, 1978), p. 184.

33. Author's interview with former PCF Central Committee member and historian François Hincker, October, 1987.

34. Robert Schneider, *Michel Rocard*, pp. 241-242.

35. Author's interview with PS *comité directeur* member Maurice Benassayag, June 1984.

36. Martinet, *Cassandre et les tueurs*, p. 152.

37. *Le Nouvel Observateur*, June 21, 1980.

38. Author's interview with Jacques Julliard, June 1984.

39. *Le Monde*, December 23, 1978.

40. Schneider, *Michel Rocard*, p. 272.

2

Twenty-one Months on the Left

THE THIRD ROUND

Giscard d'Estaing had defeated Mitterrand in 1974 by a narrow margin, almost certainly because many voters feared the PS alliance with the Communists. Promising "change without risk," he spoke of governing France from the center. Giscard would attempt to be simultaneously conservative and socially progressive.

Under de Gaulle the Fifth Republic had been a *dirigiste* welfare state. Claiming to speak for all classes, it offered them stability, modernization, and prosperity. Georges Pompidou continued the welfare state, but politically and economically he moved to the right, discarding some of de Gaulle's interclassist claims (especially after 1972), and evolving toward a fully conservative regime.

Giscard's progressive ideas were translated into law by the legalization of abortion and lowering the voting age to eighteen, but stopped there. A badly prepared effort to introduce a capital gains tax failed for lack of support in the president's majority. That majority was in any event disparate. Giscard chose Jacques Chirac as prime minister in part because this young Gaullist politician had helped him to defeat the official Gaullist candidate Chaban-Delmas. An even more powerful motive was his belief that Chirac would deliver Gaullist parliamentary support for his policies, which explains why he did not attempt to create his own presidential majority by dissolving the year-old National Assembly, where Gaullists outnumbered Giscard's own Independent Republicans.

Two years later Chirac had taken over the Gaullist party and organized it as his own. He resigned in 1976, and his newly renamed Rassemblement pour la République (RPR) became a troublesome ally for Giscard, especially after the 1978 parliamentary elections when it again outpointed Giscard's forces, now embodied in the new Union pour la Démocratie Française (UDF).

Giscard's election coincided with the onset of the economic crisis set off by OPEC's steep hikes in the price of oil, a crisis which this experienced and long-time economics minister (with most of his contemporaries) thought would be serious but short-lived. Magnified by a second oil shock in 1978 and by stagflation throughout the western world, the crisis worsened throughout Giscard's term in office (with a few remissions). The French had grown accustomed to full employment. By the spring of 1981 there were 1,700,000 unemployed.

Giscard was further confronted with a resurgent Left convinced that most of the effects of the economic crisis had been brought on by the selfish and shortsighted behavior of French capitalism. When the quarrels of the Left after 1977 seemed to guarantee Giscard's re-election in 1981, many Frenchmen gloomily predicted intense social disorder arising from a blocked political system unable to cope with social and economic crisis. Mitterrand was elected in 1981 because of that crisis, because doubts about Giscard's leadership were intensified by the presidential campaign waged against him by Chirac, and because a large Communist vote defected to Mitterrand on the first round and relieved much of the anxiety prevalent in 1974 that he would owe too much to the Communist party leaders. The crisis was now Mitterrand's, to cope with according to Socialist ideas.

The American constitutional system stipulates a ten week interim between an election and the inauguration of a new president. France knows little delay. On May 21, 1981, ten days after the election, Giscard departed the presidential palace, the Elysée, and François Mitterrand became the fourth president of the Fifth French Republic. He now faced the hostile National Assembly elected in 1978. His first political choice was whether to compromise with it in some way, temporizing, or to use his presidential powers to dissolve it immediately and hope that new elections would bring in a Left majority.

Mitterrand wasted no time. He appointed the veteran Socialist politician Pierre Mauroy as prime minister, and immediately dissolved the National Assembly. Mauroy formed a ministry composed almost entirely of Socialists, designed to handle the immediate concerns of government until the new Assembly could be elected. Again, there was little delay; the two-stage parliamentary elections were scheduled for June 14 and 21. Some politicians thought Mitterrand's campaign promise to dissolve a risky one. Mitterrand's former Socialist rival Michel Rocard is said to have advised against it (thereby confirming Mitterrand's long-standing doubts about Rocard's political intuition).

Even before Mitterrand announced dissolution the "third round" had begun — in the ranks of the old majority. Giscard's own Independent Republicans (renamed the Parti Républicain, or PR) were now part of the umbrella coalition called the UDF (Union pour la Démocratie Française), of which the other members were the Centre des Démocrates Sociaux (heir to the briefly powerful Christian Democratic MRP of the Fourth Republic), a remnant of the once-powerful Radical Socialists, and a right-wing Socialist splinter group. Giscard and his Republicans had been allies of de Gaulle; the smaller parties had entered government only under Pompidou or Giscard.

Giscard's rival Jacques Chirac led the larger and better organized RPR, the neo-Gaullist party. The RPR, with 150 seats in the Assembly elected in 1978, had frequently frustrated Giscard and his prime minister Raymond Barre; the UDF had only 138 seats. The Socialists, for their part, had had only 104 seats in that Assembly.

The UDF was the president's movement, and when he fell there was confusion in its ranks. In his first public statement after the election Giscard addressed himself to the more than fourteen million voters who had supported him, promising to show them the way to defend the essential interests of France. He advocated what he had always endorsed but never accomplished, "democratic assembly at the center of French political life." But in his bitterness at Jacques Chirac, the rival who had consistently undercut him and had cost him re-election, Giscard attacked those who had committed "premeditated treason."

The UDF deputies, however, were already worrying about their chances in the oncoming election. They needed not recrimination but unity for the parliamentary elections and hastened to approve a plan advanced by Chirac for a united conservative ticket. Even before he had left the Elysée, Giscard had lost the leadership of the opposition to Chirac.

Chirac talked confidently of victory, but may not have expected it. Polls already showed that the surprise of Mitterrand's victory was not unwelcome even to many who had voted against him. "It's not good to have the same people in forever. I didn't have the nerve to vote against Monsieur Giscard, but somehow I would have been disappointed if he had won," one young woman told a reporter. The question remained whether a Socialist presidential victory could create a solid parliamentary majority for the Left — or for the Socialists alone. One of the most experienced Socialist election specialists estimated in late May that his party might hope for 210 to 230 of the 478 Assembly seats, with minor leftist allies adding another twenty, and the Communists holding fifty to sixty seats.

Here was the big question: could the Socialists and their smaller allies win the 240 seats needed for a majority, or might the Communists hold the balance in the new legislature? The Communists hoped so. Rapidly rallying to the standard of Left union they had earlier abandoned, they hastened to "catch a moving train" (as *Le Monde* put it), declaring that they had their share in the victory and were ready to assume responsibility "at all levels of national life." The Socialists gave them a cautious welcome, reminding the PCF that the Socialists had not altered the positions criticized by the Communists for the past three years. Nevertheless, the PS was ready to deal with a humbled and inferior PCF. Knowing that they would still need electoral help, they renegotiated the traditional agreement to support the best placed candidate of the Left in the second round.

The voting in the first round of the parliamentary elections suggested that the electorate remained wary of Socialist dependence on the PCF. The Communist vote barely rose above the level to which Marchais had brought it in May (16.12 percent instead of 15.34 percent). Where 144 Communist candidates had come in ahead of Socialists in the first round of the 1978 elections, there were now only sixty-five, many of whom could not expect to be elected.

The second round confirmed and exaggerated the results of the first. The Socialists alone had a clear majority—269 seats plus another twenty held by smaller allies. The Communists had lost half their seats, sliding from eighty-six in the old Assembly to forty-four in the new. The conservative forces were also reduced by half. Jubilant, still incredulous, the Socialists saw themselves the masters of France, carried along by a wave of support they had long hoped for, but had never before received. After twenty-three years in the political desert, the Socialists had finally won their victory.

THE NEW MEN

During the five years when Mitterrand governed with an overwhelming Socialist majority, the French public became familiar with a new set of leaders, not altogether different in family background and education from Gaullists and Giscardians, very unlike their predecessors in attitudes and outlook. The first Mauroy government handled current affairs until the legislative elections. The second government, formed immediately afterward, saw the addition of four Communist ministers and some reshuffling of posts. With a few changes, this group endured through another government reshuffle in March 1983, ending with Pierre Mauroy's resignation in July 1984.

Mauroy as prime minister was by constitutional definition "chief of the government" and number two man in the new governmental system. He proudly traced his proletarian descent from a long line of woodcutters in the old forests near the northern city of Cambrai. Mauroy *père* became a teacher, rising to be an inspector of schools. His son, born in 1928, became a professor of technical education and a militant of the SFIO, which was traditionally strong in the north country. A protege of Guy Mollet, he was national secretary of the Socialist Youth from 1950 to 1958, then head of the SFIO federation of the Nord, one of the largest in the party, and deputy first secretary of the SFIO. Mauroy thought himself Mollet's heir until 1969, when he was passed over in favor of Alain Savary. Mauroy remained deputy first secretary, and in 1973 succeeded another mentor, Augustin Laurent, as mayor of Lille. He was elected a deputy in the same year.

Mauroy had led the old SFIO forces which combined with Mitterrand's CIR and the CERES to make Mitterrand leader of the PS. He had sided with Michel Rocard in 1979 and found himself in the minority at the PS congress of Metz. His SFIO past and alliance with Rocard inclined the more inquisitorial members of Mitterrand's entourage to treat Mauroy as a moderate (a dirty word in French Left usage). The label was neither accurate nor easily suffered; both as prime minister and thereafter Mauroy was at pains to stress that he was very much on the left. Tall, broad shouldered, outgoing, an orator overly given to length and flowery Socialist cliches, the new prime minister was to prove a hard worker and courageous leader in facing the bitter choices which would soon present themselves.

Another leading figure in the new government was economy and finance minister Jacques Delors. Born in 1925, early active in progressive Catholic youth organizations, Delors took an economics degree and worked for seventeen years at the Banque de France. He was a key adviser to liberal Gaullist prime minister Chaban-Delmas in 1969-1972. ("Take away Delors and what have you got? " asked Marie-France Garaud, the Dragon Lady of French politics.) He joined the PS in the early 1970s and became a Mitterrand partisan, even though his economic views were close to Rocard's. Able, ambitious, and cautious, he was still an outsider in the first year of Socialist power. Later his prestige rose as his predictions came true. He annoyed Mitterrand by frequent complaints and threats to resign, but the president came close to making him prime minister in 1983. After Mauroy resigned, Delors did not care to serve under Laurent Fabius, who had been his too insubordinate junior minister for the budget, and Mitterrand rewarded him with a prestigious nomination for president of the the European Community Commission.

The new interior minister and minister for decentralization, Gaston Defferre, was at seventy-one the oldest man in the government. He was a Protestant lawyer from the south, a Resistance hero, a rich newspaper-owner and yachtsman. Defferre was the Socialist mayor of Marseilles (the Chicago of France) and had been boss of that tumultuous city for over forty years. An aspirant to the presidency in 1965, bruisingly defeated in the 1969 presidential campaign, he was a respected elder statesman and powerful Mitterrand ally.

Foreign Minister Claude Cheysson, born in 1920, was an ex- diplomat and ambassador, aide in 1954-1955 to Prime Minister Mendès France, and former European Community commissioner. A strong believer in aid to the Third World, a good linguist with excellent English and German, Cheysson would carry plain speaking to the lengths of foot-in-mouth disease, as in the uproar immediately after General Jaruzelski's coup against Solidarity in late 1981, when he said, "Of course, we shall do nothing." (No one did do anything, of course, but Cheysson won no admirers for truth-telling.)

Charles Hernu, born in 1923, the new defense minister, had been a journalist, politician, and a Mitterrand admirer since the early 1960s. Son of a gendarme, Hernu in the early 1970s was one of the few leading Socialists convinced that the new PS must support a strong nuclear defense. He won the party over in 1977 (with Mitterrand cheering him on but leading from behind), when the PS finally abandoned its traditional pacifism. Hernu was to be popular with the military, but torpedoed himself in 1985 with the *Rainbow Warrior* affair, when intelligence agents acting on his authorization blew up a ship in a New Zealand harbor belonging to the ecologist organization Greenpeace. In the scandal that followed discovery of the French role, Hernu denied knowledge of the matter but was forced to resign.

Justice Minister Robert Badinter, born in 1928, was a close friend of Mitterrand but not a member of the PS. The appointment of this wealthy and successful trial lawyer at first scandalized doctrinaire Socialists who protested the nomination of this non-comrade and *"grand bourgeois"* to the cabinet. He became a Socialist hero as the minister who brought about the abolition of the death penalty (which he had long opposed) and as a champion of judicial reform. Badinter also became the target of bitter attacks, sometimes covertly anti-Semitic, by an opposition which accused him of being soft on crime. In 1986 Mitterrand named him president of the Constitutional Council (the closest French equivalent to the United States Supreme Court) for a nine-year term.

The new minister of education (who in France controls the teaching personnel and much of the curriculum at all levels) was Alain Savary, born in 1918, who had been displaced by Mitterrand as first secretary of the PS in 1971. A Resistance fighter from the earliest days, Savary became governor of St. Pierre and Miquelon at twenty-three when de Gaulle's forces took it from Vichy (to the annoyance of the U.S.). As a deputy and minister in the Fourth Republic he was deeply involved in decolonization in North Africa (a major street in Tunis is named after him), but resigned in disgust from Guy Mollet's cabinet when the prime minister did not disavow the hijacking of Algerian leaders over international waters. As education minister, Savary tried to steer into safe harbor a bill reconciling state-financed church education with the secular state system, only to fail when intransigent Socialists provoked intransigent Catholics and a monster demonstration opposed the government in the streets of Paris.

Law professor Jack Lang, born in 1939, minister of culture, had first become known as the founder of an innovative theater festival in Nancy and then as director of the Chaillot National Theater in Paris. Tall, immensely energetic, Lang made himself a name in the early years as a noisy Left nationalist who attacked the United States for its "cultural imperialism" (*Dallas* was a major sinner). He ended as one of the most popular Socialist ministers, who delighted his constituency by doubling the cultural budget.

CERES leader Jean-Pierre Chevènement, born in 1939, was a graduate of the Ecole Nationale d'Administration and an ex-civil servant in the finance ministry. A deputy at thirty-four, he led the most leftist faction in the PS. He was minister for scientific research and technology in 1981, and took on the industry portfolio as well a year later. His frequent intervention into the management of nationalized industry infuriated managers, and in the cabinet reshuffle in 1983 Mauroy offered him a different portfolio. Chevènement chose instead to resign, letting it be known that he opposed the new austerity policies. He returned to office however in July 1984 as education minister, reintroducing the singing of the *Marseillaise* in schools and taking a strong "return to the three R's" line.

Michel Rocard had made at least pro-forma peace with Mitterrand. He was still the head of a faction in the party which doubted the wisdom of many current Socialist ideas, and his continuing though frustrated ambitions to take over the party caused most of its leaders to regard him with deep distrust. Born in 1930, a brilliant technocrat versed in economics, Rocard was made minister for economic planning and development. This seemingly important post had little staff and no independent funding; it turned out to be a gilded cage. In 1983 Rocard successfully took over the agriculture portfolio, previously mishandled by an overly doctrinaire minister who had offended the powerful farmers' lobby. He would resign in 1985 to pursue his presidential ambitions, renounce them again, and become prime minister in 1988.

There were six women in the new government. (Under Giscard, two women had been appointed ministers for the first time.) The two most important posts went to Nicole Questiaux, born in 1930, whose title as minister of national solidarity covered social affairs, and Edith Cresson, born in 1934, minister of agriculture. Questiaux, a senior civil servant, soon found herself in disagreement with government policy and left the cabinet in June 1982. Cresson quarreled with the farmers' lobby, and was moved in 1983 to the post of minister for foreign trade, where she was more successful. One other woman had the title of minister: Catherine Lalumière had the portfolio for consumers' affairs. Two others were junior ministers: Yvette Roudy for women's rights, Edvige Avice for youth and sports, and another, Georgina Dufoix, was state secretary for family affairs.

Communist leader Charles Fiterman was the most senior of the four Communist ministers in the government, and the only one who was a member of the PCF Politburo. As minister for transport (the sector for military transport was removed from his ministry) he proved an effective executive. His PCF colleagues were Civil Service Minister Anicet Le Pors, Health Minister Jack Ralite, and Minister for Professional Training Marcel Rigout. Former foreign minister Michel Jobert, who had quarreled with Giscard but was not a Socialist, became minister for foreign trade. He left the government in March 1983. One minister and one state secretary represented the Left Radicals, the PS' small satellite. In all, there were forty-three cabinet members. Seventeen ministers were under fifty. Six were graduates of the prestigious Ecole Nationale d'Administration (ENA). Only one minister had engaged in private business, but fifteen were or had been teachers, and ten others members of the civil service. Only three had been ministers before. Collectively, their principal administrative experience came from their jobs as mayors. Twenty-three of them held this post (and as is permitted by the French system, remained in the job while serving as ministers).[1] Some of these mayors came from large or good-sized towns: Prime Minister Mauroy's Lille, Interior Minister Defferre's Marseilles, plus Rennes, Pau, Villeurbanne, Clermont-Ferrand, La Rochelle, Caen, Chartres, and other smaller towns.

The Socialist party organization was stripped of many of its experienced leaders as its chiefs became ministers and took their aides with them. Lionel Jospin, to whom Mitterrand had confided the leadership of the PS when he became a candidate, was confirmed as first secretary. Two key Mitterrand lieutenants, Louis Mermaz and Pierre Joxe, remained outside the second Mauroy government, becoming respectively president of the National Assembly and chairman of the Socialist parliamentary fraction, while another key lieutenant, Pierre Bérégovoy, became secretary general of the Elysée (roughly equivalent to an American president's chief of staff). With the exception of the four Communists, Michel Jobert, and two Left Radicals, the entire government and an overwhelming number of its staff came from the Socialist party. Its power and consequent responsibility were now enormous.[2]

GOVERNING IN A HURRY

The new occupant of the Matignon palace, seat of the prime minister, was not a man from the president's own clan. Leading Mitterrandists had looked askance at Mauroy since he opposed Mitterrand in the 1979 Metz congress. Mitterrand intimate Pierre Joxe, chairman of the PS group in the Assembly, waged incessant guerrilla warfare against him. Pierre Bérégovoy, also a Mitterrand cohort, functioned for over a year in the job of secretary general of the Elysée as another power center uncontrolled by the prime minister, until Mitterrand was persuaded to give him an important ministry.

These were problems for the future. The ministers of the first Mauroy government did not know whether they would be confirmed by the elections or kept in office by their president, and were primarily concerned with the election of a strong Socialist group in the National Assembly, from which everything else would follow. They therefore assembled only skeleton staffs to carry on current affairs for the month intervening before the parliamentary elections.

The new president and his prime minister had additional concerns. The franc had been declining even before the election. It began to fall more rapidly in the days between the election and Mitterrand's entry into office, as nervous capitalists took their money out of the country. Some technicians asserted that a rapid devaluation of the franc was essential. CERES leader Chevènement was already arguing that France should shake off the constraints of the European Monetary System. Mitterrand wanted none of it. Devaluation had a political symbolism that he understood well; the economic implications were less clear to him. Defense of the franc was a strong nationalist affirmation—had not de Gaulle defended it in the turmoil after 1968? He intended to include the Communists in the government after the elections, which would certainly frighten the financial community. Devaluation smacked of unreliability. Whatever technical advantages devaluation might present, it was politically too risky.[3]

In retrospect, some economists have argued that a speedy and prophylactic devaluation would have cleared the air, while the government found itself obliged to devalue the franc in October in any case—and then twice again. Others are less sure. In any event, the decision not to devalue in May was made on political grounds alone.

The June parliamentary elections created an unhoped-for Socialist majority. Where the Socialists had earlier worried whether eventual Communist participation in the government would be needed to secure a parliamentary majority, they now saw inclusion of Communist ministers as a minor risk, largely compensated by tying the Communist-controlled CGT to government policy. Although Communist voters might think their party's entry into the government the logical result of the resurrected Union of the Left, the Communist leaders knew better. Having sabotaged what seemed like certain victory in 1978 to escape Socialist hegemony, they now saw themselves obliged to enter the government in a far less favorable position. By entering it they meant to satisfy their rank and file, draw whatever benefits they could from participation in government, and try to heal the electoral wounds of the presidential and parliamentary elections.

The first months of the new administration saw a long honeymoon with public opinion, or in the more theological French phrase, a "state of grace." But the president and his team were in a hurry. The memory of Léon Blum's government in 1936 weighed on them. They knew their majority guaranteed them a minimum of five years in full power and spoke frequently of the importance of this "long duration" afforded them by the institutions of the Fifth Republic. Subconsciously, however, they could not quite believe it. The periods when the Left had been in power had always been brief. Even though they had more time than Blum, they still had to hasten, having promised great and rapid change. Because so many of their promises meant upsetting an economic status quo now placed in limbo by the elections, delay was impossible for reasons both economic and political.[4]

Their promises included a cut in the work week, retirement at sixty, a fifth week of paid vacations, an increased minimum wage, and extensive nationalization. Communist polemics had consistently maintained that the reformist Socialist leaders were not workers, were only verbally leftist, and in practice were "trained bears" anxious to serve the interests of their secret allies in big capital. The president, the prime minister, and the vast majority of the Socialist party were determined to show "the people of the Left" that these charges were lies. Given the big majority of 1981, what economic arguments could have sufficed to block measures thought politically necessary? In retrospect, even the cautious Jacques Delors agreed: "The Left [read PS] would not have been credible if it had not taken the measures due its electorate. The sin of treason is more mortal than that of error."[5]

NATIONALIZATION

Prominent in Mitterrand's electoral platform of "110 proposals," was number twenty-one, which read: "The public sector will be enlarged by the nationalization of the nine industrial groups foreseen by the Common Program and the Socialist program, and of the steel industry and the armaments and space activities financed by public funds. The nationalization of credit and insurance will be completed." At the opening session of the new Assembly on July 8 Mauroy made this proposal the centerpiece of his general policy declaration.

Nationalization had figured large in the Common Program of 1972, although oddly enough it was not part of the ancestral heritage of the French Left. Neither Socialist founding father Jules Guesde nor Léon Blum had favored nationalization. But the idea was taken up by social planners in the 1920s and early 1930s and gained popularity at the end of World War II. The

Left coalition presided over by Charles de Gaulle then nationalized the three biggest banks of deposit, the railroads and the airlines, electricity and natural gas production and distribution. A major automobile builder, Louis Renault, was nationalized less for economic reasons than because of his collaboration with the German occupier.

Renault did very well until the early 1980s. It was the symbol of successful state-owned industry (with the state largely keeping its hands off management). Renault's plants, especially the island factory at Boulogne-Billancourt on the Seine just downstream from Paris, became redoubts of the Communist-controlled CGT. Communist success in Renault and other state-controlled enterprises explained PCF interest in extensive nationalization. (The Union of the Left broke up in 1977 when the PCF demanded additional nationalizations — hundreds of companies partially controlled by the big conglomerates on the Common Program list.)

The Socialists had espoused the idea of nationalization for a variety of reasons, not necessarily consistent with each other. For the CERES and some others, Communist advocacy might almost have sufficed: if the biggest party of the Left, the party of the workers, demanded it, then the PS could not take the side of capital. (The example of Swedish socialism, which has never stressed nationalization, made little impression on overheated French Socialist thinkers in the 1970s.) The Socialists agreed to nationalization in 1972 for one set of reasons, and then found others. The original purpose was "to seize the commanding heights of the economy." The major conglomerates built up under Pompidolian capitalism must be removed from the control of big money. Under public ownership, key industrial sectors would become show-windows of economic democracy and social innovation. As time went on Socialists also argued that French capitalists were not investing enough. They were building or buying plants outside of France and therefore, in their selfishness, causing unemployment. French industry must be restructured, made more efficient, more competitive — and capable of employing more workers. Mitterrand stressed a nationalist argument in a September 1981 press conference:

> The nationalizations will give us the tools for the next century. If that were not done, instead of being nationalized these enterprises would speedily be internationalized. I refuse an international division of labor and production decided on far away and obeying interests other than our own. Nationalizations are an arm of the defense of French production.[6]

The French public was not opposed to nationalization in 1981; a SOFRES poll of early October 1981 showed fifty percent of the population favoring it. De Gaulle had set a precedent for such action, which could not be branded as intrinsically leftist. The French state had bulked large in the economy ever since the time of Louis XIV's finance minister Colbert, and state action since 1944 had rebuilt the French economy from the abyss of defeat and wartime destruction.

Opponents of nationalization, like its proponents, had arguments both doctrinaire and practical. Opponents feared its indefinite extension, although Mitterrand insisted that those firms not on the list would be let alone "at least until a national decision by popular consultation (parliamentary or presidential elections) should decide otherwise."[7] Almost all bosses feared the encroachment of the CGT in their businesses (some of them having previously excluded it by using company unions). They expected constant government interference, pressure to hire without permission to fire. And above all this, Renault or no Renault, they thought state control hopelessly inefficient, even if the new masters did not eject them from their positions of power.

Although everyone in the new government agreed on the principle of nationalization, there was disagreement on the manner of implementing it. Should all the industrial groups on the list be nationalized 100 percent, or would a fifty-one percent control suffice? Should all companies owned in whole or part by nationalized conglomerates be taken over also, as the Communist and some CERES members wanted? How were shareholders to be compensated? How fast should the government proceed?

Ideology and practical reasons both argued for speed: the Left wanted a display of firmness, but business executives also needed to know where they stood: the economy could not be left in limbo. Mauroy proposed nationalizations to the National Assembly in early July, but discussions concerning ways and means continued until September. Delors, Rocard, and Badinter advocated control without full takeover, and Badinter argued that full nationalization would involve lengthy arguments with the Constitutional Council and the European Community. Rocard took the position that ownership and control were separate concepts. Since the state controlled the national railways with a fifty-one percent share, why not apply this less expensive method to the current nationalizations? Mauroy wanted full nationalization, and some of the exchanges were heated. Angered by the tone of arguments against his policies published in the conservative press, Mauroy exclaimed to Delors in an August meeting: "All those people there, little bankers and high civil servants, are our adversaries. We have to cut off their hopes. Afterwards, things will go better." Arguing against the extensive nationalization of banks, Delors angrily accused his opponents of wanting to demonstrate the promised "break with capitalism" to the forthcoming Socialist congress. "You are going to smash your faces on this. Wait until

1982." Mauroy replied, "We are living an historic moment. Softness will get us nowhere."[8]

In the end, Mitterrand accepted the advice of his economic counselors and opted for full nationalization. Six industrial groups were to be entirely nationalized: the Compagnie Générale d'Electricité (electronics, naval construction, cables, computers, telecommunications), the Compagnie Générale de Constructions Téléphoniques (formerly ITT-France), Péchiney-Ugine-Kuhlman (aluminum, ferrous metals and copper, chemical products), Rhône-Poulenc (chemicals), Saint-Gobain-Pont à Mousson (glass and plastics), and Thomson-Brandt (electronics and telecommunications). Two big steel companies, Usinor and Sacilor, which had been extensively bailed out under Giscard, were taken over by conversion of their debt into stock held by the state. The Dassault airplane construction firm, whose principal customer was the state, was also on the list. The nearly nonagenarian Marcel Dassault had been nationalized before. He compromised with the government, asking only that he be left in technical control of his firm. The state also acquired control over the computer firm CII Honeywell Bull and Roussel UCLAF (pharmaceuticals), both partly owned by foreign capital (American and German). Matters were more difficult with Matra, a conglomerate prominent in the manufacture of sophisticated armaments, but with substantial holdings in publishing and radio stations. Since only the arms sector was profitable, the final compromise stipulated a fifty-one percent share for the government, thus guaranteeing the survival of the entire company. Thirty-six banks were also nationalized — most notably the major investment banks Banque de Paris et des Pays Bas (Paribas) and Banque de Suez; the major banks of deposit had been nationalized in 1945. The newly nationalized sector made up twenty percent of the gross turnover of French industrial production, and together with the older nationalizations employed twenty-four percent of the industrial labor force.

Debate on the nationalization law opened in the National Assembly on October 13. At once the minority conservatives introduced a large number of amendments and objections designed to provoke and frustrate the Socialists. After the Socialist majority had approved the bill in late October, it was rejected by the Senate, delayed when the Constitutional Council decided that the terms of payment were insufficient, and finally became law only in February 1982.

ECONOMIC PROBLEMS

While the nationalization bill was making its controversial way through the parliament a host of other economic and social measures also occupied the attention of both the executive and legislature. Mitterrand had promised a rapid reflation of the economy to increase employment. His economists told him that since the new Reagan administration in Washington intended to reflate the U.S. economy, France could launch itself on the cresting wave of a world economy. Economic prognostications, particularly OECD estimates, suggested that in 1982 the twenty OECD countries would have an average growth of two percent in GNP, while demand for French exports would rise by 6.25 percent. (The actual figures were minus 0.5 percent for GNP, 0.4 percent for exports.)[9]

The strongest element in François Mitterrand's socialism was a passion for social justice. The Fifth Republic had enlarged the welfare state, but the Left believed that much remained to be done. A famous OECD report of July 1976 on income distribution in major countries cited France as having the highest percentage of annual income going to the richest ten percent of its citizens. The raging double-digit inflation of the late 1970s had increased the inequalities felt by elderly and lower-paid citizens already hard hit by an indirect taxation that burdened food and other necessities with a seven percent value added tax.

Comforted by prophecies of an expanding world economy, the new government proceeded to follow an economic policy shaped by its political needs and social aspirations. Mitterrand had promised to raise the minimum wage and old age pensions, set retirement age at sixty, cut the work week, introduce a fifth week of paid vacations, and above all, reduce unemployment. Rapid economic growth was a necessity if all these measures were to be paid for.

The heads of the major nations met for the annual economic summit in Ottawa in July 1981. Mitterrand, making his first appearance on a world stage, added his voice to a general European demand for the U.S. to cut interest rates. Ronald Reagan was not interested. "The new administration didn't really have a policy on interest rates," remembers Henry Nau, senior National Security Council staffer for economic policy. "High interest rates were Paul Volker's policy; we went along with them."[10]

Undeterred by this setback, the new French government went ahead with an ambitious program. It had already raised the minimum wage (SMIC) by ten percent in early June, with immediate effect on one and a half million workers. Manual laborers making roughly a third more than the *smicards* felt a more gradual effect, and more highly salaried workers very little.[11] The government undertook to compensate business directly for half the increased social burden imposed by this rise.

Family allocations were raised as well. The Barre government (worried by a birth rate that had begun to sink after a period of rising birth rates unknown in France since the early nineteenth century), had raised payments to families for the birth of a third child by 5,000 francs. The Socialists not only raised this allocation by twenty-five percent, but also increased payments to families with two children. Minimum old age pensions, languishing in 1980 at 57.6 percent of the minimum wage, were raised sixty-two percent in the first two years of the Socialist administration. To these should be added increased rent subsidies, aid to poor farmers, and a rise in compensation for part-time unemployment. Altogether, the cost for all social measures was 200 million francs in the second half of 1981 and 800 million in 1982.

Mitterrand had promised in 1981 that the work-week would be reduced from forty hours to thirty-five, a measure expected to create new jobs. The CGT wanted this done at once, with compensation for a forty-hour week. Mauroy favored a gradual reduction of the work week but worried about the wage reduction. Acting without fully consulting his prime minister, Mitterrand opted in January 1982 for the thirty-nine hour week paid as forty. Only a few thousand jobs were created instead of the hundred thousand jobs optimistically estimated. The extra costs did not affect industry as much as might have been expected, being compensated by a gain in productivity. The precedent of a drop in hours worked without a drop in pay did however block further motion toward a thirty-five hour week. In retrospect, this was recognized as the kind of action the government should have left to labor-industry bargaining rather than enacting it by decree. [12]

All of the government's actions had stressed greater social justice, but PS economists also expected that the liquidity injected into the economy would greatly expand consumer spending and bring about new growth in the French economy. Here they seriously miscalculated two factors. In late 1980 and early 1981 Giscard's prime minister Raymond Barre (for reasons not unconnected with the forthcoming elections) had raised old age pensions, granted new aid to investment, and altered the practice of previous years by excluding increases in the cost of oil from energy bills paid directly or indirectly by the public. These measures alone stimulated growth by circa 0.4 percent in 1981, and were only imperfectly integrated into the Keynesian measures of the Socialist economists.

The second and more important miscalculation was the estimate made in mid-1981 that the French economy had sufficient capacity to fill the consumer demand that would result from reflation. The money injected into the economy did not sufficiently stimulate French consumer production, which was unprepared to handle it. Instead it brought a rise in imports, particularly from West Germany, which swiftly placed heavy pressure on the balance of payments.

These pressures were compounded by a drop in French exports, the result both of high French prices caused by an overvalued franc in 1979-early 1981 and the influx of highly competitive Japanese and other non-European products into German and other European markets. The French automobile industry in particular suffered a rapid loss of export markets, as its products lost the ability to compete with the Japanese cars imported freely into the smaller European countries with no automobile industry of their own.[13]

For several months the government's economists believed that their measures were successful. But December 1981 saw a steep decline in the balance of trade which continued into 1982; in October 1981, 92.3 percent of imports were covered by exports, while by the following June this index dropped to seventy-nine percent. France had devalued the franc in October by 8.5 percent (three percent devaluation of the franc, 5.5 percent revaluation of the deutschmark). In agreeing to do this, West Germany insisted that France must deflate somewhat, reducing its 1982 budget by fifteen billion francs.[14]

The devaluation did not do much to change the economic picture, as Delors himself had foreseen, when he argued vigorously in the Council of Ministers in early October for a tighter budget and slower expansion of buying power.[15] In late November Delors went public in a radio interview, advocating "a pause" in new projects. If the minister's views were good economics, they were bad politics and worse public relations. He had, deliberately or not, chosen a word with strong historical associations. Léon Blum had spoken in early February 1937 of a pause in the economic program of the Popular Front. The pause became a dead halt, and the Blum government was overthrown not long after.

This clumsy use of loaded language did nothing to raise the minister's credit with an angry François Mitterrand, whose eye was still fixed firmly on his political problems. He told Delors, "The people who voted against Barre's austerity policy won't quickly accept a return to constraints. . . . In any case, the Right will do everything to capsize the policy of change which is backed by public opinion."[16]

The economic news grew worse in January and February, as both Delors' and Mauroy's economists had warned them. The president's advisers preferred to believe that the tardy world economic recovery would begin within six months. (In December 1981 the OECD was still predicting an average two percent growth in 1982 for its member nations; the real figure was minus 0.3 percent.)

Meanwhile the whole process of reflation set in motion in summer 1981 continued inexorably into 1982. Only one quarter of the new expenses had been pumped into the economy in 1981, and the economic effects of Barre's reflation were slightly more important to the economy in 1981 than those undertaken by the new government.[17] Barre's injections of liquidity into the economy had however been temporary measures, like a reflation attempted by Chirac in 1975. The Socialist government's reflationary measures could not be easily abrogated; they were designed as permanent social ameliorations. Unable to stop a process it had set in motion for political and social reasons, the government would find itself condemned for the next three years to continue releasing buying power on the one side while sopping it up on the other.

Mauroy was not convinced of the need for drastic action until the spring of 1982.[18] Meanwhile, his economic advisers, together with two of the top economists of the presidential staff (now alerted to the crisis) met constantly with Delors' men to plan a counter-attack on the economic front. The president's attention was riveted on the economic summit to be held at the palace of Versailles. Hoping to convince the leaders of the United States, West Germany, Japan, Canada, Great Britain, and Italy to approve an ambitious program of worldwide economic expansion, Mitterrand resolved to impress Western leaders (and especially Ronald Reagan) with the splendors of France, as if to imply that the heirs of the French monarchy could not be thought of as untrustworthy, or as the accomplices of Communists. The president insisted that nothing be done to diminish the Versailles summit, at which he appeared so regal, so solitary in his splendor that an irreverent minister, remembering Giscard's predilection for Louis XV, whispered to his neighbor, "I never knew that Louis XIV had succeeded Louis XV."[19]

A SLIGHT CASE OF HUBRIS

The Versailles summit marked the end of phase one of the Mitterrand presidency, when the Socialists basked in unwarranted self-assurance, displaying an arrogance based on misreading the election results. Their victory had been too big. Returned on the flood tide of Mitterrand's victory and an unprecedented parliamentary majority, many Socialists thought in 1981 that their new power might last for twenty years.

Simultaneously they overreacted to the bitter language of a conservative opposition quite unused to loss of power. Its world turned upside down, the Right gave full expression to its indignation and its fears. In the early months it had still another reason for strong language: the spokesmen of the Right were not yet preaching entirely to the converted, but were also intent on winning back those moderates who had voted for Mitterrand and had to be brought back into the fold.

A Socialist government was bad enough, but a Socialist-Communist government! "The trouble-makers of 1968 have taken power," exclaimed Gaullist baron Olivier Guichard. Unused to opposition, the Right freely employed wild language charging the new government with collectivizing or sovietizing France, and cried out that a government taking such measures was not legitimate.

Ever since they had signed the Common Program with the Communists the Socialists had proclaimed their attachment to the principle of alternation in power. Leninist tactics were not for them; power won through the ballot box would be yielded if the ballot box went against them. To be told that they were dangerous to French democracy, society, and institutions was an insult, an idea to be entertained only by unspeakable reactionaries. The Socialists naturally reacted with resentment and a self-satisfied assertion of good conscience.

Thus feeling themselves provoked, and armed with a happy sense of destiny, the Socialists let power intoxicate them, and foolish words issued from their lips: "The frontier which we crossed on May 10, which separates the light from darkness. . . . " (Culture Minister Jack Lang); "Its [the Right's] supreme value is money." (Pierre Mauroy); "The French people know quite well that freedom is on the Left." (PS deputy leader Jean Poperen).[20] Most damaging of all was a phrase uttered by a young Socialist deputy, the diminutive and dogmatic André Laignel. Replying to the objections of former Justice Minister Jean Foyer during the nationalization debate, Laignel said, "You are legally wrong, because you are politically in the minority." His words would go echoing down the years of Socialist power.

On top of this, the Socialist party congress held in Valence in late October 1981 displayed an ugly triumphalism which shocked the country. A speech by PS leader Paul Quilès drew the most attention. He demanded a purge of those persons who were resisting or obstructing the new regime. This would not be a systematic purge of high civil servants and chiefs of industry, but:

> It would be naive to leave in place people who are determined to sabotage the policy desired by the French: rectors, prefects, the heads of national industry, senior civil servants. We should not say "heads will roll," like Robespierre in the Convention, but we must say which ones, and quickly.[21]

Not that many heads did roll, although conspicuous ones had already fallen. The Socialists had constantly complained over the years about tight government control over radio and television, and Mitterrand had promised a pluralist media. But if the new government wanted a free media, it also thought that many television officials and editors who had risen in the Pompidou and Giscard era were its enemies. The result was a rapid purge of the directors of the three national television networks, of news editors and anchormen. Communists had always been excluded from television. The party now pressed for the hiring of Communist journalists. Some were taken on, although not always the ones at the top of the PCF preference list.

No government action could be more conspicuous than one which caused the disappearance of familiar faces from the tube. By purging TV personalities, by permitting themselves to use arrogant and imprecise language, by playing the Jacobin, 1793 style, the Socialists accredited the accusations of the opposition. The hubris of Valence was not easily forgotten; even *Le Monde*, friendly to the government, would write in 1984 that the phrase "Valence" still symbolized a sectarian image which had stuck to the Socialists.

The government continued to alienate powerful special interests. Agriculture minister Edith Cresson tried to buck the farmers' association, the FNSEA, by giving preference to an insignificant alternative organization, and a similar attempt to bypass the CNPF, the employers' association, was a useless provocation. The meaning of such gestures for many people suspicious of but not yet hostile to the new government was that the Socialists were both incompetent and sectarian.

Mitterrand declared on the day he took office that "the political majority has rejoined the sociological majority." He meant that an electorate which should have voted for the Left in 1978 had now taken a fundamental decision to shift left and stay there. In other words, the Socialists had been swept into power not merely by a few percentage points in the presidential race and given full control of the Assembly by thirty-eight percent of the vote, but by the ineluctable forces of history and sociology. Socialists could not believe that once the country went for them it would ever again wish to vote against them.

With this blithe assumption that History had taken out a PS party card, and a serene confidence that they were the party of freedom (though unsure of this virtue in their Communist partner), the Socialists made the grave error of believing that a temporary plurality of votes conferred nearly unlimited legitimacy for change.

From Laignel's concept of "politically in the minority, thus legally wrong" it followed that a Socialist legitimacy emerging from a relatively small majority at the polls made conservative objections illegitimate. Small wonder that conservatives already inclined to shout "sovietization" found their fears confirmed.

In fact, the Socialists had mistaken a delirious honeymoon for a stable marriage. The honeymoon soon ended. Confidence in Mitterrand's ability to resolve France's problems was measured by polls at seventy-four percent in June 1981, but began to decline in September, and dropped below sixty percent by December. The index of satisfaction with Mauroy's week-to-week conduct as prime minister dropped from a high point of fifty-three percent to forty-four percent in December 1981, and was only above fifty percent for two brief periods in 1982. In January 1982 by-elections for deputies whose elections had been invalidated for irregularities returned the one opposition member previously elected, and unseated three other deputies elected on the PS ticket. All four had won earlier by a margin of a few dozen votes; the by-elections gave the opposition candidates much larger majorities. The March 1982 cantonal elections for *conseillers généraux* (delegates to departmental assemblies) confirmed this pattern. In 1979, not a good year for the Socialists, the PS had won twenty-six percent of the vote in cantonal elections. Now, nine months after their big victory of June 1981, they won only twenty-nine percent.[22] The honeymoon was over.

Had the PS ever had a chance to create a new majority on the basis of the results of May and June 1981? Probably not, for as electoral analysis has shown Mitterrand won in 1981 by rallying almost all the Left vote and gaining nearly a million votes from disgruntled neo-Gaullists who refused to vote on the second round for Giscard d'Estaing. The subsequent legislative elections were marked both by heavy abstention and a desire on the part of moderate voters to give the new president a workable majority. When this majority did not show itself as moderate, the momentary fellow-travelers of June 1981 promptly redefected to the Right.[23]

Yet any serious attempt to hold them would have collided with the political necessities that ruled out cautious economic policies in the first months: the new government felt obliged to meet the expectations cherished by the Left electorate. Even if the Socialist tribunes had held their tongues, their acts would not have pleased the fringe voters of 1981. If the government had done what sober hindsight identifies as the rational thing, it would have been untrue not only to its promises but to itself, not gaining another electorate but losing its own. Mitterrand retained the trust of his core electors in the increasingly difficult times of 1982-1985 by keeping his early promises.

PARENTHESIS WITHOUT AN END

Socialist self-confidence did not last long after the Versailles summit; the economic realities the Socialists had rejected were about to demand recognition. Still unpersuaded of the need for drastic economic measures, Mitterrand reluctantly agreed to a devaluation—after Versailles. The French watched the concluding scenes of the conference on their television screens, as horsemen of the Garde Républicaine emerged from the twilight to sound a fanfare along the banks of the grand canal. "France pretended to be rich and powerful, though if the Fifth Republic had been a parliamentary regime the crisis would have burst and the government would have been overthrown."[24]

Immediately after the summit, Mitterrand gave a press conference still suffused with optimism. Four days later France devalued by ten percent (with the mark re-evaluated by 4.25 percent, the franc by 5.75 percent). Mauroy was applauded when he told the congress of the CGT that prices would be frozen, hooted when he announced a four-month wage freeze. The Communist party and the CGT chiefs went along with the plan — reserving their criticism for later.

The full plan for *"rigueur"* (as austerity was prudishly baptized) was composed of three measures: a wage and price freeze until the end of October, and a one percent rise in value-added taxes (the VAT on food, which Mitterrand had promised to abolish altogether, was reduced from seven percent to 5.5 percent). Finally, social spending was cut, in part by the price freeze on pharmaceuticals and doctor bills, in part by a minimum payment for hospitalization expenses.

Mauroy's polls showed that the French people understood the need for a more realistic policy and would welcome it, but the new policy was clumsily presented and extensively misunderstood. Mitterrand himself had not been convinced that a change of course was necessary, or if it was necessary, that the one chosen would do the job. The new measures were set forth as short-range ones and presented to the country as "a parenthesis in the process of change." The PS deputies did not understand these new necessities, resented the new language, and by showing their resentment, braked change. Both Mitterrand and Mauroy felt the need to go easy on their own troops and on the PCF — or rather on the CGT. Meanwhile French businessmen were still doubtful of the social measures of 1981, deeply suspicious of the price freeze, and resentful of Socialist charges that their reluctance to invest was willful sabotage of the economy.

If Mitterrand had fully engaged himself in the program of attenuated austerity begun in June 1982 he might have explained it more clearly to the country. Instead, the government went on emphasizing that the policy of reforms would continue. Mauroy had worked easily with Delors in convincing the president that a change was necessary in June. Now he disagreed with the minister of economy. He wanted to downplay *rigueur* and emphasize that the government had not really changed or abandoned its program.[25]

Business circles and the press predicted a price explosion when the freeze ended. Mitterrand looked for a way out. The outline of a new policy had been suggested to Mitterrand by some of his advisers in the crisis of June 1982. They argued for boldness, a severe but salutary jolt to the economy. The rules of the European Monetary System made dramatic and competitive devaluations almost impossible; France must leave it to regain full economic independence. Had not Giscard twice left its predecessor arrangement, the "snake," and returned? Mitterrand, they argued, could do the same. This advice came both from members of the government and from old friends of the president who had his confidence. The Delors-Mauroy course was wrong, they said; France must follow another policy.

THE LEGISLATIVE RECORD

Socialist success depended on economic policy, and Socialist failures were ultimately rated by the voters as preeminently economic. But the new government also hoped to be judged on its ambitious reform program. In attempting a great deal, it undoubtedly dissipated its energies. Convinced that things left undone in the first two years risked not being done at all, the government introduced bills on judicial reform, new labor laws, and important new laws on decentralization, plus much lesser legislation — meanwhile fighting the time-consuming nationalization bill through the National Assembly. The conservatives systematically opposed most new legislation with a flood of amendments, some substantive, some silly, like one to the law on retirement at sixty: "Plant coconut trees in every town in proportion to the population sixty and over, and make it compulsory for all the adult population to climb them at least once a year."[26]

Not all new laws were controversial; some were passed with little or no opposition. The abrogation of the death penalty was approved in September 1981 by three-fourths of the deputies, notably including Jacques Chirac. Other legal measures which received high priority were the abolition of the special court set up at the end of the Giscard administration to hear security cases and the repeal of a severe 1970 law directed against rioters. Legal reform had long been high on the Socialist list, but once achieved these reforms met with a mixed reception. As the incidence of crime increased, abolition of the death penalty became unpopular; in 1984 polls showed that sixty-one percent of the French wished to reintroduce the guillotine.[27] The opposition found much approval for its charge that the Socialists were soft on crime and terrorism, although this topic was more successfully exploited in 1983 and thereafter by the emergent National Front of Jean-Marie Le Pen.

Another top priority was decentralization, to which Interior Minister Defferre devoted so much attention that he neglected the law-and-order functions of his office. (An interior minister is habitually referred to in the breezier newspapers as "France's top cop.") A series of decentralization laws first limited the power of the prefects, no longer to be chief executives of the departments, and then transferred central powers, responsibilities and resources to the towns, departments, and regions. (See Part IV below for a fuller treatment.)

A series of laws known by the name of Labor Minister Jean Auroux introduced extensive changes in industrial relations. A new authority for television and radio was created to loosen the government's grip on the electronic media; abortion became reimbursable by social security; a whole series of grandiose public works was announced; and a new savings system indexed modest bank accounts.

The public's awareness of all these laws was not great, and its enthusiasm hard to detect. Worries about taxes, unemployment, and harder times ahead remained as always the bread-and-butter issues. As 1982 wore on discontent and pessimism were everywhere evident. In July, the monthly SOFRES poll on satisfaction with the prime minister registered a dip to thirty-nine percent of persons satisfied with Mauroy. Except for a slight rise in September-October, the curve would continue to decline. The president's public relations adviser Jacques Séguéla, famous for coining Mitterrand's meaningless but highly effective campaign slogan "Mitterrand, the Quiet Force," had been telling him since spring that Mauroy had been the man for a time of dreams but was out of place in a time of austerity. Other advisers agreed. Mitterrand hesitated, believing that he could afford only one change of prime minister during the life of the legislature, a change which must signal a new period. In August he summoned Mauroy to Latché, his country hideaway in the pine downs south of Bordeaux. The two men talked at length, as the president sought to reassure himself that the new economic policies would work rapidly. In the end he told Mauroy that he would give him four more months to succeed.[28]

The polls told Mitterrand that although his prime minister was rapidly losing popularity he himself still retained the confidence of more than half of the electorate. But the government had much to worry about. By-elections for *conseillers généraux* and the occasional mayor continued to register a tilt toward the Right. The Socialists had vowed to solve unemployment, which instead had increased by 14.9 percent in the first year after they gained office. The government was obliged to raise gas and electricity prices to meet the rise in world prices and make employees pay more to balance a threatening social security deficit. Popular confidence in the government as a whole was eroding. (A SOFRES poll in early August 1982 registered fifty-seven percent who thought that the government reacted from day to day, without knowing where it was going; worse, thirty-three percent who called themselves PS voters agreed.)[29]

Despite Mitterrand's unquestioned authority, the government's day-to-day conduct frequently produced an impression of confusion and dissension. The Mitterrandists did not easily accept the authority of Mauroy, "the loser at Metz," and an eager press fed full on rumors of arguments within the government assiduously leaked by bickering ministerial staffs. Declarations by ministers were frequently contradicted by the prime minister or the president. Mauroy's style, orotund and eagerly optimistic, met frequently with skepticism and sometimes with scorn.

The opposition was powerless to defeat bills in the National Assembly. The Senate possessed delaying powers only. For an opposition accustomed by twenty-three years of power to feel that its ranks constituted the natural leaders of the country the frustration was immense. The only vent for it was in bitter speeches, and in the columns of the conservative press. Press lord Robert Hersant's newspapers, particularly the Paris *Le Figaro* and *France Soir*, plus the independent Paris tabloid *Le Quotidien de Paris*, the weekly news magazine *L'Express*, and to a lesser extent its rival *Le Point* abounded in criticism that descended frequently into invective.

In the opposition the Socialists had not been too restrained in their own vocabulary of criticism; had not the president himself written a book twenty years earlier in which the whole Fifth Republic was derided as a "permanent coup d'état"? But Socialist thin skins betrayed inexperience in office. When the crowd at the Fourteenth of July parade hooted Mitterrand, no fewer than three top PS leaders issued communiques (uncoordinated) denouncing plots by factious elements and evoking the memory of the fascist leagues of 1934.[30]

As polls and by-elections alike indicated ebbing confidence in the Left government, an opposition which had been stunned by defeat plucked up its spirits. In 1982 a wave of rumors traversed Paris-in-the-Know: Mitterrand was dying of cancer; a new presidential election would come soon and the Right would return to power. Chirac meanwhile allowed his lieutenants to fire away at the new government. He himself was at first concerned to build up his stature as the unquestioned leader of the opposition, a bit above the daily fight in the trenches.

All this ended in the summer of 1982, when the government produced a new law designed to diminish his position as mayor of Paris. In the name of decentralization the twenty arrondissements of the capital would each become a town in itself, with the mayor of Paris (master of a multibillion franc budget and boss of 40,000 employees) reduced to the role of a senior coordinator. (Though gentrification had pushed most of the old Parisian working class and much of the lower middle-class into the suburbs, the Socialists still hoped to take over a number of town halls within the city.)

"Suicidal cranks, professional liars and tricksters," sputtered a Chirac lieutenant. The mayor of Paris took the high road, accusing the government of balkanizing the city. Why Paris only, and not (Socialist-ruled) Marseilles, demanded the opposition. The Socialists retreated — Paris, Marseilles and Lyons would have multiple mayors but would each remain one city. The government ended by showing itself both heavy-handedly partial and politically clumsy. It succeeded only in uniting the RPR with an UDF still resentful of Chirac's takeover of Paris in 1977. In the 1983 municipal elections the

Socialist maneuver proved a spectacular failure, as Chirac's partisans took all twenty Paris *arrondissements*.

The autumn of 1982 saw no economic improvement. The American economy was barely beginning to take off, too late to help the French, while the other European economies were nearly stagnant. French exports to West Germany sank steadily throughout 1982.[31] Unemployment leveled off as a result of reflations and other actions, but did not diminish. Inflation decreased slightly, but remained in double digits.

The government was slowly losing the confidence of its own inner constituency and not gaining any from French businessmen. Enjoined by a Socialist-Communist government to invest at a time of high inflation and falling profit margins, company directors not unreasonably chose to wait. Rapid rises in the minimum wage, the fifth week of paid vacation, the thirty-nine hour week paid as forty did not endear a Socialist-Communist government to businessmen whose attitude already ranged from suspicious to hostile. A darkening economic picture in 1982 did nothing to lessen their doubts about a government they neither liked nor trusted. When the government declared that the measures it had taken toward *rigueur* (austerity being a taboo expression) were temporary, a "necessary parenthesis" which once closed would permit further steps on the march toward socialism, the business class believed them, though the workers did not. Businessmen nourished only the gloomiest views of the future.

Given this climate, it was hardly surprising that the twice-devalued franc came under increased attack in the autumn and winter of 1982, as the need for a long-range austerity policy became plainer and the government continued to issue confusing statements. Through the cloud of language the French people perceived that the situation was growing no better, and feared it might grow much worse. Meanwhile, there was no consensus within the Socialist party on what to do, and none in the government. Mauroy, more and more under the influence of his economists and in general agreement with Delors, understood clearly that a new and greater austerity was necessary. But his intellectual acceptance of this necessity warred with his visceral dislike of it. Furthermore, he had every reason to believe the president far from ready to approve more austerity, and quite ready to entrust whatever new actions might be taken to a new prime minister.

As always, Mitterrand was thinking in political and not economic terms. While he had told Mauroy in August that he gave him four months to succeed, he had not meant to replace him in December—because his eyes were fixed on the municipal elections set for early March. France holds all municipal elections simultaneously every six years, with two rounds, as in legislative and presidential elections.

In the 1977 municipal elections the Union of the Left at its most united had won city council majorities in 159 of the 221 cities which had more than 30,000 inhabitants. Seventy-two big city mayors were Communists. All signs suggested that in 1983 the Left would not do well. Thirty-four members of the Mauroy cabinet were also running for election or re-election as mayors; severe losses for them would be a disavowal of the government. Mitterrand reasoned that if this should happen he would need a new prime minister. But any new chief of government would also need to embody new policies, if the old ones seemed rejected. The ideas of those who favored a break with Delors' version of conventional austerity appealed ever more strongly to him. These plans were bold, different, dramatic; if successful, they would permit a dramatic breakout from the trench warfare in which Mitterrand felt entrapped. Their advocates were old friends, ministers, personal advisors. Mauroy often met them in the presidential antechamber as he left Mitterrand's office at the end of the day. He gave them the name of the spectral presences in a famous René Clair film of the 1940s, *les Visiteurs du Soir*, the "night visitors."

SOCIALISM IN ONE COMMON MARKET COUNTRY

Pierre Mauroy's intellect had conquered his instinctive aversion to austerity, but was still at war with his sentiments, and his oratorical style served sentiment rather than intellect. The collection of his speeches as prime minister, significantly titled *A Gauche*, demonstrate that although he did not hide the problems presented by the policy of *rigueur* his desire to be optimistic got him into trouble. One celebrated example came in a television interview in February 1983. "I will try to show tonight that finally the big problems are behind us. In June, we had to make choices. In November, we had to fix governmental policy. But now governmental policy is fixed, and I will show you that all the traffic lights for governmental policy, or practically all, are finally showing green."[32]

If Mauroy was referring to a hard battle won he was disingenuous at the least, for he knew that the battle as he conceived it was not finally won. Municipal elections in three weeks might remove him from office and open the way to a change of policy if a much-feared swing against the Left was too great. Nine months after the first decisions on austerity, François Mitterrand was still hopeful that other roads might be found. "The night visitors" were pressing him to switch to their "other policy." They were Jean Riboud, president of the giant multinational Schlumberger, publicist and sempiternal idea-man Jean-Jacques Servan-Schreiber, Industry Minister Jean-Pierre Chevènement, top adviser Jacques Attali, plus two ministers personally very close to Mitterrand, Pierre Bérégovoy and Laurent Fabius. Their advice was appealing to a man who detests feeling trapped: that France need not remain in the European Monetary System and accept its constraints. The way to regain growth and pursue a Socialist course was to go it alone, pursue a partially protectionist course, cut interest rates and do everything to build up French industry and its internal market. Later, France might return to the EMS, or like Great Britain, remain outside. Mauroy regarded all this as both anti-European and terribly risky; he did not think that French industry had the elan to fill the role assigned.

The polls had gloomy news for the Socialists in the election month of March: only thirty-nine percent of respondents gave their confidence to Mauroy, forty-eight percent to Mitterrand. The first round of the municipal elections on March 6 seemed to confirm PS fears, but in the second round the Socialists rallied. Worst hit were the Communists. The Socialists lost Nantes, Grenoble, Brest, Chalons-sur-Saône, but were happily surprised to hold embattled Marseilles. Indeed, those cities where ministers were also mayors (or candidates, like Bérégovoy and Edith Cresson) almost all ended in the Socialist column. Except for Marseilles, the biggest cities had gone against the Left, with a crushing defeat in Paris. The balance of the country had shifted to the right. But since they had expected worse results and more humiliating ones, the Socialists could think that a glass they had feared more than half empty was really almost half full.

Mitterrand's reaction to the second round was relief; the vote had not obliged him to jettison Mauroy. The "night visitors" had, however, convinced him to change economic policies. He felt constrained by an austerity policy that tied him to the European Monetary System, to humiliating negotiations with the Germans, and to a policy of slow growth. "At the rate the external deficit is going, plus the difference between our inflation rate and that of our partners," whispered the night visitors, "France will be a colony of the deutschmark in two months. By January 1984 the IMF will call the tune in Paris."[33]

The adventurer in Mitterrand was excited by ideas suggested by Riboud, an old friend and a big capitalist who was also a man of the Left. Riboud believed he could re-establish the dynamics of growth within three years. France would then be independent and free of the fetters of its capitalist partners. Severe but temporary austerity would permit imaginative and successful policies.

The morning after the municipal elections the Paris daily *Libération* published what seemed an authoritative story by its chief editor Serge July, based on diligent leaks from Mitterrand's staff. It asserted that Mauroy would soon depart to make way for "the other policy," which would begin by floating the franc and proceed to stronger action against imports. Arriving at the Elysée, Mauroy was not surprised to find that these were indeed the president's ideas — but Mitterrand wanted him to remain as prime minister to carry them out.

The prime minister asked for a few hours to think it over, consulted with his disapproving entourage, and returned a negative answer. "I do not know how to drive on an icy road," was his comment. But the news was already out that the president would speak on television the next evening. Having nothing to announce, Mitterrand was obliged to cancel the broadcast and deny that one had been planned, or that any change of prime minister was in the offing. He announced that he would speak to the nation ten days later. Together with the *Libération* story, these actions implicitly told the country that the government was without a prime minister and hesitating between two policies.[34]

The crisis of March 1983 was the hinge event of 1981-1986. In May 1981 and June 1982 policies had been suggested that might have taken France out of the European Monetary System and turned her toward a go-it-alone policy. In 1983 the president decided to take this course. Then for ten days he hesitated, as he consulted with his closest advisers, with the most famous French economists, and with a variety of other pundits political and economic.

Mauroy had declared his opposition to the president's plan and was packing his bags. Delors, supported by most of the government's economists and key advisers at the Elysée, produced a continual series of memoranda on the precarious state of French finances. Budget Minister Laurent Fabius, a proponent of the "other policy," was briefed by Treasury chief Michel Camdessus that French monetary reserves were only thirty billion francs, not enough to survive the hammering of speculators once the franc was allowed to float. A devaluation of twenty percent would automatically send the foreign debt from 330 billion francs to 400 billion. Close presidential advisor Jacques Attali had rallied to the camp of caution, as did many of the president's technicians. They warned him that if the franc were set free to float it would immediately sink by twenty and perhaps thirty percent. No one would lend to France. The effect of higher prices on imports would be immediate, while any positive effect on exports would be much slower in coming. Once out of the European Monetary System, France could expect no support from its European ex-partners. The only defense of the franc would then be to hike interest rates from the prevailing fourteen percent to twenty percent or higher. No one would invest at such rates.

The advocates of the "other policy" had told Mitterrand that the arguments of the orthodox faction seemed plausible only because they had the computers to extrapolate results. If we had the same resources, they argued, we could show why our ideas are better. But "their ideas were so vague," charges former Mauroy top aide Henri Guillaume contemptuously, "that they had no details to back them up."[35] Nor were all advocates of the new policy agreed among themselves. Chevènement favored a protectionism that meant closing French borders to other European goods, which Bérégovoy and some others termed "Albanian" tactics.[36] The "other policy" was clearly a leap in the dark. Once Mitterrand had recognized the political danger he agreed that conventional austerity must continue. But he was still looking for a prime minister.

For a week, Jacques Delors thought the nod would go to him. He knew that Mitterrand detested the idea of going to the West German government cap in hand to ask for a favorable devaluation/revaluation. Negotiating feverishly with the West German government, Delors arranged for Bonn's finance minister Gerhard Stoltenberg to come secretly to Paris to prepare the next meeting of the European Community countries. To reassure Mitterrand, Delors reported that he had pushed frankness with the Germans to the point of insult, accusing them of causing monetary disorder in Europe.[37] In Brussels, he let it be understood that if he failed to get the devaluation agreement, Mitterrand might revert to the "other policy."

Where Delors had demanded a major German revaluation, he had finally to content himself with a 2.5 percent devaluation for the franc, the mark rising by 5.5 percent. To accompany devaluation, the French government would be obliged to extend the policy of austerity, not for a few months, but for years. To carry out this policy Delors believed he must be not only prime minister but also have the economics and finance portfolios, like Raymond Barre under Giscard.

This gesture of distrust toward Mitterrand's intimates Bérégovoy and Fabius was a tactical error. Delors, they charged, was "too greedy." Besides, he had no following in the Socialist party. He was a late comer, the brains behind the policies of Gaullist prime minister Chaban-Delmas. Mitterrand listened. He did not feel comfortable with Delors, and disliked his frequent offers to resign when decisions went against him. For a day, Bérégovoy may have hoped to be prime minister. Mauroy prepared his formal letter of resignation, which he delivered to the president on March 22. Half an hour after leaving the Matignon he was back. At the last minute, Mitterrand had decided to name him prime minister again.

By March 1983, Mitterrand should probably have taken the advice given him by his image artists to get rid of a prime minister unsuited to the new dispensation. The president's difficulty was that he did not have a candidate available who could assume the symbolism of the new policy—and Mitterrand was perhaps not certain exactly what the new policy was to be. He had thought of Delors and rejected him. Louis Mermaz, an old Mitterrand friend who was president of the National Assembly, was rather lackluster. Pierre Bérégovoy was loyal if not exciting, but he had been an advocate of "the other policy" until the end. So had Laurent Fabius, who according to most accounts had only changed his mind in the decisive last week of the crisis. Besides, he was young and needed more experience; he had never headed a major ministry. Michel Rocard was not to be trusted, a choice of last resort. Mauroy was faithful, diligent, honest . . . and when his usefulness was ended he could be trusted to go quietly.

The new austerity plan, still called *rigueur*, was designed to sponge up the excess demand which the government's earlier measures had continued to spill into the economy. It aimed at equilibrium in the balance of payments in two years — and in so doing accepted what the Socialists had violently rejected two years earlier — low growth or none. Buying power was siphoned off by a ten percent obligatory loan figured as a surcharge on income tax (for households paying more than 5,000 francs in tax), a surtax of one percent on income, taxes on alcohol and tobacco destined to refloat social security (Bérégovoy had already set a twenty franc per day fee for hospital stays in November 1982), and higher electricity and gas prices. Railroad tickets and telephone rates were raised by eight percent in April, instead of the habitual rises later in the year. The state also scaled back or delayed its outlays by twenty-four billion francs and took some measures to encourage savings.

The most visible and instantly irritating new measure was a ban on the purchase of foreign currency, limiting tourist expenses to 2,000 francs per adult per year, with the use of credit cards abroad restricted to business trips. In a country where vacations are sacred and every year millions plan to travel abroad, this irruption of state power into private family planning dramatized the question of the government's foresight, planning, and honesty. An already skeptical public had watched Mauroy saying "all the stoplights are green" and "there is no secret plan for more austerity in the files." If that was not exactly what he said or what he meant, that is what people retained. After a year of semi-rigor explained as a parenthesis there had come a new crisis, a third devaluation of the franc, new taxes, and austerity without a visible end.

If the economic policy adopted in June 1982 involved long-term austerity, why had the government not explained this to the country? If the policy of March 1983 was new, people wanted to know how it was to be distinguished from the old one, and how long it would continue. Those already hostile to the government found the confusion of March 1983 just one more example of incompetence, and said so loudly. A leading Paris Socialist remembers: "We didn't admit to ourselves that the changes of 1982 were real. In effect, we were lying to the country, which was much too smart not to see it." Mauroy's satisfaction rating in the SOFRES poll fell from forty-five percent to thirty-three percent between March and May.

Before the crisis of March 1983 it had been possible for some Socialists to think that the economic constraints weighing on France were temporary and contingent, to be conquered by bold measures and a firm will to prevail against all difficulties. The great lesson of March was that a middle-sized capitalist country with a network of economic and political ties to its neighbors in the European Community could ignore or shake off these ties only at extreme peril both economic and political – in fact, could not shake them off at all. Once the lesson sank in, only the Communists could be found to dispute it.

Mitterrand himself may not have understood this completely at first; there is some evidence that he continued to hope that an improvement in the Bank of France's reserves would permit him to go back to the "other policy" later in 1983.[38] But by early June Mitterrand began to adopt the new dispensation as his own. When in September 1982 he had mysteriously declared, "I do not make socialism my Bible," he had not specified what new scriptures he had adopted. On June 8, 1983 he declared, "There is no other possible policy," and admitted that mistakes had been made. "It's true, perhaps we were dreaming in 1981."[39]

Slowly, the country began to believe that the new economic severity was a real change and not a patch. That did not make it more palatable to Socialists. Jean Poperen, number two man in the PS, attacked the government: "Jacques Delors has hit the wrong target again. He has undertaken a program of classic deflation, while making it easy for entrepreneurs, bosses, and farmers, who would never vote Socialist. He demands the most from salaried workers, specialized workers, white collar workers, [who were] the support and the electorate of François Mitterrand in May 1981."[40]

This was a single-mindedly political discourse. Other Socialists began openly to admit their failure to understand the workings of the economy. Looking about them for a familiar conceptual framework to explain the setback and to discern the outlines of the future, they found little guidance. Was socialism *à la française* to be nothing more than any policy conducted by a government composed of Socialists? Individuals, party, prime minister, president – everyone began to search for some larger meaning, and came up with diverse answers.

SURVIVORS IN THE ICE AGE

To understand the confusion and dejection in Socialist ranks after the disappointments of 1981-1983, we must look at the changes in the intellectual climate that had nourished and conditioned the French Socialist revival. The socialism of François Mitterrand's PS relied on a conception of the Left profoundly affected by the intellectual climate that had set in after World War II.

From the Liberation until the early 1970s the winds of political and intellectual fashion in France had blown steadily from the Left. The ideological climate turned in the mid-1970s, though as often happens with climatic change it was not immediately recognized. In 1981 the Socialists could think their triumph the natural culmination of a long struggle by the Left. In reality, Socialist victory was the belated result of causes that were ceasing to operate, a fact the Socialists were slow and exceedingly reluctant to discover.

The PS that Mitterrand took over in 1971 had no unitary ideology, but all its members drew on the traditions of the Left. Some of them retained the SFIO's deep suspicion of the Communists. Others, themselves ex-Communists, knew that party too well to trust it. Mitterrand himself was a pragmatic anti-Communist who believed in the necessity of working with the PCF. Only the CERES (composing about one quarter of the PS in 1971-1975) was philo-Communist, though it rejected Communist organizational ideas. Building a new party on the ruins of an SFIO largely discredited by its opportunism and competing actively with the PCF within the framework of their alliance, Mitterrand's PS needed to refurbish its leftist rhetoric. Advocacy of nationalizations, denunciation of capitalism at home and abroad were obligatory. Competition with the PCF also obliged the PS to craft an ideology of its own. The doctrine of the "class front," bringing together salaried workers of all descriptions to oppose wicked capitalists domestic and foreign, was set against the Communist doctrine of the class struggle.

The leftist rhetoric of the PS necessarily drew on the common fund of Left ideas in France, and particularly on those enunciated by the intelligentsia since World War II. For many years after 1944, a French intellectual was almost by definition a man of the Left. Intellectuals took as their concern what society should be and was not, and the model that most of them adopted in 1944-1945 was the Soviet one. Not until the mid-1970s did this intelligentsia admit that the Soviet experiment had created a society that offered nothing to the West, and at the price of immense injustice and suffering. Admiration for the Soviet Union and for Russian communism might or might not mean admiration for or membership in the French Communist party, might or might not mean uncritical praise for Soviet actions in all fields. Its lowest common denominator was a belief in the purgative and creative powers of revolution, the elemental force born in France in 1789, reborn in Petrograd in 1917.

Paris, with a few thousand intellectuals centering on St. Germain des Prés on the Left Bank, has always been the epicenter of intellectual opinion-making. This Paris mandarinate of the upper intelligentsia also influences hundreds of thousands of lesser opinion-makers throughout the country, not least in the lower intelligentsia typified by secondary schoolteachers. The powerful Fédération d'Education Nationale (FEN) groups among its half-million members three independent teachers' unions – primary and secondary school teachers and university professors. The latter two were and are dominated organizationally by Communists. Not all or even a majority of teachers were Communists, but the vast majority of them were and remain on the left. Like *haute couture* from the Paris *salons* descending to the mass garment trade, opinion fashioned in Paris spread to the provinces.

Leftists of all stripes agreed in the early postwar years that a gradual and reformist course was impossible for France. "A serious effort at economic renewal would have such broad social and political consequences that only the partisans of revolutionary change could accept them," wrote a reproving critic of Raymond Aron's *Opium of the Intellectuals* in 1954.[41] For most leftists, therefore, the Communist party remained the only agent of change. The parties which vied with the Communists were in their eyes either hopelessly bourgeois (that much used Marxist obscenity) or, in the case of the Socialist party, about to betray the cause of the Left. The leftist language used by the SFIO in 1945-1946 did not convince many Frenchmen attracted by Communism. The opportunist practices of Mollet's SFIO repelled them throughout the years of the Fourth Republic and well beyond.

Uncritical admiration of the Soviet Union for its role in World War II was commonplace in Europe until the onset of the Cold War, and Communist parties won appreciable percentages of the vote in a number of countries throughout the 1940s. But a powerful leftist ideology bolstering a massive Communist vote persisted thereafter only in France and Italy. In the United States and in most of Western Europe optimism about the Soviet Union faded as formerly innocent or willful ignorance confronted Soviet brutality in bringing the Eastern European countries under their domination. Defectors brought out more and more details on the horrors of the 1930s, now being repeated in the postwar world.

Why did French intellectuals refuse to credit testimony that so impressed their peers elsewhere? There are a number of explanations, but the root cause was a passionate desire to believe in the thaumaturgic October revolution. That revolution, incarnate in the Soviet Union, could perhaps make mistakes, thought the French intellectual. It could not commit crimes – or else the world made no sense. This deformation of reason into rationalization forged an almost impenetrable armor against unpleasant reality. The armor easily repelled information printed in the conservative or gradualist press, treated axiomatically as disinformation serving the ruling class. Anyone who lost the faith and wrote of his disillusion in the bourgeois press was necessarily an enemy, a traitor, had "sold out." Concentration camps were education camps, and victims of repression were at best casualties in a class war that was by definition pitiless, or more likely criminals rightly punished.

Communists best exemplified this philosophy, but in the immediate postwar years it possessed almost all those who considered themselves to be on the left. The Soviet Union, and in France, the Communist party, might err—but one should not dwell on it. In the polarized world of the Cold War they were the only sources of hope. "We must not destroy hope in Billancourt," said Jean-Paul Sartre in 1952 (the Renault auto workers standing for the proletariat in general).

The year 1956, bringing Nikita Khrushchev's secret speech and the Hungarian revolt, should have marked a definitive change in intellectual fellow-traveling, whose essence was revolution-worship. But revolutions could be found outside Europe, and many left-wingers reinforced their belief by support of the Algerian revolt. They also discovered the Third World. Its hundreds of millions of impoverished non-whites had been exploited by white Europeans and North Americans; they must for this reason be purer and better than their oppressors. Salvation might be found in the blood of their revolutions. Fidel Castro's Cuba became a beacon, together with the abortive revolutions which Castro and Che Guevara supported in Venezuela and Bolivia.

Unwilling to renounce their central tenet of revolutionary salvation, French intellectuals thus enlarged their devotion from Muscovite monotheism to a pantheon of revolutionary causes. Most of these were in any case supported by Moscow. Where they were not (the Algerian case), this troubled sincere Communists but not the fellow-travelers. The PCF attacked French government policy in Algeria, but left domestic support for Algerian liberation to non-Communist leftists.

By multiplying the number of revolutionary causes, revolution-worshipers deflected the critical attention they might otherwise have directed to the Soviet Union. After Sino-Soviet disagreement became increasingly apparent in the mid-1960s, some revolutionary purists tilted toward China. But most looked away from the problem, concentrating on a cause backed by both China and the Soviet Union. In Vietnam a revolutionary government that had already defeated French imperialism was struggling against "the center of world imperialism," the United States. Here was the perfect cause for the French Left, all tendencies combined. It offered the chance to assuage their residual guilt as Frenchmen for France's battle against the Viet Minh, to overlook Sino-Soviet problems, to support an ex-colonial people in its revolutionary struggle, and to execrate the United States.

Left-wing opinion was consolidated and even comforted in the mid-1960s by a new foreign policy consensus with the Right. Denunciations of Soviet policy and practices in the moderate or conservative press had not touched

Left opinion; such things were well known to serve the class interests of the bourgeoisie. But the intellectuals were not insensible to agreement with their own views. When Charles de Gaulle's government spoke well of the Soviet Union, or attacked American policy in Vietnam or Latin America, left-wingers concurred. Even the bourgeois French government, they told themselves, has seen the light; the worst anti-Communists are isolated and in France, at least, powerless.

The left climate of opinion in the 1960s survived the move of many non-Communist leftists away from the direct political engagement of an earlier decade. The new intellectual cults springing up around the structuralism of Claude Lévi-Strauss, the semiology of Roland Barthes, the post-Freudianism of Jacques Lacan, and the deconstructionism of Jacques Derrida attracted the left-wing intelligentsia, but its members were not explicitly bound to or engaged in political action by virtue of their interest in these new movements, as they had been earlier with Sartre and the *engagé* movement. Many of these intellectuals were not so much cured of revolution-worship as partially distracted from it.

Decreased political engagement on the Left Bank did not mean a change in the direction of political opinion, and the most admired intellectuals remained men of the Left, ready to sign manifestoes for important causes. Since the most prominent cause in international affairs during the 1960s was Vietnam, where a large national consensus reigned, the left climate and its revolution-worship continued throughout the decade substantially unchanged.

Events in the 1960s nevertheless prepared the way for a change in climate. The French people began to feel the benefit of economic changes fostered by the fallen Fourth Republic and pursued under de Gaulle. By 1960 French industrial production (in 1938 still at the 1911 level) had increased 242 percent over pre-World War II levels. By 1965 it had risen to 310 percent and by 1970 to 410 percent. Personal consumption went up accordingly; only twenty-one percent of French households possessed an automobile in 1953. By 1972 fifty-nine percent of households did, and seventy-two percent ten years later. Eleven times as many households had refrigerators in 1972 as in 1954, ownership of washing machines increased sevenfold in the same period to sixty percent.

The rise of consumerism left revolutionary intellectuals unhappy and suspicious. Consumer goods, thought the left intellectuals, were becoming the new opium of the people; the bourgeoisie was corrupting the toiling masses with radios and vacuum cleaners. Caught in the race of *métro-boulot-dodo* (subway-job-sleep) to pay the installments on his automobile and appliances, the worker could lose interest in revolutionary change.

A revolution – or something that for a moment looked like one – came in 1968, sparked by the discontent of largely middle- class students. When the workers belatedly joined in, they demanded not revolution but better pay. Although de Gaulle's prime minister Georges Pompidou skillfully blamed the Communist party for the fright suffered by right-leaning France, May 1968 had in fact taken the Communists by surprise. As confused as the government by the unexpected situation, the PCF reacted at first with shock and hostility.

Some young left-wingers intoxicated by the spirit of 1968 took careful note of this Communist reaction. They found in it fresh evidence that the version of Communism preached by the Soviet Union and its dependent parties had strayed from revolutionary grace. The Chinese example with its dramatic new Cultural Revolution was more to their taste. Some of these Maoists were aided in gaining a larger notoriety by the aging Sartre, now disabused of Soviet-style Communism but still obsessed by the revolution. Usage began to distinguish between *gauche* (left) and *gauchiste* (leftist), i.e. those who criticized the Soviet and sometimes even the Chinese revolutions. This criticism of course antedated the Sino-Soviet split and 1968, but had been confined to small groups. May 1968, however, was the *gauchistes'* own movement and therefore made an immediate impact on French left intellectuals. The new leftists helped to break the taboo that had forbidden any rigorous criticism of the Soviet Union and the PCF.

The events in France of May 1968 not unnaturally seized the attention of the French left-wingers at the expense of events in a country far away. The Dubcek experiment of reform Communism and its suppression by the Soviets evoked a mixed and complicated reaction on the French Left.[42] Before August 1968 the Czech reformers had troubled parts of the non-Communist Left by their insufficiently Marxist language: they praised the "bourgeois" values of individual liberty instead of those of some potentially "pure" revolution. The suppression of Czech reformist Communism evoked at best mitigated indignation on the non-Communist Left. The PCF reacted to the Soviet invasion by announcing its severe disapproval, which was almost instantly watered down to mere disapproval and followed by rapid acceptance of the Soviet fiction that a settlement of the Czech question had been negotiated and not imposed.

PCF reactions to Soviet behavior in Czechoslovakia posed problems both political and ideological for Mitterrand's new PS. The visceral anti-Communism of the SFIO had proved a handicap, and alliance with the PCF was now a necessity. But aside from this political requirement, the leaders and militants of the new PS could not fail to be affected by the ambient leftism. Particularly because they had abandoned Cold War tactics and were now competing for leftist and Communist votes on grounds staked out by the

Communists, Socialists had to adopt a more leftist language, and in the vast majority of cases had come to believe in it.

The aftermath of the Czech events was a test for the new Socialists. They could not be comfortable with Soviet actions and PCF reactions. However, the 1972 Common Program gave them a powerful motive to believe or pretend that their new ally was sincere in "disapproving" the Soviet action in Czechoslovakia. Mitterrand felt compelled to keep a leftist, parallel course with the PCF, and to proclaim it a democratic and trustworthy partner in the opposition and in future government.

The Prague spring nevertheless threw its shadow over Mitterrand's program. If the PCF did not genuinely condemn Soviet behavior in Czechoslovakia, and backed Husak's repression in Prague, what kind of democracy did it want for France? This was a question too uncomfortable to face. Proclaiming support for the Czech exiles and resistance to normalization, Mitterrand and most of his friends also continued to pretend against much evidence that the PCF was not backsliding on Czechoslovakia. The events of 1968 in Czechoslovakia thus did not rapidly change the attitudes of many *gauchistes* or Communists, and Socialists had their own blinkers.

In 1973 the coup in Chile against Salvador Allende's government gave the Left a new martyr and a new occasion for hatred of western imperialism. Events in Chile comforted all those on the Left who saw the U.S. as the main devil in the world. Yet they did not suffice to shore up revolution-worship in its old function as a prop for pro-Sovietism. Slowly the old attitudes were changing; the once bright image of the Soviet Union was now tarnished by too many revelations, too much criticism by Chinese or dissident Communists. Post-1968 Czechoslovakia was far too dreary, discouraging, and repressive to suggest even the relative hope of Kadar's post-1956 Hungary. The Soviet Union under Brezhnev did not glitter with hope; it was instead a consumption-oriented society offering very little to consume.

THE SOLZHENITSYN EFFECT

The seizure by the KGB of the manuscript of Alexander Solzhenitsyn's *The Gulag Archipelago* in September 1973 was the first event in a revision of attitudes in the French left intelligentsia that would occupy the rest of the decade. *The Gulag Archipelago* had a catalytic effect on the French intellectual Left. A rapidly popular phrase, "the Solzhenitsyn effect," denoted the considerable controversy and lasting impression the book engendered. Perhaps nowhere outside France could a book have such striking and rapid effect — but one must add in the same breath that this same France had ignored a very long list of earlier books — often with less literary merit and detail, and by lesser figures, but making essentially the same point.

The French Communist party sensed a new spirit of anti-Sovietism in the air and quickly opened an attack designed to bully the non-Communist Left into a conformist account of Solzhenitsyn's new work, targeting first the left weekly news magazine *Le Nouvel Observateur*, then *Le Monde*, and finally the PS itself. The PCF campaign continued amid great verbal violence into the early spring of 1974. Mitterrand worried about the political effect of an anti-Soviet campaign. Although some of his friends were willing to attack the Soviet Union, he preferred a careful dosage of tut-tutting mixed with hope addressed to the USSR and still more to his Communist ally. In early February 1974, just before the Soviet state bundled Solzhenitsyn onto an airplane and shipped him off to exile, he wrote: "I am persuaded that the most important thing is not what Solzhenitsyn says but that he can say it."[43] What Mitterrand really thought about the matter is undiscoverable, in this as in so much. What he was repeating was the new Socialist line: the French Communists have changed and so has the Soviet Union, even if much remains to be improved; but in any case we Socialists are democrats.

The publication of *The Gulag Archipelago* did not change left opinion in a thunder clap. Witness *Le Monde's* cautious treatment of the book in its June 1974 review: a double-page spread in the review pages bracketed Solzhenitsyn's book with two others under the sub-title, "three books, using indictment, satire, or witness launch anathemas against totalitarianism" (nuances of distaste here). On the other page appeared a discussion of four other books, two written by French Communists, subtitled "positive approaches to Soviet reality." Discussing this and other early reactions in France to Solzhenitsyn's book, the Sovietologist Alain Besançon concluded gloomily in the summer of 1974 that nothing had changed in the French Left's refusal to see Soviet reality.[44]

Change came in 1975. April saw the complete victory of the Communist cause in Vietnam and in Cambodia. Post-Watergate America appeared strangely weakened, powerless to aid its friends in Asia or in Angola, where Cuban troops helped the National Liberation Movement to triumph. The European Security Conference met in Helsinki, confirming the borders of the Soviet empire, but also dramatizing the question of human rights within them. The crisis in Portugal sharpened, with a threat of Communist takeover that continued until September. The Soviet Union continued its pressure on the European Communist parties for a regional meeting designed as a pendant to the Security Conference, where it hoped to condemn Chinese heterodoxy and bring the Europeans into line. And in Italy, where the Communist party had taken the lead in distinguishing its positions from those of the Soviet party and in resisting the conference, regional elections saw a sudden bound of the Communist vote from twenty-eight to thirty-two percent.

By the end of the year new noises were emerging from the French Communist party. Secretary general Marchais was persuaded to adopt a partial imitation of the Italian approach to Communism, a shift encouraged by Italian electoral success and the failure of the Sovietophile Portuguese party to take power. Meanwhile, French left-wing intellectuals were excited by the publication of a diatribe against the Soviet Union by André Glucksmann, a young ex-Maoist and frequent contributor to *Les Temps Modernes*.

The contribution of ex-Maoists to the attack on the Soviet Union is a notable one. Glucksmann, Bernard-Henri Lévy and other young writers who rapidly became known by the collective title of "the new philosophers" had been led by reflections on 1968 and their initial excitement over the Cultural Revolution to a deeper criticism of Stalinism. Their faith in the Cultural Revolution had also waned (mandarin-hazing being essentially un-French).

As it became more fashionable on the Left to criticize the Soviet Union and even Marxism, more and more disquieting news arrived from the Far East. In Vietnam the victors were not behaving well. In Cambodia the Khmer Rouge had begun a systematic and insane campaign of genocide against its own people that cost millions of lives. As the news seeped back to Europe the Left refused to believe it, then began to cede before the overwhelming evidence.

Solzhenitsyn had won, on the charnel ground of Pnom-Penh. Under the hammer-blows of repeated disillusionment, non-Communist left intellectuals finally began to lose their belief in revolution—Russian, Chinese, Cuban, or Cambodian—as the continuation of French history and example for the future. Revolution had been shown up as Cyclops, a brutal one-eyed eater of men. Even the myth of the French Revolution could now be re-examined, no longer "a bloc," in Clemenceau's famous phrase, but only a series of events where violence had often not paved but obstructed the way to a better society.

The Communist party had done its best to block change by attacking Solzhenitsyn's defenders. The 1974 presidential campaign then demanded a stress on unity, which gave way in the autumn to a violent attack against the electoral encroachments of the Socialists. And in yet another tactic, the PCF suddenly emerged in late summer 1975 from an anti-Socialist stage and moved almost without transition into its Eurocommunist phase. One of the first signals was its discovery that there were indeed concentration camps in the USSR.

There was a logic behind these successive shifts. They began with an attempt to keep the Socialist alliance and simultaneously please the Soviet Union. Next followed a campaign to tell Communist voters too much impressed by Mitterrand that the Socialists were only momentary and untrustworthy allies, followed thereafter by an attempt to patch up the alliance (at least for the municipal elections of 1977) by imitating the successful tactics of the Italian Communists. In all this the implicit Communist assumption was that the electorate and left-wing public opinion was so much clay which it could mold as it wished — an assumption reasonably justified by past experience. Instead, the shift to Eurocommunism weakened the party. By dropping its automatic adulation of the USSR, the leadership permitted and sometimes encouraged those numerous party members who had doubts about the Soviet Union to speak out, both in party and in public meetings. A member of the Politburo even shook the hand of the exiled Soviet dissident Leonid Plyushch at a Paris meeting organized by the non-Communist Left.

The opportunistic electoral tactic of Eurocommunism could be justified by success, but as parliamentary elections approached, the Communist leaders were forced to examine the nature of a future victory. Deciding that entry into government with the Socialists meant junior partnership on unequal terms, they broke the alliance.

Having abandoned the idea of immediate electoral gains, the party had little use for the Eurocommunism it had adopted to achieve them. Political wisdom might have suggested that rapid switches from almost unconditional pro-Sovietism to Eurocommunism and back again would end by alienating advocates of both policies and confuse large numbers of present or possible future Communists. Political wisdom was however in short supply. Jean Kanapa, architect of French Eurocommunism, died in September 1978. Shortly thereafter PCF leader Marchais declared that the balance-sheet of Soviet achievements was "in general positive." By early 1980 Marchais had backslid the entire way from Eurocommunism to approval of the Soviet invasion of Afghanistan. And in 1981 the PCF approved General Jaruzelski's crackdown on Solidarity.

Pro-Soviet French Communists had been outraged by Eurocommunism, but party members harboring some doubts about the Soviet Union were probably more numerous. Once the party admitted that the Soviet Union was highly imperfect a taboo had been broken, and taboos, like Humpty-Dumpty, are hard to mend. The anger of many in the party ranks at the PCF's sabotage of the Union of the Left in 1978 did not abate. The PCF score in the European elections of June 1979 remained at twenty percent, but two years later a quarter of the Communist electorate abandoned Marchais to vote for Mitterrand in the first round of the presidential elections. The hemorrhage thus begun continued in 1984 and 1986. With its electoral losses, the PCF also increasingly lost the capacity to bully the Left into silence, even as admiration of the Soviet Union was dropping to an historic low.

Two interlinked ideas central to the French Left — the cult of revolution and admiration for the Soviet Union — thus underwent a number of attacks within a relatively brief period. The desire to believe had resisted the assaults of Khrushchev's secret speech and the Hungarian revolt, and had rationalized and trivialized the suppression of the Prague reformers. The edifice of belief was battered but had resisted. It could not hold against the fresh battering of the 1970s, against an accumulation of attacks striking it from all directions. The myth of the Soviet Union had been shaken by Maoist China and by the *gauchisme* of 1968; the justification of revolution was called into question by Solzhenitsyn and the horrors of Cambodia; and the surrogates for Soviet revolution were devalued by the Khmer horrors and the collapse of the Cultural Revolution with the fall of the Gang of Four. All these and the other influences already mentioned conjoined within a few years: it was too much.

French reaction to the Soviet invasion of Afghanistan in December 1979 provides a remarkable example of new attitudes. Afghanistan had never occupied a high rank in French geographic consciousness — as it had in that of Britain, for example. If there was a country in the world that for France exemplified the phrase "a small country far away of which we know very little," Afghanistan was it. The old leftist mentality would have had no trouble rationalizing the struggle of the Afghan Moslems as the retrograde battle of feudal forces against progressive modernity. This was precisely the line taken by the Communist party — and it proved unacceptable to the French Left. Afghanistan became and remained a burning topic in the consciousness of the Left, and the PCF defense of Soviet actions there did the party far more harm than it may have reckoned. Probably the Afghan issue carries with it in Left consciousness an extra weight, guilty awareness of previous issues to which it had reacted inadequately.

By the spring of 1977 the historian François Furet noted that the criticism of Soviet totalitarianism and more generally of all power calling itself Marxist had ceased to be the monopoly of the Right and was becoming a central theme for reconsideration on the Left as well. "The important thing is that Left culture, once it has brought itself to reflect on the facts, which is to say the disaster that is the Communist experiment in the twentieth century, is led in the name of its own values to criticize its own ideology, its interpretations, hopes, rationalizations."[45]

The PS could hardly ignore the changes taking place in the Left culture; neither did it speedily embark on the process Furet described. The reasons were entirely political. Until the March 1978 parliamentary elections the PS was busy being "unitary for two," fending off Communist accusations that rightist deviation in the PS had provoked the break in the Union of the Left. Polls consistently showed a potential majority for the Left coalition in 1978 despite Communist behavior, and the Socialists still needed the PCF. François Mitterrand had no time to re-examine first principles, an undertaking potentially subversive to his claim that the Communists were a fit coalition partner in government.

After the defeat in 1978 Mitterrand's whole strategy was called into question by Michel Rocard, with the charge that current policy was "archaic." Mitterrand won out, but the price of his victory was a renewed alliance with the left-wing CERES faction, accompanied by a kind of official mindlessness toward new challenges both economic and ideological, summed up in his followers' slogan "we are all archaic." Paralyzed by Rocard's challenge in 1979 and his ambition to be the party's candidate in 1981, the PS organization stood pat. It looked to Mitterrand, and Mitterrand chose to be a sphinx.

*   *   *   *   *   *   *   *   *   *   *   *

Having ignored all warnings by Rocard's friends and other intellectuals that the Left climate had changed, Mitterrand seemed justified by his triumphant election. In the days after there was much puzzled press comment about the lack of popular excitement, but no one suggested that the shift in attitudes would go on to bedevil the Socialists throughout their term in office. The elections seemed to have taken place entirely on the political plane to which François Mitterrand had devoted his entire attention, with no reference to the intellectuals and their changed ideas.

The Socialists thus entered office too little aware of new problems, whether ideological or economic. Three years later, they had found more sharp critics than defenders among intellectuals on the Left. In July 1983 government spokesman Max Gallo called for an outpouring of intellectual support for the now embattled government. Gallo, himself a respected novelist and historian, was treated to a series of letters in *Le Monde* explaining why intellectuals could not give a support they now found comparable to that of tame intellectuals in totalitarian states.[46]

Ideological change did not cause the economic woes of the Mauroy government, which would have existed even if nothing had affected the intelligentsia. PCF criticism of government policies in 1982-1984 would have had much greater impact on the government and the Socialist party, however, if the PCF had not been electorally weakened and intellectually discredited. (In fact, independence from the PCF might not have been possible at all.) Ideological change did help to precipitate the electoral collapse of the PCF in 1981-1986, though sociological change also obviously played a major role. The change in the intellectual climate affected the Socialists in more subtle ways than it did the Communists. The latter were devastated by the disintegration of belief in the Soviet Union. The analogous effect afflicting the Socialists was loss of belief in the curative power of revolution and in the watered-down Socialist version of this idea expressed as "breaking with capitalism," *changement de société* (a change of society, not just in it). In this fashion, banal economic difficulties brought about by the imprudent but essentially Keynesian policies of 1981 (and not by the more Socialist nationalization policy) suggested to both the country at large and many of the Socialists themselves that their program had failed.

The Socialists (and particularly Mitterrand, with his convert's glibness) had taken insufficient account of the structural causes of the economic crisis, but also of the new political agnosticism that replaced revolution-worship. Their beliefs of the 1970s had asserted the possibility of a profound change that was never called revolution but owed a good deal to pre-Marxist and Marxist ideas of revolution. Once the Socialists discovered that the measures of 1981-1982 could not reverse unemployment or restore prosperity, disillusionment set in, encountering and fitting well with the new and ideologically disabused ideas abroad in the country. A non-ideological party might have been less affected by failure.

By 1984 the French Socialists had a certain sense that their ideology had run dry. The Communist alliance had ceased after mid-1984 to guarantee a Left majority and was increasingly offensive on ideological grounds to an influential intellectual community that was now anti-Left. With the resurgent Gaullists and UDF baying at their heels, abandoned by the opinion-makers, with an economy unresponsive and ailing, the Socialist government faced a seeming infinity of problems.

LEGISLATION AND ITS DISCONTENTS

By late 1983 many French Socialists began to find the institutions of the Fifth Republic an unexpected burden. Before Mitterrand's election they had distrusted a presidentialized system designed permanently to exclude them. In June 1981, the guarantee of five years in control of the state seemed a marvelous dream realized. At that time, they were still guided by the aims expressed in their 1977 language for the revision of the Common Program:

To break the domination of big capital and set in motion a new economic and social policy, rejecting the policy of the present government, the government will progressively carry out the transfer to the collectivity of the most important means of production and financial instruments now in the hands of dominant capitalist groups.[47]

Two years after they had attempted to put these brave words into action some Socialists yearned for the irresponsibility of the Fourth Republic, which would have dismissed them from office after the setbacks of 1983, leaving behind the monument of their legislation. In two years the Socialists had introduced laws concerning almost all of the promises Mitterrand had made in 1981. As *Le Monde's* chief political writer noted: "Concentrating so great a number of reforms in the first months of the *septennat* — nationalization, decentralization, workers' rights — so-called structural reforms, the Left rapidly exhausted itself: suddenly it found itself without projects."[48]

In one sense the Socialists had done their work. In any event they were weary and without further ideas they could call their own, just at the point when they had to adopt unwelcome economic policies.

The existence of these temptations to lay down the burden exemplified a widely-shared and formalistic conception of government as the power of prescriptive law — one that reached back to the great Revolution and the celebrated night of August 4, 1789, when the whole fabric of feudal France came crashing down all at once. Yearning for the freedom of the Fourth Republic bore the impress of the long years of opposition, the notion that the Left was the force of innovation, the Right that of administration. Not all Socialists shared this view, of course, and least among them the tenant of the Elysée palace, who was intensely conscious of the fact that his lease ran for seven years.

The myth of the Revolution and experience in short-lived Left governments of the Third and Fourth Republic suggested that the power of the Left to alter France lay in massive doses of legislation, rapidly injected. It followed also from the myth of 1789 that those favorably affected by such legislation would support the party or forces that had introduced it (although the evil forces of money always intervened to deprive them of power.)

The Socialists were therefore surprised and disappointed, as they watched their popularity steadily diminish, to find that their laws and measures weighed so lightly in the balance of popular approval. Here was naivete. Apart from actions that put money immediately into people's pockets (but raised the danger of inflation), many of their measures were too technical, complicated, or far-reaching to affect or even influence the general public in the short run. Decentralization had no daily effect on the average citizen, nor did legal reform. Some legislation on civil liberties actually became unpopular — notably abolition of the death penalty and restriction of police freedom to stop and search. As crime mounted, it did no good for professors to demonstrate in the pages of *Le Monde* that its cause was not abolition of the death penalty but rather deep seated sociological problems. It was far easier for the opposition to charge that the Left government was soft on crime.

The mass of substantive legislation that had occupied the attention of government and parliament in 1981-1982 was also slow to excite enthusiasm. Announcement of new legislation was usually followed by a long parliamentary debate, and many months later by a brief notice that the law was actually in effect. Whereas the nationalizations announced in 1981 and carried out in 1982 occupied the complete attention of the managements affected, they made much less difference to the workers involved, and no obvious difference at all to those not immediately affected.

Against the strenuous efforts of the opposition, the government enacted extensive new labor laws. They were designed to increase workers' ability to discuss issues with management, oblige small employers with fewer than fifty workers to admit unions into their enterprises, and to institute annual obligatory firm-level wage bargaining. Separate enterprise committees on health, safety, and working conditions were amalgamated, giving the new committees greater powers, with greater rights of expression at the shop level. In the public sector, workers' representatives were to be represented on the board of directors.

The Auroux laws were backed most strongly by the CFDT (Confédération Française Démocratique du Travail), the formerly Catholic federation which had "deconfessionalized" itself in 1964, first moving left, then moderating its stance. The least ideological labor confederation, Force Ouvrière (FO), opposed the Auroux laws, fearing that factory councils would be dominated by Communists and become so many factory "soviets." The Communist-controlled CGT thought the laws were not strong enough.

Because the unions were no more in agreement under a Socialist government than they had been under the Right, they did not and could not work easily with it, and the government ended by talking to the unions in only the most formal sense. FO chief André Bergeron remarked icily, "Close consultation (*concertation*) is not just for idle chatter," while Edmond Maire, head of the CFDT, who was apparently not even informed in advance of the austerity measures of March 1983, noted (in 1987) that the CFDT found it easier to talk to leaders of the Right than those of the PS.[49] The CGT was on its best behavior at first, but became less and less restrained after March 1983. Although polls continued to show that workers favored the government more than did any other social class, their union representatives were not to be found in the cheering section.

If the government had been dealing with a unitary union system like the German DGB or the LO in the Scandinavian countries some of these frictions would certainly have been reduced. As it was, close cooperation was a near impossibility both for suspicious unions and a government wary of the several union leaders and anxious not to show itself too close to any of them.

The other major reform of 1981-1982 was decentralization, proclaimed by Interior and Decentralization Minister Defferre as "the most important issue of the president's term." Not all Socialists were enthusiastic decentralizers — there was an implicit contradiction between increasing state power by socialist measures and lessening it by devolving powers on local government. But precisely this contradiction appealed to a composite majority in the party. Some of them (particularly Rocardians) distrusted the Jacobin state. Others thought there was no real contradiction in practice between democratizing from below and increasing state control of the economy, while decentralization could in any case serve to correct some undesirable statist aspects of their own policy. Socialist advocates took pride in undoing the centralizing work of Napoleon and the Bourbon kings. Yet their reform, however praiseworthy, was relatively limited in scope, extremely technical in nature, and decidedly unlikely to elicit either enthusiasm or gratitude from the larger public, for which immediate results from decentralization were likely to appear in higher local taxes.

Here was the dilemma: immediate measures improving the lot of the socially disadvantaged affected a relatively small part of the population, which voted for the Left in any case. Once implemented, the new statutes aggravated the economic crisis, provoking an austerity that restricted further social legislation and increasingly collided with the pocketbook interests of the lower-middle and middle classes. Ideas on social, judicial, and governmental reform that conscientious citizens on the Left (and not the Left alone) had cherished over the years produced limited electoral resonance once they had been enacted into law.

Could the Socialist government have managed things otherwise, and would a more participatory variation of Left government have evoked greater enthusiasm and support? Certainly workers' enthusiasm even in 1981 was less than that displayed for the Popular Front. But enthusiasm in 1936 had taken the form of factory occupations, which scarcely aided the Blum government. It is easier to note that the Mitterrand government consulted too little and decreed too much than to know whether a more determined and skillful effort at participatory government would have made a major difference. Indeed, commenting on French Socialism's lack of integral ties with labor, a PS economist remarked wryly in a private conversation in 1987, "If we had had ties to the unions like those of the Labor party or the SPD, we would never have been able to do the things we had to do in 1983 and 1984."

The Socialists had entered into office in 1981 without a completely clear and unanimously held definition of socialism *à la française*. They held unrealistic expectations that their electorate would value as highly as they did the measures they promised and delivered. Despite the successful passage of much legislation, they disappointed their electors.

Nevertheless, if Left voters did not get all they expected, it was not the shortfall in genuine socialism that hurt the government worst. Mitterrand and the Socialist deputies owed their elections to the accident of an electorate more determined to reject Giscard and company than to choose socialism. Mitterrand's "sociological majority," the wage-earners who were the vast majority of French men and women, did not have a majority of workers. The Socialists had briefly constructed a majority which included a significant fraction of the middle class, and rapidly lost much of it again.

As noted above, the Socialists had excellent reasons to give priority to their core constituency. In the hubris of the first year they also quite unnecessarily provoked business and farmer organizations by favoring splinter groups thought to be pro- Socialist. Yet arrogance and a bias toward the underprivileged were not the principal reasons why they lost much of their temporary middle-class constituency. Much of it would have remained loyal to the choice made in 1981 only if the Socialists had been able to do everything right, making a rapid dent in unemployment, meanwhile cutting inflation and improving the economy. The mistakes and bad luck of 1981-1982 ended this possibility.

Voters also shift their loyalties in the short or long term according to their choice of alternatives. In Spain, the Socialist government of Felipe González has attempted to avoid some of the mistakes made by the French Socialists. González nevertheless owes his longevity in office in considerable part to the great confusion in the ranks of his conservative opposition. Margaret Thatcher has displayed a single-minded determination to stay the course she has set—but she owes her parliamentary majorities won in the general elections of 1983 and 1987 to the division of an opposition that collectively possesses a majority. In France, the conservative opposition rallied as early as 1982—after an initial stunned incredulity. A small majority of Frenchmen had not wanted conservatives to govern France forever, but the opposition still benefited from a cultural prejudice that held the politicians of the Right to be the natural forces of government. Naturally, the outs also benefited from the very French pleasure of savagely criticizing the ins.

Adopting a new free enterprise philosophy gilded by the 1983 upturn in the American economy and made relevant by the failures of the magic wand of Socialist *dirigisme*, the Right found a newly pleasing language to use with the French electorate. Jacques Chirac triumphed in every *arrondissement* in Paris in the 1983 municipal elections. A seemingly discredited Raymond Barre, his policies revalidated by reluctant Socialist imitation, moved up in the polls as Mauroy's ratings sank, and began to prepare himself for the challenge of the 1988 presidential race. Polls showed that an electorate grown doubtful of the Socialists was skeptical of the opposition's ability to do much better—but was nevertheless inclined to test its claims. By mid-1983, as the government grew visibly weary, the opposition in France—unlike that in Britain or Spain—increasingly appeared a viable alternative.

THE PROBLEMS OF PIERRE MAUROY

Weary and short of ideas the government might be, but under the Fifth Republic it had to persevere. It had squeaked past the test of the municipal elections, but everything else seemed to be going badly. An opposition press now in full cry and charging universal incompetence cheered on the numerous demonstrations of the late spring and summer of 1983: by farmers in Brittany and elsewhere, by hospital interns and clinic chiefs, medical students, small businessmen. The streets of Paris and numerous other cities were frequently blocked by the protesters. The pro-government papers spoke of "right-wing gangs," and some leading Socialists wondered if force might not be needed to break up demonstrations, while the rightist *Le Figaro* gleefully accused the government of seeing plots everywhere.

The period from spring 1983 to the change of prime ministers in July 1984 was a transitional period within Socialist government. The Socialists were attempting to understand the changes in policy which events had forced on them, trying to cope with an economy still in decline, an opposition on the rise, and an ideology in tatters. President and prime minister reacted differently to these problems. François Mitterrand had begun as early as September 1982, though hesitantly and with many contradictions, to take his distance from "socialism, which I do not take as my Bible."[50] His interest in "the other policy" in early 1983 was not necessarily proof of a diehard attachment to socialist ideas; one of the chief influences on him at that time was Jean Riboud of Schlumberger, who believed that French business needed an electric shock to waken it to competition. The very socialist Pierre Mauroy opposed the idea in part because he did not believe French business capable of responding to the challenge.

By mid-1983, Mitterrand was in search of a new theme. He wanted to give the lie to opposition charges of incompetence, to reassure the French that austerity would not last forever, and talk up growth as the way out of the nation's troubles. But he also knew that the high taxes needed to support the social costs of more than two million unemployed and of all the other expenses he had inherited or incurred had exasperated a middle class which thought itself pinched.

The sophisticated politician's eye roved over political successes achieved in other countries. Whatever the French president's opinion of Ronald Reagan, he saw that American tax cuts were popular. In June 1983 Mitterrand told a radio audience that the total burden of taxation and social security had gone from forty-two to forty-four percent, which was the outer limit. Meanwhile the Treasury wanted to raise social security contributions by another one percent, although with a tax credit to aid small taxpayers. To offset the general rise, the president opted for a surtax hitting big taxpayers, which risked bringing in too little. The budget announced for 1984 contained new surtaxes, continuation of the extra one percent tax for social security, and a rise in some value-added taxes.

An IFOP poll in autumn showed that sixty-three percent of those polled thought the government's economic record was negative. In mid-September 1983 Mitterrand went on television and showed himself the last of the Laffers. Announcing that too many taxes asphyxiated the economy and cut back tax income, he declared that the 1985 budget would have to come down by one percent at least. (In preparing the 1984 budget, Mauroy and Delors had assumed that fiscal pressure would unfortunately have to increase again in 1985.) Mitterrand had not adopted Reaganism, far from it, but he had shown that in searching for new ways to appeal to the nation he was not to be hemmed in by the boundaries of any doctrine.[51]

Mauroy had courageously taken the lead in difficult economic decisions both in June 1982 and early 1983. Now he was suffering from the stings of all the nettles he had grasped. The logic of long-term austerity meant a revision of optimistic plans to reopen declining coal mines in his native North, as well as major cuts in the work force of the deeply deficitary steel industry of the North and Lorraine. Mauroy wanted to soften the blow by extending the process over time. By the end of 1983 the emphasis in the Elysée was again on shock tactics. A rapid operation, cutting where surgery would be necessary sooner or later, might at least gain credit for courage. The positive action accompanying these cuts was to seek growth by aiding new industry and investing in high technology, described as the road to future job creation. These were the ideas of the president and his advisors — particularly his chief idea man Jacques Attali and his protege Laurent Fabius, since March 1983 minister of industry.

Mauroy, on the other hand, saw the working class of his own industrial north as the core constituency of the Left. Anything but pro-Communist, Mauroy believed that the social forces shoring up the Communist party represented a part of the electorate that the Socialists would never be able to reach. The support of voters from this irreducible Communist minimum would in his view always be necessary for a genuinely social democratic policy. Believing that the intransigent leadership of the PCF would ultimately have to accept the fact that their party could no longer grow and might well continue to shrink, the prime minister opposed an industrial policy that would burn PS bridges to the PCF and its electorate.[52]

Both arguments were as much political as economic, and were affected by considerations of timing. Mitterrand and his advisors had their eyes fixed on the legislative elections of March 1986. If the economy continued to lose speed, they would end in disaster for the PS, and perhaps force the presi-

dent to resign, ending the whole Socialist era with a whimper. But in almost
three years much could be done to retrieve the situation, even perhaps to
win these elections. Consciously or unconsciously, Mauroy looked at a different perspective. He knew that his stewardship as prime minister would
terminate by the end of 1984 at the latest, and while he certainly did not
desire defeat in 1986 his thinking was not centered on this date.

Mauroy was furthermore whipsawed by the contradiction between his
need to defend austerity policies to the Left constituency and his natural ten-
dency to sound as optimistic as possible. Mitterrand watched his prime
minister's credit diminish, and waited. The next electoral contest was the
election for the European parliament in June 1984. Some time thereafter a
change in prime minister might be necessary.

As 1983 dragged on, bringing new crises in the important automobile industry, where nationalized Renault and privately held Peugeot-Citroën were
both fast losing their market share in France and in Europe, the political
logic of rapid and dramatic action appealed increasingly to Mitterrand. Not
only Fabius and Attali, but also Delors now argued that the government must
not appear to be bogged down and defeatist. Mauroy's go-slow ideas inevitably fell into this category.

In pursuing the logic of dramatic action Mitterrand was implicitly breaking with the policy of alliance with the Communists which he had followed
since 1965. In mid-1983 he seems to have to persuaded himself that since the
PCF had not left the government after the municipal elections (their most
logical departure point) they would "eat their hats," and remain in the
government until 1986.[53]

Pushing the Communists this hard was a gamble, for the president could
not be sure Mauroy was wrong in thinking that the PS would still need a coalition partner, and in 1983 another precipitate drop in PCF fortunes was still
far from certain. In July 1984, when Mitterrand chose Laurent Fabius to succeed Mauroy and the PCF left the government, its share of the vote had already fallen to 11.28 percent. Mitterrand may have hoped that the
Communists would remain in the Fabius government, but he could not logically have expected them to do so, since both their political and social
reasons to remain in the government had disappeared.

The political decisions made in 1983, well before Fabius' appointment,
led toward a new policy. The government could no longer describe itself as
the engine of social change. In future it would need to appear as the agency
of strong and sensible orthodox administration, dedicated to the modernization of the French economy, socialist only because more sensitive than
the Right to the pain caused by inevitable surgical operations. The new
economic policies meant that the Socialists were unable to do much more
for the core Left electorate. To have a presentable record in the March 1986

elections they were obliged to go in chase of the mildly left-center voters whom they had disenchanted in 1981-1983. This was in any case the electorate most likely to be pleased by their new economic policies.

The period between March 1983 and Mauroy's resignation in 1984 is both confusing and confused; neither Mitterrand nor Mauroy was ready to face the logic of the president's choices. Mitterrand should have taken a new prime minister in March 1983, one who could pursue austerity while giving it the new goal of modernization. Instead he temporized, choosing Mauroy again rather than Delors (Fabius seemed too inexperienced) because he thought Mauroy safer. He also thought that he could afford only two prime ministers in the five year lifespan of the legislature, and wanted to keep his options open for 1984. The new industrial logic of closures and austerity risked an imminent break with the PCF, which the president hoped to avoid or postpone. Retaining Mauroy helped him to manage the Communists.

Mauroy, however, was seen by the country and by himself as a champion of orthodox Socialist ideas. Unwilling to appear merely as an administrator, and unable to find a conspicuously socialist agenda in economic measures, Mauroy began to emphasize other promises made in Mitterrand's 110 points. His policy was to please and remotivate a dispirited Left. Meanwhile, the new economic policies directed by Delors might win back left-center voters. Mitterrand assented to this double-tracked scheme. In retrospect, it is clear that Mauroy's tactics would have worked only if each constituency involved had listened to the right tune, and remained deaf to the appeal not meant for it. Master politicians (and Mitterrand is one) can sometimes bring off such a stratagem. But evidently neither Mitterrand nor Mauroy had yet understood in autumn 1983 that they (and particularly Mauroy) had lost the strength essential to this maneuver, which is the ability convincingly to define a policy to the country on one's own terms. The next months would show that this capacity had passed instead to the opposition.

Mauroy's first target was the press empire of Robert Hersant, the French Rupert Murdoch. De Gaulle's government in 1944 had decreed a limit on the number of newspapers which could be owned by one person, a principle largely infringed by Hersant's growing press acquisitions. Like Murdoch, Hersant was something more than a rich man with an appetite for gobbling up papers — French newspapers (like the old *Le Figaro* which he acquired in the late 1970s) were slackly and wastefully run. Hersant had understood how to modernize both administrative and printing operations. But the Socialists hated him as an ambitious press lord of the Right with aspirations to acquire still more titles and radio stations — and eventually television channels when this became possible.

Hersant in extreme youth was tainted with charges of collaboration — although these had not excluded him from membership in Mitterrand's own small party, the UDSR, when he was a deputy during the Fourth Republic. In the Fifth Republic, he and most of his papers moved to the right, and after May 1981 his flagship, the Paris daily *Le Figaro*, had become the most vociferous and frequently violent media opponent of the government.

Nevertheless, Mitterrand's old friend and aide André Rousselot had negotiated with Hersant in 1981-1982, hoping to purchase the popular Paris daily *France Soir*, which he believed the press magnate wished to sell. Without a daily press outlet of its own the Socialist government and party found itself frequently frustrated by the way in which the independent press of both Left and Right explained and criticized its actions. The Socialists believed in a free press. They also wanted to be understood, lovingly.

Many Socialist leaders, including Mauroy and his entourage, noted that no French party had been able to sustain a profitable Paris daily (the Communist *Humanité* was no exception, being heavily subsidized). They would have preferred to acquire provincial newspapers to support the party. In any case, Hersant was not negotiating seriously with Rousselot. He had his eye instead on a prestigious Grenoble daily, *Le Dauphiné Libéré*, with wide circulation in the Isère department and much of the important Rhône-Alpes region. Mitterrand lieutenant Louis Mermaz, Socialist boss of the Isère, would have liked to acquire the title or at least dissuade Hersant by denying him credit from the nationalized banks. For whatever reason, nothing was done to block Hersant's acquisition of the paper in 1983. Thereafter, he lost interest in negotiating the sale of *France Soir*. Thus mocked, the Socialists found the Hersant empire an ever more tempting target.[54]

When Mauroy told the Socialist congress of Bourg-en-Bresse in October 1983 that "the exercise of democracy demands pluralism and clarity . . . a halt to the creation of ever more powerful and monolithic press monopolies" he was wildly applauded. A month later the government adopted a bill "to guarantee freedom of the press and readers' free choice by limiting concentration." Immediately baptized "the Hersant law" and violently criticized by the right-wing press (not Hersant's alone), the bill was passed by the National Assembly after lengthy and stormy sessions, during which the opposition introduced no fewer than 2600 amendments. An appeal to the Constitutional Council produced the Solomonic verdict that the law was constitutional—but could not apply retrospectively, a judgment glossed by the satiric *Canard Enchaîné* as declaring that no one but Robert Hersant might possess a press empire.

The Socialists therefore failed to force Hersant to cede a part of his empire either to them or to neutral forces. Worse, they played directly into the hands of an opposition now trumpeting the superiority of economic liberalism (Adam Smith or Reagan style) over stumbling socialism. Blindly confident that civil liberty was their own exclusive property, the Socialists did not see that in backing a bill designed to curb the powers of a press lord they were giving their opponents a means to link the cry of freedom for the economy to freedom of the press, and thus accredit the blanket charge of "collectivism."

THE BIGGEST DEMONSTRATION EVER

In 1981 Mitterrand had included in his 110 propositions the rash promise to erect a "unified and secular public education system." The pursuit of a highly modified version of this pledge ended in June 1984 in a fiasco that brought down the Mauroy government.

In the 1980s approximately sixteen percent of French children attended private schools. Perhaps half of their parents were practicing Catholics. Church schools (especially secondary ones) had grown increasingly popular as French public education battled unhappily with the same intractable problem that confronts American secondary education in the late twentieth century: the lack of any philosophical consensus on the minimum content of general education in a mass society where the old classical curriculum seems of uncertain relevance. Doubts abounded on the value and content of experiment and innovation, while disciplinary problems spread in often overcrowded classes taught by increasingly underpaid teachers.

A poll commissioned by the Education Ministry in 1982 showed clearly that all these factors influenced the parents who sent their children to private schools. While two-thirds of them wished their children to receive religious instruction, only ten to fifteen percent considered this the principal reason for their choice of institution. They named instead discipline, quality of instruction, ease of contact with the teachers, and the assurance that their children would receive an education respecting traditional values.[55]

The church schools were regarded by the adepts of secular education as a throwback to a period before universal, public, and secular education had been guaranteed in France. The village schoolmasters had in the late nineteenth and early twentieth century been the shock troops of republican socialization in a pre-modern France where the ordinary people, easily manipulated by pro-clerical government under Napoleon III, were to be educated in sound republican values by men immune to reactionary clericalism. The quarrel with the church had simmered down by the mid-twentieth century, but secular education as the supreme value of the republic remained a dogma for many on the Left.

In 1959 Prime Minister Michel Debré had brought in a law providing government funding for teachers' salaries in Catholic schools, even though a petition against it gathered eleven million signatures. The Guermeur law of 1977 gave church schools rights that state schools did not possess, and sometimes accorded them funds for subject-matter they were unable to teach. However, in 1978 only thirty-three percent of respondents in a poll desired integration of private schools into the public system.

With Alain Savary, Mitterrand and Mauroy had chosen an education minister with a long record as a principled and patient Socialist able to negotiate with all parties. The PS leader most identified with the claims of lay education, Louis Mexandeau, was significantly passed over for the education job and given another ministry. In 1981 the Catholic hierarchy could believe that if the extravagant language of Mitterrand's promise was not meant literally, then the strength of support for church schools might enable the Catholic educators to sign a peace treaty with the paladins of secularism, and resolve the church-state education question once and for all.

Nevertheless, in retrospect the shipwreck of Savary's law reforming the status of Catholic schools assumes an air of inevitability. To promise an educational system that was both unified and secular was clearly a major error. Formulated in the heat of the campaign, the promise had been drafted to please a powerful PS constituency, the Fédération de l'Education Nationale (FEN). Oddly enough, in view of the enormous fuss aroused in 1984, the education plank played no great role in the 1981 election campaign. To counter rumors that the Socialists intended to cut off payments to private schools or rapidly absorb all Catholic schoolteachers into the state system, Mitterrand promised in an open letter of May 1, 1981 that the new dispensation would result from "negotiation and not from a unilateral decision," and that nothing would be done abruptly.[56]

The negotiation proper began in 1982 and lasted for two years, during which Savary and his staff worked hard to frame a compromise law that could accommodate the demands of moderates on both sides of the question. On the Left, the leaders of the National Committee on Secular Education (CNAL), allied to but not identical with the FEN, refused to believe that public opinion supported public aid to church schools. "Public funds for public schools, private funds for private schools" was their war cry. On the Right, deep suspicion of the real intentions of the government was fed by the declarations of the CNAL and excited by politically inspired denunciations of the government's whole educational policy.

Savary's attempts to reform state education centered on the idea of increased decentralization to promote initiative in individual schools. He ran into a wall of mistrust constructed over fifteen years by ever increasing criticism of French education in the mass age. The years 1983-1984 saw publication of a number of "why Jeannot can't read" books, with titles like *Your Children Don't Interest Me Any More*, *Do You Really Want Idiot Children?*, *The Massacre of the Innocents*, etc. Denouncing lowered teaching standards and laxity in discipline, such books sold well and were publicized in television discussions.[57]

Savary's pedagogic reforms were thus easily confused by the general public with an increase in laxity, while the opposition's politicians denounced the introduction of a tutorial system suspected of being ideological. Against all this, the private, Catholic school (known in France as the "free school") offered an alternative which parents might or might not choose, but was at least reassuringly present.

To these factors must be added the immigrant question, which by 1983 emerged in the political consciousness as the most acute social problem of contemporary France. In the 1960s French industry had freely imported more than a million low or unskilled foreign workers to help it in the boom years. A favorite recruiting ground was the Maghreb—the North African countries of Algeria, Morocco, and Tunisia. By 1984, there were some two million *maghrebins* living in France. The young men who had come alone to find work in France between the late fifties and 1974 had sent for their wives or married once they were employed. Products of a birthrate still governed by the customs of a peasant society, their numerous children moved into the schools of the large inner cities, and especially those along the Mediterranean coast. With little cultural baggage, often speaking limited French, they filled already crowded classes and slowed the process of instruction. Mitterrand had promised in 1981 that maximum class sizes would be reduced to twenty-five, but this was possible only in private schools.

Mauroy emphasized the Hersant law and the Savary school bill to placate a Socialist party badly in need of some nourishment other than the distasteful fodder of *rigueur*. The opposition, no less political, rapidly saw that both bills fit neatly with its tactic of denouncing the Socialist-Communist assault on liberty. By early April 1984, when the Council of Ministers adopted the Savary law, the *Figaro* was attacking the "murder of the church schools," while the talented polemicist Jean-François Revel heaped wood on the fire by announcing that "all education in the proper sense is from now on positively forbidden."[58]

The temperature rose as the Savary bill approached its National Assembly reading. In the course of negotiations, the idea of the unified secular service had melted away. The bill made concessions to the church schools which the CNAL found intolerable; guaranteeing state payment of the teachers in church schools and basic school expenses, leaving only upkeep to the diocesan authorities.[59] The church hierarchy in turn was troubled by an article stating that teachers in private schools who had passed their state certification examinations could, if they so wished, apply for civil service rank (*titulaires*) in the state teaching establishment. This provision was objectionable because Catholics feared it might open the way for complete state control of private teaching, allowing the state to assign private school teachers (like their public school colleagues) anywhere in the country. This could break up the free schools. However, the hierarchy quietly let the Elysée know that it would not oppose this point if guarantees were given that the state would not push hard to implement the provision.

On March 5, a rally against the Savary bill sponsored by the well-organized private Parent-Teachers Associations drew nearly a million persons to Versailles. Leading opposition politicians were conspicuous among them. On April 25, the CNAL organized a counter-demonstration in Paris — also against the Savary bill — that drew 75,000 people. In the front ranks marched not only the CNAL leaders, but also PS first secretary Lionel Jospin, PCF secretary general Marchais and part of his Politburo, and Pierre Joxe, Socialist leader in the National Assembly. In mid-May, Joxe and other Socialist leaders in the Assembly told Mauroy that they would not vote for the bill as it stood; amendments were needed.

Carefully steering between two opposing extremisms, Savary had produced a bill supported by the government, the church hierarchy, and the Catholic PTA leadership. Challenges came not only from the lay side but also from Catholics and from politicians of the Right uninterested in successful compromise. Warned by Mauroy that Socialist deputies would insist on amendments, the church negotiators repeated their opposition to absorption of private school teachers into the state system. The prime minister attempted to appease them. Both sides threatened new mass demonstrations. European elections, which would be fought on almost exclusively domestic questions, were scheduled for June 17; the government seemed trapped between two forces. Mauroy asked for Mitterrand's advice. "Work something out" (*débrouillez-vous*), advised the president unhelpfully.

In the night of May 22 the National Assembly passed the Savary bill with amendments reluctantly accepted by Mauroy. One amendment stipulated that towns were not obliged to finance private nursery schools, and tied creation of new ones to the prior existence of public nursery schools in a town. A second stated that towns need not pay their share of school expenses until a majority of teachers in private schools had — after a six-year discretionary period — accepted the status of state employee. Although the state would guarantee to meet such payments for eleven years, it would not guarantee them forever (as Mauroy had allegedly promised the church negotiators).

The amendments did not seriously alter the thrust of the Savary bill, affected only a small proportion of state payments for church education, and left a great deal of room for future adjudication. But they tilted a precarious balance in the Catholic camp. The cardinal archbishop of Paris told *Le Monde* in an interview on June 5 that Mauroy had broken his word. The prime minister consulted the president, then hotly denied this on television.

The European elections of June 17 further weakened a stumbling government. In balloting marked by a 43.3 percent abstention the PS vote fell to 20.76 percent, the PCF to 11.28 percent. The combined list of the Right had done less well than it hoped, but with 42.88 percent it still outweighed the combined Socialist and Communist vote. The unwelcome surprise of the elections was the sudden rise of Jean-Marie Le Pen's racist National Front, with eleven percent.

One week later came a great Parisian demonstration against the Savary bill organized by the Catholic PTA associations. (The bill still had to go before an obstructionist Senate.) Both the government and the Catholic forces had worried about the dangers of a mass demonstration in Paris degenerating into clashes, but the impressive organization of the march and the quiet determination of the marchers thwarted any such dangers. Its good temper, discipline, and sheer size astonished a government and a nation well accustomed to mass demonstrations. Wave after carefully timed wave of demonstrators, between a million and a million four hundred thousand of them, emerged from metro stations, buses, and trains, marched to the Place de la Bastille and dispersed. They kept coming for twelve hours, Bretons in costume shepherded by their priests, Alsatians, southerners, each group with its own flag and a common slogan, "The free school will live!"

Paris had seen immense street demonstrations before, the great crowds of May 1968 (the biggest being some 200,000) or the pro-de Gaulle response to May 1968 on the Champs Elysées (500,000). But with the exception of the passionate manifestation of joy that brought nearly two million Parisians and suburbanites spontaneously together to welcome de Gaulle on the morrow of liberation in August 1944, the Catholic forces had mobilized the biggest demonstration ever known.[60]

The Savary law had sowed discontent both on the secular Left and the Catholic Right. It was also judged severely by the general public. Polls in June 1984 showed that fifty-five percent of the French thought the bill infringed liberties. Almost certainly many people thought the Left mistaken in reopening the church-state question, which was widely perceived as anachronistic. Furthermore, as Serge July has pointed out, the government made a serious error in allowing the debate to be framed in terms of uniformity, by emphasizing the idea that teachers should all be government officials, and in speaking of a state monopoly over the schools. These were the values of the old Jacobinism which the opposition had now abandoned and condemned in the Left. By incurring once again the charge that the Left wanted to collectivize everything, the government revived all the old doubts and fears.[61]

After so stunning a show of disapproval immediately after the disavowal of the European elections, the government would have great difficulty in continuing as if nothing had happened. But how could it extricate itself from the situation into which it had blundered?

Mauroy, ever the optimist, continued to believe there was some way out. At the end of June he took advantage of a visit to Rome originally scheduled for much earlier to sound out the pope, hoping he might issue a statement that would soften the French episcopate. John Paul II may have found ironic amusement in this spectacle of an agnostic French Socialist prime minister seeking ultramontane aid to cope with the Gallic clergy, but all he offered Mauroy was a specially blessed chaplet for the prime minister's aged and pious mother.

In the meantime, the opposition announced its intention to fight the Savary law in the Senate all summer long, and suggested that Mitterrand should consult the people in a referendum on the matter. Mauroy opposed any such idea, keeping to an interpretation of the constitution that permits referenda only on questions of the "public powers." He toyed with the notion of a giant secularist counter-demonstration. The Senate was impotent to kill the education bill and would have to release it by September. And while the ultras of the RPR were talking of "a pre-revolutionary situation," the president, however embarrassed by the drop in Socialist fortunes, reaffirmed his support for the Savary bill in televised remarks on July 5.

Mitterrand was spending more and more time traveling outside France as his domestic popularity dwindled. He now departed on an official visit to Jordan. On July 11, when the prime minister went out to Charles de Gaulle airport to greet the president on his return (a procedure Mauroy had grown to detest), he was dumbfounded to learn that Mitterrand had suddenly adopted the idea of a referendum — with a difference. Mitterrand announced his intention of going on television the next day to propose a double referendum, one to permit votes on general questions, followed by another affording a popular vote on the school question. Mitterrand sought however to appease Mauroy's fears for the future of the Savary law. Not until a television interview two days later, on Bastille Day, did he admit that the process of a referendum was incompatible with urging passage of the law by the Senate. After praising the honest effort made by Savary, Mitterrand concluded, "But it is evident that my opinion is not shared by a very large number of French people. Thus, as I have just said . . . I worry about what the people who don't agree with me are thinking, and I take it into account."[62]

Mitterrand had not thought it necessary to inform either his prime minister or his education minister that he was withdrawing the Savary bill. Savary immediately told the prime minister that he had been disavowed and would resign. His decision determined Mauroy not to serve Mitterrand for a last few months as the president desired, but to resign immediately on a political issue, to "fall on the left." His resignation and the appointment of thirty--seven year old Laurent Fabius as his successor was made public on July 17.

These details of a ministry's fall are a striking illustration of François Mitterrand's idiosyncratic mixture of indecision and sudden resolution, his unwillingness to share his thoughts even with close collaborators, and finally a resourcefulness very lightly ballasted by ideology. Having backed Savary until the end in a course which required delicate maneuvering, the canny tactician can scarcely have overlooked the danger of new amendments. He apparently did nothing to stop his liege man Joxe from pushing these resolutions in the Assembly, nothing to urge Jospin to hold off the wave of anachronistic secularist sentiment that had broken out in the PS. He seems to have confined himself (between trips out of the country) to hoping that the probable would not be the inevitable, and when things turned out badly he did not even trouble to forewarn the laborers in his vineyard that he was about to reject their harvest.

Seizing the opposition's idea of a referendum to turn it against them was exceedingly clever, but the scheme itself might in practice have greatly increased the powers of the president, enabling him to frame all sorts of direct appeals to the country in pure Second Empire style. The young Mitterrand had opposed such tactics. But it may be that Mitterrand the president foresaw correctly that the opposition would refuse to give him such powers, blocking them in the Senate, which by law had to concur on the text of a referendum. So it turned out. Mitterrand's game of mirrors dazzled everyone; the president was quit of the Savary law, and could still tell himself and the country that he had first tried to save it and then bowed honorably to the weight of public opinion.

The imbroglio forced Mitterrand to change prime ministers slightly ahead of his planned schedule and humiliated him despite the skill he showed as an escape artist. In the end, however, he came out better than one might have expected at the time. The leaders of the opposition had marched in the ranks of the protesters, but they did not command them. The wave of protest against a perceived Left threat to liberties swelled up, broke, and did not rise again. June 1984, with the European elections and the school demonstration, was the low point for the Socialist administration.

Mauroy had provided much ammunition to his critics. He left behind him a blurred impression of his record in office. Despite his courage in retreating from policies he had advocated and desired, his misleadingly optimistic television performances were held against him to make him appear ridiculous. His attempt to inspire the old Left coalition by attacking Hersant and pushing a compromise education bill unloved by both Socialists and Catholics had played straight into the hand of the opposition. Fabius the modernizer would manage to symbolize better than Mauroy many of the older man's accomplishments. With a better sense of public relations, he was also able to present himself as a new man with new policies.[63]

NOTES

1. Cf. Monique Dagnaud and Dominique Mehl, *L'Elite rose*.

2. The biographical information in this section has been drawn from *Who's Who in France* 18th edition (Paris: Jacques Laffitte, 1981).

3. Philippe Bauchard, *La Guerre des deux roses*, pp. 25-31; Pierre Mauroy, *C'est ici le chemin*, p. 19; author's interview with Mauroy adviser Thierry Pfister, October 1984.

3. *Le Monde*, June 26, 1981.

4. Cf. Thierry Pfister, *La Vie quotidienne à Matignon au temps de l'Union de la Gauche*, p. 221.

5. Quoted in ADA, *Bilan de la France*, p. 61.

6. Quoted in *Le Nouvel Observateur*, September 26, 1981.

7. News conference of September 24, 1981, cited in *Le Nouvel Observateur*, September 26, 1981.

8. Pfister, *La Vie quotidienne*, pp. 170-171.

9. Alain Fonteneau and Pierre-Alain Muet, *La Gauche face à la crise*, pp. 95-96.

10. Author's interview with Henry Nau, August 1987.

11. Fonteneau and Muet, *La Gauche*, pp. 97-98.

12. Ibid., pp. 97-107.

13. Ibid., pp. 156-162.

14. Cf. Peter Hall, *Governing the Economy*, p. 199.

15. Cf. Jérôme Vignon, "Le Delorisme en économie," *Les Cahiers français*, no. 218 (October-December 1984), p. 61.

16. Quoted in Bauchard, *La Guerre des deux roses*, p. 86.

17. Fonteneau and Muet, *La Gauche*, p. 127.

18. Author's interview with Pascal Lamy, Mauroy and Delors aide, October 1985.

19. Nay, *Le Noir et le rouge*, p. 9.

20. Christian Jelen and Thierry Wolton, *Le Petit guide de la farce tranquille*, passim.

21. For quotes from the Valence congress, see *Le Monde*, October 25-26 and October 27, 1981. For the continuing echo, see Jean- Marie Colombani, "Faire oublier Valence," *Le Monde*, July 4, 1984.

22. Cf. Alain and Marie-Thérèse Lancelot, *Annuaire de la France politique, Mai 1981-Mai 1983*, pp. 33-34; p. 81.

23. Cf. Alain and Marie-Thérèse Lancelot, "The Evolution of the French Electorate 1981-1986," in *The Mitterrand Experiment*, eds. George Ross,

Stanley Hoffmann, and Sylvia Malzacher; and Jérôme Jaffré, "De Valéry Giscard d'Estaing à François Mitterrand: France de gauche, vote à gauche," *Pouvoirs* 20 (1982).

24. Pfister, *La Vie quotidienne*, p. 250.

25. Ibid., pp. 250-255.

26. Ibid., p. 191.

27. Cf. *Quid 1987* (Paris: Laffont, 1986), p. 696c.

28. Pfister, *La Vie quotidienne*, p. 255.

29. SOFRES poll in *Le Nouvel Observateur*, 28 August 1982.

30. See *Le Nouvel Observateur*, July 24, 1982.

31. Fonteneau and Muet, *op. cit.*, p. 158.

32. Pierre Mauroy, *A Gauche*, p. 109.

33. Serge July, *Les Années Mitterrand*, p. 85.

34. Ibid.

35. Author's interview with Henri Guillaume, May 1985.

36. Author's interview with Pierre Bérégovoy, October 1987.

37. Bauchard, *La Guerre des deux roses,* pp. 141-150; author's interview with Delors aide Pascal Lamy, March 1986.

38. Cf. July, *Les Années Mitterrand*, pp. 96, 99, 107 ff.

39. Ibid., p. 111.

40. Quoted in Bauchard, *La Guerre des deux roses*, p. 162.

41. Raymond Aron, *Mémoires*, p. 328.

42. For a detailed account, see Pierre Grémion, *Paris/Prague, la gauche face au renouveau et à la régression tchécoslovaque, 1968-1978.*

43. *L'Unité*, (Paris) February 8, 1974, cited in Grémion, *Paris/Prague*, p. 284.

44. Alain Besançon, "L'Affaire Soljenitsyne: deux 'approches positives'," *Contrepoint* 15 (September 1974), p. 137 ff.

45. François Furet, *Penser la Révolution française*, p. 28.

46. *Le Monde*, July 1983, passim.

47. *Le Programme commun de gouvernement de la gauche, propositions socialistes pour l'actualisation* (Paris: Flammarion, 1978), p. 58.

48. Colombani, *Portrait du Président*, p. 82.

49. George Ross, "From One Left to Another, *Le Social* in Mitterrand's France," in *The Mitterrand Experiment*, eds. Ross, Hoffmann and Malzacher, p. 202, and Edmond Maire, "A l'épreuve de l'expérience," *CFDT Aujourd'hui*, no. 86 (September 1987), p. 33.

50. Mitterrand's remark that *"socialisme à la française"* was not his Bible was made at a speech in Figeac on September 27, 1982; quoted here from *Le Nouvel Observateur*, October 2-8, 1982, p. 21.

51. On Mitterrand's behavior in early summer 1983, see Bauchard, *La Guerre des deux roses*, pp. 167-176.

100 *Twenty-one Months on the Left*

52. Cf. Pfister, *La Vie quotidienne*, p. 300, where the author is clearly expressing Mauroy's ideas.

53. Cf. Bauchard, *La Guerre des deux roses*, p. 165, quoting a private interview with Mitterrand.

54. On Rousselot and the negotiations to buy *France-Soir*, see Jean Michel Quatrepoint, *Histoire secrète des dossiers noirs de la gauche*, p. 23, and Pfister, *La Vie quotidienne à Matignon*, p. 133. My information on the *Dauphiné Libéré* affair comes from a February 1986 interview with Grenoble journalist Pierre Frappat.

55. See Alain Savary, *En toute liberté*, pp. 122 and 126.

56. Ibid., pp. 15-17.

57. Cf. the discussion on the pedagogical debate and the Savary law in general by Antoine Prost, "The Educational Maelstrom," in *The Mitterrand Experiment*, eds. Ross, Hoffmann, and Malzacher. Prost was himself the author of a controversial report on lycée reform.

58. *Le Point*, May 21, 1984, quoted in Prost, "Educational Maelstrom," in *The Mitterrand Experiment*, eds. Ross, Hoffmann, and Malzacher, p. 233.

59. The text of the bill and the subsequent amendments may be found in Savary, *En toute liberté*, p. 220ff.; the amendments appear on p. 163.

60. Cf. the detailed account in *Le Monde*, June 26, 1984.

61. Cf. July, *Les Années Mitterrand*, p. 173.

62. Pfister, *La Vie quotidienne*, pp. 285-287; p. 343; and for the details of Mitterrand's dealings with Mauroy on July 11-17, pp. 336-354.

63. In this section I have drawn on the accounts given in *Le Monde* for late May, June, and July 1984, *Le Point* of April 30 for the CNAL march, and on my discussions with a number of French intellectuals immediately before and after the events described, as well as on personal observation of the June 24, 1984 march. I have used Pfister, *La Vie quotidienne* for an inside view of Mauroy's thinking and his relations with the president, and drawn on an interview with Pfister on July 12, 1984. I have also used Alain Savary, *En toute liberté* as well as interviews with Savary and with former Jesuit provincial Henri Madelin in October, 1987. Also see *Le Monde Aujourd'hui* May 19-20, 1985 for Alain Vernholes' reflections on Mauroy a year after his resignation.

3

Thirty-six Months at the Center

FABIUS SOCIALISM

During the curious interim between the June 24 demonstration against the Savary law and Mitterrand's retreat on July 12 — another interregnum like that of March 1983 — *Le Monde's* chief political writer Jean-Marie Colombani asked in a front page analysis-editorial: "What does one do when one is in power and has just been disavowed, and when less than two years remain before the real rendezvous with the public's verdict?" Since votes lost by the PCF were no longer moving to the PS column, it was clear, he wrote, that to remain viable the PS must conform its rhetoric to its policies and seek to build a social democratic bloc — a party sure of at least thirty percent of the vote.[1]

Always resistant to exterior constraint, Mitterrand had been putting off the moment for conforming economic policy and political rhetoric. When Mauroy's resignation faced him with an immediate need to choose a new prime minister, he picked the person most in tune with his new ideas, Laurent Fabius.

The "young prime minister whom I have given to France," as Mitterrand referred to Fabius in his paternalistic way, had been very much on the Left when this was Mitterrand's stance. In 1979, when Mauroy and Rocard challenged Mitterrand at the PS congress in Metz, Fabius had lectured Rocard on the meaning of socialism. Until March 1983 he had been an advocate of high taxes for the rich and of the "other policy" of leaving the EMS, changing his mind late in the day after an alarming briefing on the state of French reserves.

Fabius had been a member of the PS for ten years when he was named prime minister, the youngest man to hold the job since the reign of Louis XVIII. Son of a rich Parisian antique dealer, the precocious young man graduated from both the Ecole Normale Supérieure and ENA, taking high honors and opting for the *grand corps* of the Conseil d'Etat. An accomplished horseman and man about town, he seemed destined to join the gifted and gilded *énarques* clustering around one of their own, Valéry Giscard d'Estaing. Instead he joined the PS, where he rapidly impressed its first secretary.[2] Mitterrand has always liked to surround himself with bright young men, pushing forward their careers more rapidly than those of their elders. Among the most prominent were Jean-Pierre Chevènement, Pierre Joxe, Jacques Attali, Lionel Jospin — men who in their different ways aided and complemented Mitterrand without posing any threat to his position. Fabius was first in this class. Beginning as a member of the PS Economic Commission, Fabius rapidly became director of Mitterrand's cabinet, then a national secretary of the PS. In 1977 he was "parachuted" into the Socialist constituency of Le Grand-Quevilly, an industrial suburb of Rouen, to replace its aged and popular mayor. Working hard at his new job, passing out leaflets at factory gates, the Paris *énarque*, who "had learned to speak Socialist language quite correctly" also succeeded the mayor as a deputy in 1978.

Named budget minister in 1981, Fabius was promoted in March 1983 to minister of research and industry. He headed a superministry to which telecommunications had been added, a move which brought more independent access to funding than this ministry has usually possessed. Industrialists who had disliked his interventionist and dogmatic predecessor Chevènement were pleased. Others were not. *Le Monde*, more critical of the Socialists than in 1981, entitled one article on Fabius' nomination, "A Mysterious Young Man" and another on Fabius' record as industry minister, "The Art of Dodging."[3]

The unanimous opinion, however, was that Fabius was his master's voice. "Mitterrand appoints himself prime minister," said the conservative *Quotidien de Paris*, echoed on the Left by *Libération*: "Mitterrand prime minister." Having taken as his first prime minister a man who symbolized the ideas of traditional socialism, the president was now choosing a close collaborator who had no following of his own but symbolized the change in Socialist policy. Fabius stood for only one thing — modernization, the new leitmotiv of the Mitterrand administration.

The Fabius ministry itself was only partly new. Jacques Delors departed for Brussels to become president of the European Community Commission. He was replaced as minister for economy and finance by Pierre Bérégovoy. Michel Rocard, agriculture minister since 1983, remained in his post. Claude Cheysson remained at the Quai d'Orsay (which the Socialists had renamed External Relations) for some months yet, before departing to become once again an EC commissioner; his replacement was Mitterrand's close associate Roland Dumas. Mauroy's top aide Michel Delebarre became labor minister, a post in which he would make a mark. Pierre Joxe moved from leadership of the Socialist fraction in the National Assembly to become interior minister and take a new hold on the government's troubled dealings with the police. And Jean-Pierre Chevènement returned to occupy the siege perilous of the education ministry.

The new prime minister declared his program in late July: heavy emphasis on modernization amid continued austerity. Growth presupposed a solid production apparatus, but modernization might cost jobs before it produced new ones. Investment, reduction of the burden of social costs falling on industry, a move toward freeing industrial prices, lower taxes — these were the main points made by the new Socialist chief of government.[4]

The country reacted well to the change: Fabius' initial poll ratings were far higher than Mauroy's had been towards the end. The government's core constituency was still sulking and the Communists had begun to hammer away at government policies, but at least policy and rhetoric were in line again. Chevènement and Fabius sought a quick compromise on the church education question. Negotiating quietly, they worked out a compromise by which the government would finance private education (the principle of which, of course had never been at issue, except in the superheated rhetoric of some secularist fanatics). The concessions of the 1977 Guermeur law, which even many churchmen thought indefensible, were rescinded, and the Debré law of 1959 was reaffirmed.

Chevènement then made himself improbably popular in circles where he had been a *bête rouge* by promoting a return to the three R's in education. The singing of the *Marseillaise*, dropped for many years, was reintroduced into schools. Discipline and classroom authority were emphasized. Many teachers were displeased, but the public loved it. At a minimum, Chevènement had hit on a brilliant stroke of symbolic politics. Part of Savary's problem had been that too many people believed that experimentation (begun long before 1981) had wrecked public education. Therefore Savary's innovations were suspect and government interference in private education automatically bad. Chevènement's back to basics was understood as "no experiments" and met approval.

Pierre Mauroy's thirty-seven months as prime minister had begun with boundless optimism. They were filled with the actions of a government first in a hurry to make its mark, then to correct a slide, and finally with frenetic attempts to please the Socialist deputies by veering to the left.

Laurent Fabius' twenty months began at the low point of July 1984, with a nearly mathematical certainty that the PS would lose control of the National Assembly in March 1986. A dejected PS was still only beginning to come to terms with the idea that too many of its old ideas had been illusions.

Fabius' mission was to present the new face of the Mitterrand administration. In the 1970s, the Left had rejected the idea that it should "manage the crisis." Now the task was to show that the Socialists *could* manage the crisis — better than the Right had done, more humanely, and with more vision for the future.

Accordingly, the achievements of the Fabius government have a largely non-Socialist flavor. His economics and finance minister Pierre Bérégovoy is proud of having created a financial futures market — a good idea, but not one he would have propounded at the Metz congress in 1979. The government also discovered a means of bringing private capital into nationalized industry, by selling up to fifteen percent of the stock of certain companies owned by nationalized conglomerates. With a renewal of business confidence, the Paris stock market took off.

In keeping with the new honor paid to profit and the entrepreneur, Fabius declared it scandalous that the creation of new businesses in France should be crippled by formalities lasting up to a year. He compared the combination of administrative expense and bureaucratic complexity in France to the ease of incorporation in the United States. The goal, said the prime minister, was a process lasting not more than a week, and in fact, it was reduced to approximately a month.

BITTER MEDICINE

The principal task of the new government was to show that the Socialists, now governing alone, were above all modern administrators of the enterprise called France, and Fabius hastened to set the tone of a new beginning. At his first meeting with the Council of Ministers as prime minister, after a brief homage to his predecessor "pronounced with the warmth and human feeling of an ENA graduate listing the structural causes of inflation" he concluded, "but that is the past, and we are here to prepare the future."[5]

Before modernization could make much progress the government had to continue reconstruction, which meant further job cuts and continued austerity. Austerity meant holding down consumption, which in turn guaranteed low growth at least for the period devoted to drying out the economy.

Nationalized industry had been discovered to be in far worse shape than the Socialists had originally suspected (in 1984 only one of the major conglomerates which had been taken over in 1982 was in the black). Having precluded any private investment in these industries, the government had in effect bought the privilege of investing large amounts of money in nationalized industries just to make them profitable again. At the same time, it was trying to encourage investment in private industry by businessmen reluctant for both economic and political reasons to invest. Since the policies of 1981-

1982 had already raised taxes and social costs, and the social security system required a larger budget to cope with unprecedented unemployment and early retirement, the government found that its total control of credit gave no new freedom to invest and expand. Expensive bailouts of dying industries like coal mining had to be reconsidered in terms of cost, not just jobs saved.

By 1983 the Socialists had discovered that the French economy was weak and could hardly bear the additional social burdens they had placed on it. If it was to grow, they must spend government money selectively and encourage private investment more successfully than they — or Raymond Barre — had done. Profit, which had been a dirty word to Socialists, suddenly became a favorable reference, and entrepreneurs (formerly known as capitalists) the new heroes.

How serious was the condition of the French economy in 1981? No extensive analysis can be presented here. But a number of factors are clear, though they were ignored by the Socialists before 1981 and were played down by conservatives who wished to put all the blame for the problems of the 1980s on the Left government. The French economy had grown rapidly in the 1960s thanks to initially low labor costs — which rose rapidly at the end of the decade. While oil was cheap until 1973, the fact that France imported a larger share of its energy than other European countries placed it at a disadvantage (later alleviated by a heavy investment in nuclear power). Inflation was consistently higher than in neighboring and competitive countries, obliging France to have recourse to frequent devaluations. The French industrial export product was characteristically standard, medium-level technology, with markets especially in less-developed countries. During the 1970s, when some of the oil-producing countries were at the height of their boom, France was a major supplier. But when these countries ran short of cash (or as in the case of Iraq, went to war) then France's exports dropped off, except for armaments.

As French export markets shifted to the Common Market countries (the locus of nearly half her imports and exports in the 1980s) France experienced increasing competitive difficulties, running a trade deficit in 1985 with all EC countries except Greece. Thirty-one percent of the total national trade deficit was in commerce with West Germany alone.[6] The low and almost flat level of investment sustained throughout the 1970s had by the 1980s cut French productive capacity. French industry thus turned out to be unable to satisfy the wave of demand unleashed by the reflation of 1981.

By 1983 the government had realized that intravenous feeding of dying industry was not really good politics and very bad economics. Laurent Fabius, shortly after he had become the minister for industry, wrote in May 1983 that the stake in modernization (henceforth his favorite word) was "the fate of our youth, the rank, the weight, and the independence of France in the next twenty years."[7]

But the human cost was terrible. In Lorraine alone, 20,000-25,000 jobs in steel production were suppressed. (The industry had already lost thirty-eight percent of its jobs between 1974 and 1981; this blow cut another half of the region's jobs.) The total cut in steel employment was some 30,000 jobs nationally.[8] Demonstrating Lorraine workers marched through the streets of Paris, backed by the CGT. Three PS deputies from Lorraine demonstratively resigned from the party (and quietly rejoined it).

An overmanned automobile industry hard hit by Japanese competition in its export markets found it necessary to cut 20,000 jobs, while the ailing tire industry, despite the entry of Japanese capital, lost another 10,000 jobs.[9] The government was obliged to authorize more firings at Renault, where 4,500 workers lost their jobs in 1984 and another 12,500 in 1985. While Peugeot-Citroën-Talbot was not allowed to fire all the personnel it desired, the Fabius government authorized another 2,000 firings in August 1984 and 10,700 in 1985. Peugeot recovered before Renault, making a profit in 1985, while Renault, undergoing process of profound reorganization, did not see black ink until 1987.

Another crippled industry was shipbuilding, hard hit by Asian competition in a shrinking market. Public money flowing into the shipyards, which employed some 25,000 workers, cost the state an average 100,000 francs per worker per year by the 1980s. The plan for cuts in shipbuilding (part of the private sector) called for the gradual loss of some 6,000 jobs.

These cuts were only part of the jobs that French industry was losing. But they were concentrated regionally, in Lorraine, the Nord, in Auvergne, and the industrial upper Loire, areas where the Left in general and the CGT in particular had traditionally been strong.

To provide jobs and hope in these regions, the government announced the creation of special zones, called *pôles de conversion*, where special financial incitements would draw new investment. A plan worked out together with the unions was proposed to lighten the blow for workers thrown out of their jobs.

With the announcement of all these measures, the Left government had undertaken a whole series of actions which it would have condemned severely, had a conservative government dared to put them forward. The Socialists had been elected on the promise of reversing the advance of unemployment. Instead they were now deciding the cessation of dozens of thousands of jobs. The decision to act quickly rather than to drag out a painful process over a period of years may have been affected by Mitterrand's political desire to present a fresh, new balance by 1986, but it was by any reckoning a difficult and courageous step. It struck directly at the Left constituency, and was followed by fiscal measures which, encouraging new investment, inevitably favored a constituency belonging to the Right. Unemployment soared in 1984, from 2,181,000 to 2,456,700, leveling off in 1985 before rising again by an additional 103,000 at the end of 1986.

In September 1984 the Council of Ministers kept Mitterrand's promise to reduce taxes by proposing a budget designed to lower individual taxes by five percent, abandon the one percent surtax for the social security funds, and cut business taxes. The political effect of this was however dampened by the concurrent rise in consumption taxes, especially on gasoline and telephones. In October, the government also financed special measures aimed at relieving poverty by raising income tax on the very rich by half a percent.

At the same time, the stringent measures undertaken in 1982-1983 began to produce beneficent effects. The inflation rate in France had consistently been high throughout the 1970s. Prophets of gloom had announced that Socialist policies would kick it from the 13.6 percent rate in Giscard's last full year of office toward twenty percent. The wage and salary freeze of 1982, followed by the deindexation of wage increases, broke the vicious circle of inflation linking wage and cost increases.[10]

What conservative governments had feared to do, a Socialist government accomplished. As a consequence, inflation rates began to fall. In the year of discontent 1984 they were still at 7.4 percent, down from 9.6 percent the preceding year. In 1985 they had receded to 5.8 percent, and in 1986, for the twelve month period ending in October, had sunk to 2.2 percent, lower than the European Community average. The falling price of oil accelerated this last drop, but a dawning perception that inflation was finally sinking helped to redress the credit of the Socialists as capable administrators. An annual poll asking whether the past year seemed good, bad, or average for Frenchmen as a whole showed a steady rise in 1983 and 1984 over the fifty percent who thought it bad in 1982. The 1985 figures dropped to forty-two percent. Asked about inflation, seventy-six percent of respondents said in 1982 that they expected more than eight percent for 1983; forty-nine percent adhered to this opinion for 1984, and only thirty-four percent for 1985. At the end of 1985 only six percent remained this pessimistic. Writing at the end of 1986, two leading pollsters and political scientists fixed the change in the reigning climate of pessimism in the first half of 1985, noting however that the French remained uncertain and apprehensive about the economic future.[11]

The change in prime ministers thus provided a caesura for a period perceived confusedly at the time as a failure in almost all its economic decisions. In fact, the decisions taken in 1982-1984 (particularly after March 1983) were slowly achieving results, and very gradually became evident to the public.

But the real break came in March 1983 – the Socialists spent only twenty-one months on the left, thirty-six moving toward the center.

THE PS IN 1984

The Socialist party by mid-1984 was groggy, like a spirited but inexperienced fighter who has led too often with his chin. Had the institutions of the Fifth Republic permitted it to retreat and nurse its bruises, it might have been happy to subside into resentful opposition. Since it could not, individual Socialists began to examine what had gone wrong, often with amazing candor. It was relatively easy to explain that Giscard and Barre had left them with an economy in far worse shape than they had expected. (The secretiveness of French business had hardly facilitated detailed knowledge.) On the other hand, they had persistently argued before 1981 that the crisis was largely the result of selfish and incompetent behavior by French capitalists and their friends in government. They had genuinely believed that they could turn the situation around, creating social justice and fuller employment at the same time.

The Rocardian faction of the PS had always argued that the crisis was real, but Rocard had been beaten at the 1979 Metz congress, obliged to withdraw his presidential candidacy in 1980, and confined to an unmeaningful cabinet post. As woes mounted, he and his friends continued to say "we told you so," which was humanly understandable but did not endear them to their fellow Socialists. In mid-1983, a year before the misfortunes described above, the Rocardian magazine *Intervention* published an issue entitled "Do the Socialists believe in their myths?" "Yes and no," replied the magazine's director Jacques Julliard, recounting a parable:

> The Dorzé are a small tribe in Ethiopia who are persuaded that the leopard is a Christian animal which respects the fasts imposed by the Coptic Church on Wednesdays and Fridays. Accordingly, the flocks have nothing to fear on these two days; however, they are brought [to the corral] just in case. The Dorzé simultaneously believe and do not believe in their myths.[12]

Julliard concluded that the French Socialists did not entirely believe in their myths either. The events of 1984 showed that he was right: the Socialists lamented that they had waved what they themselves called "the magic wand" of socialism – and nothing had happened. What was to be done? What did they need to jettison? What had they already thrown overboard? What did they really believe in?

The PS was still divided into its constituent factions, although the necessities of government muted their clash. The Mitterrandists led by first secretary Jospin followed the president's lead (not always without misgivings). The Rocard faction was badly represented in government and hampered by its leader's position as a minister — until he seized the chance to break out of his cage in opposing Mitterrand's 1985 decision to adopt proportional representation. The CERES too was restrained by its leader Chevènement's intermittent presence in the government. The same problem held back the Mauroy faction until July 1984. The weight of the factions could not be ascertained by the vote on their propositions at party congresses, since this procedure was left in abeyance in 1981 and 1983. So the factional movements stirred restlessly, their contours visible but their exact sizes only vaguely discernible, like bodies under a blanket. They only knew that some day—soon, if the president were forced out of office in 1986, or perhaps somewhat later— they would struggle again to determine the course of the Socialist party.

As the young prime minister incessantly celebrated the virtues of modernization, a certain number of leaders who had always been on the left of the party suggested, like Jean Poperen, that the question had to be viewed "from a class viewpoint," which presumably meant that the spirit of enterprise and the new cult of the entrepreneur were not their highest values.

Other Socialists were determined to marry the spirit of enterprise to socialism. They included both Rocardians and those who saw Laurent Fabius as a future leader. Two authors close to Rocard wrote an article significantly entitled "For a Liberalism of the Left" (i.e. liberalism, continental style), in which they argued that the nationalizations, social achievements, and labor legislation of the Socialist government were in the direct line of French tradition. The real cultural break, they said, lay in Socialist reorientation of savings away from real property and into industry, and in rehabilitation of the enterprise. A Rocardian deputy commented: "Taking enterprise into account is not a temporary concession. It is one of the axes around which our socialism will be built."

But others were not so sure. A deputy from the Nord declared: "No one is calling into question the values of socialism, liberty, justice, solidarity, responsibility. Our values remain true, but we are now in a situation where we cannot translate them into action in a period of change." She found that Fabius "lacked utopia, lacked breadth."[13]

The PS, and not just Fabius, had lost the utopian spirit. As long as the party seemed condemned interminably to the snowy wastes of the opposition, regular draughts of utopian brandy had kept socialist ideas alive. But utopian intoxication collided with the sobering tasks of administration, with its daily compromises and inevitable discouragements. Its replacement (non-intoxicating) was to be the pleasure of good management. The idea that money and profit are intrinsically dirty, which had migrated from Catholic doctrine into French socialism, now had to be abandoned. Once the Socialists had understood that the goose of capitalism did not automatically lay golden eggs, either in private or public hands, they began to revise their ideas of the importance of enterprise, the entrepreneur, and profit. Mitterrand had brought back from a visit to Silicon Valley in early 1984 a new fascination with the electronic revolution, no doubt implanted originally by his universal idea man Jacques Attali. He was fascinated by the idea of the "third industrial revolution." France would march toward this new horizon, and escape from the crisis. And since the ideal type of high-tech enterprise was small, the cult of the entrepreneur did not need to collide head on with ancestral suspicion of the big capitalist.

The Fabius government would witness the reconciliation of most of the Socialist party to the notion that it was really social democratic. French Socialists had objected violently to the idea of accepting social democracy until the early 1980s. Some also argued that social democracy was impossible without close cooperation with a unitary trade union, something impossible in France. But this was a taxonomic argument, not a political one. The real objection was that social democracy, even in Sweden, implied a compromise with capitalism that they had proclaimed unacceptable.

Here was the central Socialist myth. When Mitterrand told the editor of *Libération* in May 1984 that the idea of a mixed economy played a central role in his economic thinking, many commentators interpreted this as a key change.[14] Some Socialists scoffed, pointing out that the PS had never intended to wipe out the private sector. Nor had they, but they had over-emphasized the importance of the public sector, believing that control over it would place a Left government "on the commanding heights of the economy." Instead, they had bought the privilege of bailing out failing industry and the responsibility of cutting thousands of jobs. The new cult of enterprise — among the Socialists, but also on the Right — came from an increasing recognition of the fact that *dirigisme* either of the Left or of the Right was no longer capable of creating productive employment for the 1980s or beyond.

Celebration of the entrepreneurial spirit might be necessary, but it did not make a socialist. Could the PS strip away its myths, lose its illusions, and still be socialist? The Rocardians thought so. The Mitterrandists were uncertain, yet this was the implicit course of their president, the explicit course of their young prime minister. Was there a political majority in the country for this new Left — where the Communist party could play no real role? What would the new spirit mean in the legislative elections of 1986? And if the president were so badly disavowed in 1986 that he had to resign, what would be left them?

THE COMMUNIST PARTY OPTS OUT

The discussion of the government of the Left in this book has treated the expressions "the Left" and "the Socialists" almost as equal terms. In some senses they were. The victory of 1981 had enabled Mitterrand to speed up the process which had been central to his policies since 1972 — to make these terms increasingly synonymous. Mitterrand dealt with the Communist leaders because this was the only way to talk over their heads to the Communist voters. For the same reason he took the Communist party into the government. (They also controlled the CGT, the only Communist force he needed to fear.) The government was of the Left because two parties of the Left were in it, but it would be misleading to rephrase this sentence to say that it was a genuine coalition of two Left parties, (or three, to add in the Left Radicals). The PCF entered the government in 1981 more as a hostage than as an associate.

In 1981 the PCF had no better choice. Sulking outside would not have been understood by voters already disaffected by the Politburo's Machiavellian predilection for Giscard over Mitterrand. The party leaders hoped that participation would rebuild Communist strength and lead the way to new voter growth. But by 1984 the PCF had instead acquired more than its share of the Left's unpopularity. Laden with the memory of all their political mistakes, faced with a steady decline in the industrial working class, discredited by the new anti-Communism, the Communist leaders feared their voters would think them co-responsible for increasing austerity. The industrial restructuring of early 1984 was a fresh challenge, to which the Communists responded evasively. They persistently criticized the government's policy, but when in April 1984 Mauroy demanded that the PCF clarify its stance PCF deputies evaded the question by voting confidence in the government. Georges Marchais declared blithely that the Communists were not being critical, but merely constructive. Even when the party's vote fell to eleven percent in the June 17 European elections, the PCF proclaimed that the lost voters were merely abstentionists, not defectors. A Central Committee meeting on June 24 signaled the party's intent to remain in the government and attempt to use its influence to affect policy. The particular target was to be the 1985 budget, in order to change (or at least to denounce) the austerity policy. In mid-July, immediately before the government crisis, *Le Monde's* PCF reporter concluded reasonably enough that this tactic excluded any idea of leaving the government.[15]

A week later, the PCF announced its refusal to enter the new Fabius government. What had happened? If the party was profiting by its presence, "solidly implanted in the state apparatus, nibbling away at key jobs, one after another," as *Le Figaro* wrote in May 1984, and had not panicked at the most recent and alarming drop in votes, why should it now leave the government? If the policies Mitterrand had adopted in 1983 gave it a motive to leave, why had it been tempted to stay?

The defection to Mitterrand of a quarter of its electorate in the first round of the 1981 presidential elections had given the PCF little choice but to support him in the second round. (There were however some limited sabotage actions consonant with the original intent to destroy Mitterrand, in which trusted militants were urged to vote Giscard in the second round.) In 1981, with new legislative elections imminent, the PCF also needed PS support for its leading candidates in the second round. Its plausible hope that the Left would not have a majority without Communist deputies was frustrated when the PS won a majority on its own while the Communists elected only half their previous deputies. Nevertheless, the party believed that because of its control over the CGT it could still exercise great influence on the government. This was also the fear of the conservatives, and of a not inconsiderable number of Socialists as well.

Mitterrand and Mauroy took four Communists into the government. Only one was an important party leader: Georges Marchais' lieutenant Charles Fiterman, transport minister with the honorific rank of minister of state. The others, in descending order of party importance, were civil service minister Anicet Le Pors, an economist, former finance ministry official and Marchais advisor; professional training minister Marcel Rigout, who was a party leader in the Limousin; and party journalist Jack Ralite as health minister. None of these positions could be considered strategic. Moreover, the Socialists took care to limit the amount of patronage the Communist ministers could exercise.

Fears that Communist ministers could fill the civil service with their appointees were based on their success in doing so in 1944-1947.[16] The circumstances were in fact quite different: in the immediate postwar period the civil service had been purged of the most egregious Vichyites, leaving many openings for deserving Resistance fighters, many of whom were of course Communists. The window was not nearly so wide open in the 1980s.

The PCF might desire and receive some concessions in personnel matters, but government policy was decided by the Socialists alone. Mauroy, who believed that the PS could hardly retain a permanent majority on its own, thought the Communists were playing a waiting game. "They knew their influence would be greater later, either after they left the majority, or because the PS would need them to build a new majority in another Assembly. They could expect to see their influence grow."[17] Despite this, Mauroy kept a watchful eye on the Communists. His rule was never to create a situation where the chief of a major administration was a Communist if the CGT controlled the base. Thus when Health Minister Jack Ralite wanted to appoint a comrade as director of hospitals, Mauroy broke this office off from Health and gave it to one of his own collaborators with instructions to keep an eye on personnel changes. Similar dispositions were taken with Fiterman's transport ministry. The suburban transport system, the RATP, where autonomous syndicates were in the majority, was given a Communist president, but the Matignon's man went to the national railroads, where the Communist unions were strong.[18] The anti-Communist union Force Ouvrière, however, found itself dealing with Communist ministers in the areas where it was most concerned, and considered itself very badly dealt by.

Except for sensitive posts, the presence of party members in the government apparatus had never been taboo in the Fourth or Fifth Republics. Anicet Le Pors, well known as a Communist, had risen during the Giscard administration to the position of chief of the Finance Ministry division for economic forecasting. Personnel policy had been merely to restrict their presence and their influence. Under the Mauroy government the Communists could have left their mark on French bureaucracy — if they had had enough time and had been given the opportunity to install a large number of party members permanently in important jobs. Neither was granted to them.

Communists in high positions had no influence on defense or foreign affairs — neither did most Socialists. Their effect on governmental policy could be seen only in sectoral questions, as when Health Minister Ralite ended the usage of having beds in public hospitals available to the patients of doctors with partially private practice. Doctors were incensed.

The PCF pushed hard to have Communist journalists hired by state controlled radio and television channels. In one such case, the government chose none of the men recommended, but hired instead a Communist journalist in partial disagreement with his party. Daniel Karlin, the lone Communist appointed to the new communications commission, the Haute Autorité to oversee radio-television, was also known for his independence of mind.

Many Frenchmen objected on principle to the presence in the government of a party which made itself an apologist for Soviet actions in Afghanistan and for Jaruzelski's coup in Poland, and which called for French nuclear weapons to be counted with American ones in negotiations with the Soviets. When the investigation of Communist fraud in a number of city campaigns in 1983 caused the election of several Communist mayors to be invalidated, the opposition was (unsurprisingly) much more vociferously indignant than the Socialists. But some uneasy Socialists, mostly admirers of Rocard, thought it inconsistent with democratic principles to maintain an alliance with a party that had so clearly relapsed into its old pro-Soviet ways.

After new signs of party decline in the European elections, "reformers" of a Eurocommunist persuasion made bold to challenge secretary general Marchais, whose twelve-year tenure had seen a long string of disasters for the party. One of the dissidents was the minister Marcel Rigout. Marchais was firmly in command of the party apparatus and beat them off, using the standard Communist "any criticism approved by outside forces only proves how right I am" tactic. But when Mauroy resigned and was replaced by Fabius, Marchais and his colleagues had to decide whether to exploit this opportunity. A government presided over by Fabius would clearly continue the policies of industrial restructuring which the Communists found difficult to swallow.

Two contradictory lines confronted each other in Communist councils. Some of the Communist ministers apparently wanted to remain in the government, hoping to increase the party's influence there. Polls had also shown that a majority of the Communist electorate favored participation in the government. Marchais opted for another policy. By going into opposition, he thought to rally his troops against dissidents he could depict as pro-Socialist and opportunistic. He could also hope that opposing the government would improve party fortunes in 1986.

After the damaging zigzag tactics of 1978-1981, Marchais also had to worry about the way in which the PCF disengaged itself from the government. He could afford to look as if he had been pushed (though the Socialists did not want to push him), but not as if he had jumped. Fabius' nomination gave the party a chance to represent its departure as the result of an unacceptable Socialist demarche – a push. Thus Marchais could and did jump.

The twenty-fifth PCF congress in the following February set as new policy the establishment of a "new people's majority rally," an empty formula that could not hide the fact that no one was rallying to the PCF and that it represented a smaller minority than at any time since the 1920s. The reformers were allowed to express themselves at the congress, but were strongly criticized by the leadership. Some reformers like Pierre Juquin were not re-elected to top posts and began to move toward an open break with the party. The following months saw the resignations from the Central Committee of other reform-minded leaders. The party was turning inward on its hard core.

Communist departure from the government did the PCF no more good than its previous presence. The National Assembly elections of March 1986 saw its share of the vote sink to 9.7 percent, a regression to its position of 1924. In Paris (where the PCF had seven deputies in 1973 and three in 1978), its score fell below five percent of the vote and it won no seats at all.

The bitter criticism the PCF lavished on the Fabius government won it no credit with its former voters. In those departments where the massive job cuts of early 1984 had been most grievous the PS suffered slightly (still improving its record over that of June 1984), but the PCF continued to sink.

In the hard-hit departments of the Moselle, Meurthe-et-Moselle (Lorraine coal and steel), the Allier (rubber products), and the Nord (coal, steel, shipbuilding), the 1986 elections saw the Communist party unable to profit from its criticism of austerity. It finished well behind its 1981 vote in these departments, as elsewhere.

After the 1984 elections, and still more after March 1986, observers began to speak of an historic decline of the PCF. In five years and three elections half of the PCF's twenty percent-plus share of the vote had disappeared. The pattern of decline was nationwide. In 1978 the PCF had won twenty-five percent or more of the vote in twenty-three departments, and twenty to twenty-five percent in twenty others. In 1986 its highest score in the country was 24.75 percent in the largely agricultural Cher; only two other departments gave it more than twenty percent. The PCF vote in fifty-eight departments was below ten percent.

Particularly painful were losses in the industrial areas, and in the so-called Red belt of industrial suburbs of Paris, which had sent twenty-four of the party's eighty-six deputies to the Assembly in 1978. The most important of these was Seine-Saint-Denis, just north of Paris, where the party had won more than fifty percent of the vote in its best days, and where its 1986 vote dropped to 18.22 percent.[19]

François Mitterrand had told the Socialist International in 1972 that his ambition was to reduce the Communist vote to fifteen percent. In 1981 he had hit his mark, in 1984 overshot it, and by 1986 there was little left to shoot at. The Communists had not been wrong in 1977 when they charged that the PS wished to use them only as an electoral prop, a *parti d'appoint*. But now the prop was too short to do the Socialists any good.

The vote subtracted from the Communist column had not for the most part gone to swell the Socialist vote. It is of course impossible to determine just which voters have moved from one party to another over the past few years. But the aggregate Left, which had 50.2 percent in the first round of the 1978 legislative elections and 55.64 percent in the 1981 legislative elections (marked, however, by high abstentions), had actually dropped to 43.96 percent in the 1986 elections. In the departments of the Mediterranean littoral and in some big cities, a part of the formerly Communist vote had gone to the National Front. Some of the Communist vote had retreated into persistent abstention.

By mid-June 1984, when the Communists clearly had fallen permanently through the fifteen percent floor, the once valid arithmetic of the Union of the Left appeared dubious to both Socialists and Communists, though for different reasons. It had become clear that the PS—with or without a Communist ally—could not win a majority in 1986. It risked instead a crushing defeat that would force Mitterrand to resign. In so doing, he would brand his entire term in office as a failure, be forced to retreat from active politics, and leave behind him a shattered, embittered, and deeply divided Socialist party. A respectable score in 1986—soon set at thirty percent—was not merely a political ambition but an absolute necessity.

The Communists did not think that a serious Mitterrand defeat in 1986 would be a disaster. It might instead be the opportunity they had vainly sought in 1981, the chance to rebuild on the wreckage of the Socialist party. Their unspoken motto after July 1984 thus became again what it had been in 1977-1981: "worse is better." March 1986 showed that their retreat into opposition had neither helped them nor much hurt the PS.

The Communist departure did not merely end a coalition. That had happened in 1977, and Mitterrand had continued to pose as "unitary for two." By 1984, the inner logic of Mitterrand's policies was contradicted by Communist presence in government, even though he was unwilling to acknowledge it. Once a Communist party reduced to eleven percent left the government, the logic of a tack toward the center enforced by economic necessity could dare to speak its name. If the Communists had remained strong, no such course would have been possible. Facing a weakened PCF, a Socialist party which had lost its socialist certainties had little to fear from competition on the Left. The ideological climate of the 1970s had already disappeared, now the political weather had also changed. The president was moving increasingly away from his self-induced spell as Socialist tribune to that of defender of Left-republican values. Socialists might wish to keep to the Left, but the PCF could no longer force them to do so.

THE RETURN OF THE RIGHT

After their double defeat in 1981 French conservatives could not believe what had happened to them. At first they thought it quite possible that the Left might remain in power for decades, as they had. Hopelessly in the minority, with a total of only 155 seats—a third of the National Assembly—the younger neo-Gaullists and Giscardians fought a rear-guard action against the nationalizations, while the major conservative leaders stood aside.

During the Socialist "state of grace," the old leaders of the former majority were in discredit. Giscard and Barre were generally unpopular; Chirac was blamed by the Giscardians for bringing down Giscard and for mistakenly believing that the Socialists could be defeated in the "third round" of the

National Assembly elections. But Chirac was the strongly entrenched leader of a disciplined party, and recovered rapidly.

The first sign that the Socialist victory was fragile came in January 1982 when conservatives won all four by-elections for seats where the June elections had been invalidated, unseating three Socialists. The March cantonal elections showed a further falling away from the Socialists. The June 1982 economic crisis, triggering a second devaluation and the beginnings of austerity, gave the conservatives new hope. Election after election—the municipals of 1983, the European elections of 1984, and the cantonal elections of 1985—furnished solid proof of what polls had already shown: a strong and unprecedented swing in popular opinion away from the Left.

The defeat of 1981 evoked a need to restate the reasons for and nature of conservative opposition to the Left majority. In the Fifth Republic until 1981 an ideological Left had faced a much less ideological Right, which did not even have a name for itself. The term "Right," discredited by Vichy, had by 1945 become taboo, and the conservatives in the Fourth Republic had shunned it. From de Gaulle through Giscard they referred to themselves, like barbarian tribes whose name for themselves means simply "the men," as the Majority. This led to limp and tautological election slogans like "the Majority will win a majority!"

Conservatives in the Fifth Republic had felt no need to reverse the nationalizations carried out by General de Gaulle's government in 1945. They believed in capitalism, but with an economy directed by the state. In the mid-1970s, when Raymond Barre began to speak of liberalizing the economy, he was bitterly attacked by Chirac:

> To abandon oneself to the play of economic freedom and international competition alone is to renounce control over the future, to abandon oneself to the unforeseeable. Raymond Barre likes to quote Frédéric Bastiat . . . [who] said some very good things. But he wrote in the first half of the nineteenth century, and he accorded a religious confidence to the providential harmonies of nature. Since then, one has become much more suspicious about the consequences of *laisser-faire* and *laisser-passer*, which are not all necessarily favorable.[20]

But the Raymond Barre decried by Chirac as too much of a Manchester liberal told the editor of *L'Expansion*, the French *Fortune*, in that same year, 1978, that his liberalism was not much different from that of social democratic governments, adding that he did not exclude recourse to nationalization or to massive state aid for declining industry.[21]

This discourse was tailored for the 1970s. Both men were addressing a current of opinion influenced by the ideas of the Left, and neither thought it profitable flatly to contradict those ideas; both were also defending the record of the interventionist state capitalism of the Fifth Republic. When the victorious Socialists carried *dirigisme* further than the Gaullists had done, it became politically necessary for conservatives not just to dissent mildly, but instead to find ideas which would decry the validity of government intervention. Purely French production of new ideas was for the moment insufficient to meet this need, and recourse to imports was inevitable.

On the offensive against Giscard and Barre in 1981 and preparing to run for president, Chirac found such new ideas in the New World. Visitors to the United States reported the popularity of a newly elected Ronald Reagan, and the usefulness of a combative free enterprise ideology. Even before Mitterrand's victory Chirac had ceased to attack Giscard and Barre for espousing the ideas of nineteenth century free enterprise, and began to denounce their creeping socialism, "the cunning collectivism which has developed in the last seven years."[22] And Chirac's campaign slogan in 1981 *"Chirac, Maintenant!"* was an echo of the American "Reagan, Now!"

After the election the virtues of free-enterprise *libéralisme* were praised by Chirac's younger advisers, like the brilliant *énarque* Alain Juppé. The RPR needed to counteract a Left which spoke of liberty while allocating more power to the state. It would in future call for less state in the name of liberty. Here it departed from the tradition of Gaullism and the philosophy of Charles de Gaulle. The historian René Rémond writes: "There was no body of thought more unitary and less disposed to share power with other authorities than that of Charles de Gaulle, nor more convinced that only the state is capable of perceiving the general interest and making it prevail over the egoisms of interest groups."[23]

The Gaullist synthesis in both domestic and in foreign affairs had, however, exhausted itself by 1980. Its political heirs still wished to exploit the general's name, but they increasingly found his ideas outdated. French social scientists who analyzed responses to a questionnaire given delegates to the November 1984 RPR congress concluded that de Gaulle's name had for them an emotional and symbolic value, but that the label "Gaullist" did not commit them to a policy or an ideology.[24]

In an expanding economy when conservatives controlled the government they found a powerful argument against the Left by pointing to the welfare measures which they had introduced. In a contracting economy, the cry of "we could do it better" in social policy was clearly no way to return to power. Something new was needed.

As Suzanne Berger points out in a highly perceptive analysis, new investigation into the values of free enterprise had begun even before the Socialist victory, prompted by the crisis of directed capitalism and resentment against the *dirigisme* of late Giscardianism.[25] Henri Lepage's *Demain le capitalisme* sold 40,000 copies in 1979 and was followed in 1980 by *Demain le libéralisme*. When Socialists defeated conservatives in France, and Reaganian Republicans beat Democrats in America, the transatlantic example seemed to light the way, even before the American economy improved. Publicists described Ronald Reagan's America in glowing terms — Guy Sorman's *La Révolution conservatrice américaine*, published in 1983, rapidly became a best seller. Another best seller, François de Closets' *Toujours plus*, criticized trade union privilege, power, and selfishness, and raised the question of whether unions were necessary or even legitimate. Other books about the virtues of deregulation, supply-side economics, and less intrusive government rapidly followed. Publishers remarked that the flood of leftist literature before 1981 had nearly dried up, to be replaced by dozens of books criticizing the Left and advocating new ideas for the Right.

The new French liberals differed from the Reaganians by not attacking the welfare state. They concentrated instead on the pernicious effects of too much state power and the pervasive influence of the unions. These two themes had clear antecedents in French political thought. A newer development was their cult of the entrepreneur, no great hero in earlier French conservative thinking. (He would soon be adopted by the Socialists as well.)

As the Socialists faltered and the European elections showed that the Left would almost certainly be defeated in 1986, the conservative parties became more and more confident that they had done well to choose a new ideology — now glorified by the condition of the U.S. economy in 1984. One sign of their new confidence was a change of label: they began unabashedly to refer to themselves collectively as "the Right," with no apologies to anybody, and no adverse reaction from the country.

Though far more closely united in parliament than in the quarrelsome Giscard years, the Right was still divided on party lines. The RPR leader remained Jacques Chirac, strong despite his errors in 1981. No one in the UDF had equal prestige or power. Giscard's immediate post-election error of denouncing Chirac for treason had effectively alienated him from many of the UDF parliamentarians. Worse, as time went on his popularity did not rise as that of the Socialists sank. But Giscard's disgrace did not cling to his second prime minister. After sharing unpopularity with his president, Raymond Barre in 1983 became the most popular figure on the Right.

Why Barre, and not Giscard? The former president had dwindled in defeat. His olympian certitudes had offended too many people, especially since they had often revealed themselves to be wrong. People still remembered the early efforts at folksiness (inviting the garbage collectors to breakfast) and the later reports that Giscard had the presidential family served at table before distinguished guests. They found the folksiness phony and the snobism all too plausible. Barre had been kept out of the 1981 election campaign (too unpopular) for which he could later be thankful. But his real credit lay in Socialist discredit — and the fact that the new government had been obliged to adopt policies barely different from his.

Condemned by Chirac for liberalism in the 1970s, Barre in the 1980s refused to be swept away by the new neo-liberal enthusiasm. As a young professor he had anticipated the 1980s vogue for Friedrich Hayek by translating his *Scientism and Social Science*.[26] Having long ago assimilated liberal ideas, he refused to show the enthusiasm of the newly converted. Very likely this contributed to his renewed popularity. The French looked at the choirboys of neo-liberalism and found that an astonishing number of them had been trained in the *Ecole Nationale d'Administration*, the main nursery for the acolytes of the over-powerful state. People questioned the sincerity of their conversion.

The newly confident Right knew by 1984 that it would win the 1986 legislative elections. The real prize in the Fifth Republic is the presidency, and the 1988 presidential campaign began in early 1983. Chirac would obviously run again. Giscard wanted to avenge his defeat, but even by 1983 it was clear he might not find enough backers. Barre too had presidential ambitions; his problem, however, was that he had no party behind him. Born in 1924 on the French island of Réunion in the Indian Ocean, he had been a professor of economics and one of the commissioners of the European Economic Community before Giscard brought him into the government in 1974. In 1976 he became prime minister when Chirac resigned. Although he was elected to the National Assembly for the first time in 1978 as a UDF member, he had always taken a stance above the parties. But if he were to run for president he would need UDF support.

The UDF was not a tightly organized party like the RPR but a coalition of parties. Created in 1977 to shelter Giscard's Parti Républicain, the Centre des Démocrates Sociaux (CDS) — heirs to the Christian Democratic tradition of the old MRP, and the right wing of the old Radical party, it was named after a book by Giscard. In 1982, the Parti Républicain, the strongest element in the UDF, elected a new young secretary general, François Léotard. An *énarque*, deputy, mayor and son of a mayor of the Mediterranean port of Fréjus, Léotard soon showed that he had ambitions of his own and only limited loyalty to Giscard. He and his political friends were all deputies or were elected deputies in 1986. All in their forties, they became the leading advocates of *libéralisme* in the PR. Léotard's influence in the PR and the UDF was challenged by informal organizations loyal to Barre, which the former prime minister began to set up in 1983. His strongest support lay in the CDS, but a strong minority of influential members of the PR inclined to him also.

The power of neo-liberalism drew the RPR and UDF together. In the 1970s the Gaullist movement had moved away from the general's vague but strongly held ideas about "participation," toward Pompidou's more orthodox capitalism, while remaining interventionist. RPR adherents tended to think of the UDF as generally to the right of them (as evidenced by Chirac's 1978 disquisitions on Barre's outmoded nineteenth century liberalism). By the mid-1980s, the RPR had itself moved to the right. While RPR cadres looked down disdainfully on the UDF as incoherent and badly organized, they saw little ideological difference between the two parties.[27] There was more distance on the matter of *libéralisme* between Barre and the enthusiastically liberal *"bande à Léo"* than there was between the Léotardians and the RPR.

The approach of the 1986 National Assembly elections encouraged the Right to run joint candidates in a large number of constituencies. Agreement came more easily because it was worked out by the party leaders, with Barre standing aside and proclaiming that any "cohabitation" with Mitterrand after the election would be a mistake. Both Barre and Chirac saw the 1986 election as a proving ground for the presidential elections of 1988. Polls showed the electorate opposed to the Socialists — but skeptical that the Right would manage the country better. Barre staked out high constitutional ground when he argued that the presidency would be diminished by cohabitation; though observers speculated that he really wanted to put his new popularity to the test rapidly, after a Mitterrand resignation, rather than wait two more years. Chirac needed to forge a new popularity by serving as a successful prime minister, and had early foreseen the necessity of cohabitation.[28]

From the watershed of the European elections of June 1984 to the March 1986 elections, therefore, the parties and personalities of the Right advanced toward a battle that would decide much, but would not be decisive. The Socialists too looked beyond 1986 to 1988. The calculations of both were troubled by a new force that had suddenly arisen on the extreme right wing of French politics, the National Front of Jean-Marie Le Pen.

ENTER THE NATIONAL FRONT

The rise of the National Front came as a surprise to French politicians. From 1945 to 1953 the extreme Right had won only a minute portion of the vote. It rallied with the Poujadiste movement in 1956 (twelve percent of the vote), and collapsed again after de Gaulle returned to power. In the presidential election of 1965 Jean-Louis Tixier-Vignancour (a lawyer who had defended both Marshal Pétain and the generals who rebelled in Algeria) won 5.28 percent of the vote.

In the following years the extreme Right was divided by its internal quarrels. Jean-Marie Le Pen, one of its most talented politicians, who had been elected to parliament as a Poujadiste at twenty-eight, got 0.74 percent of the vote when he ran for president in 1974. In 1981 Le Pen was even unable to get the 500 signatures of *notables* needed to enter the presidential race. When he ran for the National Assembly in June of the same year he won only 4.38 percent of the vote in a Paris constituency. With the triumphant rise of the Left, the forces of the extreme Right seemed to have become a minority inside a minority.

Two years later Le Pen's National Front had been reorganized and made its first breakthrough when Le Pen won 11.26 percent running for a seat on the Paris city council. Proof that this was no fluke came when a supplementary municipal election in the little industrial city of Dreux fifty miles west of Paris gave Le Pen's lieutenant Jean-Pierre Stirbois 16.72 percent of the votes. Stirbois was then brought onto the opposition list headed by the RPR and UDF, which was consequently able to oust the Socialist mayor and city council in the second round. In October 1983 another such municipal election in the Paris Red belt town of Aulnay-sous-Bois ousted a Communist mayor, with the help of National Front votes.

These signs were forerunners of the gathering storm that broke in the European elections of June 1984. In France (and elsewhere in Europe) these were conducted on purely national issues. Deputies to the European parliament had little or no power, and voters felt that no great responsibility attached to their choices. The National Front received 10.95 percent of the vote, the PCF 11.2. One party was rising, however, the other sinking. Because the French were used to a much bigger and more threatening Communist party and to a negligible vote on the extreme Right, Le Pen's party appeared almost as the victor and Marchais' formation the loser.

The National Front had run as the champion of native-born Frenchmen against North African immigrants, against crime and unemployment (with the Arab presence seen as a cause of both evils), and for law and order in a France allegedly governed by a laxist and incompetent Left. Two themes which appeal to at least part of the National Front constituency—integrist Catholicism and anti-semitism—found a target in the head of the joint UDF-RPR ticket for the European elections. Simone Veil was not only Jewish, she had also as minister of health in the Giscard administration led the way to legalization of abortion.

Few thought that the National Front would disappear in the 1986 Assembly elections (and after Mitterrand decided that these would be held under proportional representation, none at all). The question remained how an extreme rightist who had been around a long time had suddenly found a hearing in 1983-1984. Le Pen is a talented demagogue, but his talents do not date from yesterday. The several themes which now win Le Pen millions of votes obviously interpenetrate and overlap in the minds of his partisans. Nevertheless, they must be analyzed separately.

The incidence of crime had climbed steeply in France with the rise of urbanization and prosperity. Between 1963 and 1983 burglary, the most common crime, was multiplied by a factor of fourteen, rising in 1983 to 392,000 reported cases and to 436,435 in 1984. Burglaries doubled in 1972-1978, and doubled again in the following six years. Violent crimes (against both persons and property) nearly doubled between 1972 and 1983, but only a small part of this involved physical violence: in 1984 the police reported a total of some 61,000 cases of robbery with physical violence, rape, kidnaping, and murder (excluding crimes of passion). Still, the figures for violent robbery had tripled in ten years. (It may be noted that in 1984 they were forty-three percent of the U.S. total. Murder however was twice as common in Holland, the U.S., and Canada as in France, and burglary rates were higher in five other European countries.) The big cities were naturally hardest hit by the rise in crime. Nearly one Parisian in five was touched by crime of some sort in 1983, and the cities of the Mediterranean littoral and Lyons were also heavily affected.[29]

The alarming rise in crime statistics had begun well before Mitterrand's election. However, a large part of the public came to believe that the Socialists were encouraging crime by their naivete and laxity. Discontent began early and increased in intensity. By May 1984 only twenty-eight percent of SOFRES respondents believed that the government's record on public safety had proved satisfactory; the statistic dipped to twenty-five percent in May 1985 and twenty-two percent in May 1986.[30]

Much of the aversion to Socialist policies on public safety was directed against Justice Minister Robert Badinter. A former criminal lawyer, author of the law abolishing the death penalty, advocate of reform in French criminal justice, and a Jew, he was a magnet for criticism. His predecessor Alain Peyrefitte went so far as to write in June 1983: "M. Badinter has continued to be the defender of criminals while being the minister of Justice. . . . For the sake of France and of justice, I only hope that the immense talent of M. Badinter, the most brilliant of criminal lawyers, will again be used judiciously, that is, in the service of famous criminals."[31] When an ex-minister and member of the Académie Française could venture to describe an honorable political opponent in such scabrous terms there was ample room for less decorated demagogues to follow.

Le Pen's views on the repression of crime are unoriginal. He wrote in 1984: "In suppressing the death penalty, they suppressed one of the most dissuasive penalties. . . . The death penalty is the assurance of the freedom of all citizens." He argued that prison discipline should be tightened and paroles accorded only rarely. "The will to repress [crime] is insufficient. . . . It is necessary to purge the justice authorities of persons who think they can use their functions in the service of a revolutionary ideology."[32]

Mitterrand had opened himself to accusations of being "soft on crime" in 1981 when he granted amnesty to 6,200 prisoners (some fourteen percent of the prison population). Among them were unrepentant terrorists of the *Action Directe* group, who were later to murder General René Audran and Renault chief Georges Besse. Such amnesties are traditional after the election of a new president. As Barre adviser Jean-Claude Casanova remarked in a critical analysis of the government's record in which he defended most of Badinter's record, the prison population usually swells to previous levels within two years after an amnesty.[33] This had happened not only in 1983, but after the amnesties of 1965 and 1974 as well.

In any case, abolition of the death penalty was badly received by a police force largely suspicious of the Left. In May 1983 three policemen were killed in one day while checking the identity of a suspicious person. The murderer turned out to have been released from prison two weeks earlier. In early June a protest organized by two Paris police unions marched to the gates of the Elysée, calling for stronger action and abusing Badinter.

The opposition's efforts to exploit fears created by the rise in crime ended by playing into the hands of the demagogue Le Pen. Peyrefitte and his friends in the RPR and UDF had not been able to reduce crime; Le Pen had the advantage of being a political outsider. He excited support by linking the rise in crime to the presence in France of some 2,600,000 North Africans.

The incidence of crimes committed by foreigners (14.55 percent of misdemeanors and crimes; 7.4 percent of convictions) is in fact higher than their proportion to the total population (somewhere between eight and ten percent; estimates vary). Analysts explain the disparity by referring to high rates of unemployment, particularly among the large numbers of young North Africans, plus inferior and crowded housing conditions. Those not disposed to be analytical found it easier to listen to Le Pen's demagogy.[34]

The North Africans, or *maghrebins*, are heavily concentrated in the working-class areas of big cities. Thus by 1981 immigrants of all nationalities made up twenty percent of the population of Paris, sixteen percent in Lyons, fifteen percent in the Paris suburban departments of Seine-Saint-Denis and Val-de-Marne, and twelve percent in Marseilles. North Africans accounted for approximately half of this number, but as they were geographically concentrated and physically distinguishable from Europeans, their presence was the more obvious.[35]

The problem in France is not precisely racial, at least not in the most obvious sense of the term. Rather it is cultural. There had long been large numbers of non-Europeans in French cities, but by the early 1980s the French had become uneasy about the apparently unassimilable Muslim North Africans. An undoubted contribution to this new fear of Islam came from the rise of fundamentalist Islam in Iran and from the inextricable tangle of Lebanon (where French diplomats and soldiers had been constant targets, and where fifty-eight French soldiers were killed in a terrorist attack on the same day in October 1983 that 239 American marines lost their lives).

The Islam France had known since Napoleon's expedition to Egypt, from its conquest of Algeria in the 1830s, and French hegemony in Syria and Lebanon, had been a culture on the defensive against aggressive Western values. Even the war in Algeria had been lost to a National Liberation Front led by a westernized elite fighting in the name of national independence. In the 1980s, however, while many Frenchmen believed that pluralist education would assimilate Moslems in France to French values, many pessimists (only a minority being intellectuals) agreed with Louis Pauwels, the rightist editor of *Figaro Magazine*, "This ignores the fact that our values are disappearing and that Islam more than ever honors its own, seeing our societies becoming sillier and decomposing ever more each day."[36]

Polls on French attitudes toward North African immigrants in October 1985 and again a year later indicated a thirty-one percent approval rating for Le Pen's views that the massive presence of immigrants posed a danger to France. The same polls showed nearly as many approving his defense of traditional values—twenty-four and twenty-eight percent, respectively.[37] What the respondents meant by traditional values is unclear; they were apparently referring to vague Le Pen slogans like "France, first of all." Other polls show that a surprising percentage of Le Pen's supporters do not object to abortion, for example.

Le Pen and the National Front exploit a confused sentiment of estrangement in one's own country, which is felt by many Frenchmen walking the streets of the North African quarter in big French cities. The *Nouvel Observateur*, not suspect of racism, described one such scene in Marseilles: "One walks along in the rue Longue-les-Capucins, in the rue d'Aix or in the rue Thubanneau as in a city in the Orient. One passes girls in veils, peddlers offer you cassettes of Kishk, the blind preacher of Cairo, and public letter-writers recite the Koran. . . . There is a radio station, called Radio Gazelle. It is secular, but announces the hours of prayer."[38]

Many Frenchmen who detest Le Pen worry about the problem of assimilating the younger generation of *maghrebins*, or *Beurs,* as they call themselves (backslang for *arabe*). Many in this younger generation are apparently unsure whether they want to be French, and whether becoming French means renouncing their cultural heritage. Even the National Front has not proposed expelling the *maghrebins* en masse. For the Front's purposes the controversy is more useful when agitated than solved, but it has campaigned against the automatic accession to citizenship of young *maghrebins* born in France. The Front wants to make naturalization a favor, not a right. Knowledge of French would not suffice; respect for French law, culture, and history would figure in. And the possibility of losing French nationality or having it stripped away would be written into law.

THE FRONT'S HOLD ON THE VOTERS

Between 1984 and 1986 the National Front electorate changed, becoming younger and less middle-class. In 1984 workers and middle-level employees made up thirty-seven percent of Front voters. By 1986 they comprised one-half, remaining at this level in April 1988. A large number of these voters are young, and have few ties with the classical Right. In April 1988, when Le Pen won an unexpected 14.39 percent of the vote in the first round of the presidential elections, his highest scores came from small shopkeepers, artisans, shop assistants, and professionals, as well as from the unemployed. His results were below his national average among women (he drew seventeen percent of the male vote, ten of the female) and in the twenty-five to thirty-five and sixty-five and older age groups. He won less than ten percent, however, only among teachers.[39]

A young journalist who spent a number of months in Marseilles posing as a National Front supporter discovered a common denominator of resentment among lower and middle level militants. "The Front is a hodgepodge (*auberge espagnole*); one enters it with his own rebellion, resentment, rage at living in bad housing, having too little money, and so many other reasons for repressed aggression. Everyone brings in his own hatreds, and then, picking from the other's plate, acquires other ones, egged on by the experienced militants."[40]

What does the rise of the extreme Right mean for French politics and attitudes? One must first distinguish between the Front's leadership and its followers. Le Pen, Stirbois, and the other principal figures are rightists of a stamp familiar from the 1930s. A broad strain of anti-semitism has always figured in their ideas. The young Poujadiste deputy Le Pen told Pierre Mendès France in 1958: "You are not unaware that you symbolize in your person a certain element of patriotic and even physical repulsion."[41]

An indication that Le Pen's all but overt anti-semitism is a handicap came in September 1987. Asked whether he thought Nazi extermination camps had really existed, he refused to take a stand and added, "I think this is a detail in the history of the Second World War." The statement caused a sharp drop in Le Pen's own and the Front's popularity. Where fourteen percent of respondents had declared a good opinion of the Front in September

1987, the rating fell to eight percent in October (though it quickly rose again). Only two percent of those asked approved Le Pen's statement, only ten percent were without an opinion, and eighty-eight percent disapproved. However, Le Pen's ratings rose again fairly rapidly. Aside from his overstepping the line in racism, however, there are clearly defined limits to Le Pen's overall appeal. An October 1987 poll showed seventy-seven percent of respondents saying they would certainly not vote for him, with ten percent more saying they were inclined against him. This is not too far from the results of the 1988 election.

The fact remains that polls have shown anywhere from a quarter to a third of the population not ill content to have Le Pen in some way as their spokesman on crime and on the immigrant question. In April 1987 (i.e. a year after the advent of the Chirac government with its "tough on crime" stance) thirty-two percent of respondents in a SOFRES poll indicated general agreement with the National Front. These polling results betray a deep uneasiness on the themes dear to Le Pen, not necessarily a political commitment to the Front. And when Le Pen shows himself a genuine right-wing extremist of the old style, he repels people.

A considerable percentage of Le Pen's voters have come from the Left. Some are former Communist voters who shifted to the National Front in 1986 — a move particularly visible in the high vote for the Front on the Mediterranean littoral, where the PCF vote crumbled. In 1988, sixteen percent of Le Pen's vote came from workers. Earlier, eleven percent of persons who had indicated that they would probably vote for him declared their party preference as PCF.[42]

The National Front is a party with extreme right-wing leaders, but by 1986 the sociological profile of the National Front was no longer that of a typical French right-wing party.[43] With its simultaneous appeal to disgruntled youth, workers, and part of the middle class, it even had some resemblance to Fascist movements before World War II. Up to now, however, the Front has largely kept to an electoral and parliamentary strategy, and is competing for votes in a healthier and more stable society than the France of the 1930s.

Most of those who vote for the Front appear to be expressing a protest vote. It is not particularly surprising that some voters already adrift or drifting away from the PCF should be pleased to find in the National Front the cult of authority and nationalism, together with xenophobia, which they had previously appreciated in the PCF. One must not, however, assume that the rise of the Front comes principally from a switch by former supporters of the Communist party. Le Pen has made inroads on the Communist or ex-Communist vote, particularly in the south, but some of these voters went for Mitterrand in 1981, and might be considered generically Left. Protest parties have had a perennial appeal both to the left and the right sectors of the French electorate — the relative novelty is to see one party grouping them together.

The respectable Right has, however, lost more voters (former or potential) to the Front than have the parties of the Left. Some of its spokesmen have charged that the Socialists' horror of the National Front was more than a little hypocritical, since its strength at the polls aided the Socialists by dividing the Right. Mitterrand's proportional voting law was designed to keep the Socialists from being wiped out in 1986, but it had the incidental effect of permitting thirty-six National Front deputies to enter the National Assembly. Under the old winner-take-all rules in single-member constituencies the Front would have won few seats, if any. Votes that might have gone to its candidates would in most cases have swelled the majority of the respectable Right. (This is precisely what happened in June 1988, after the old system had been revived — the Front won only one seat.) In 1986, the leaders of the RPR and UDF detected no Socialist displeasure in results which held the conservatives to a tiny majority.

Controversy now rages whether electoral alliances with Le Pen are permissible. After the regional elections of March 1986 the RPR and UDF accepted Front alliances in several regions in order to have a majority in the local councils. These actions brought loud cries from the Socialists. Some conservatives have asked whether alliances with Le Pen are any worse than the Socialist alliance with the Communists. The Socialists find it easiest to shout down this question.

The alliance question is crucial, but probably not for presidential or legislative elections. The Front's best chance to become a permanent feature of the French political landscape is to win as many seats as possible in the municipal elections of 1989. City council posts offer numerous possibilities for a party to spread a deep network of roots; even if denied national representation, the Front could thus perpetuate itself.[44]

NEW WORRIES FOR FABIUS

Although by early 1985 the economic picture was slowly brightening, and Fabius' image as reflected in the polls soared above Mauroy's in his last year, the government had new worries at home and abroad. The headlines were full of stories about kidnapings of French diplomats and journalists in Beirut and bombs exploding in Paris. Added to this, the long-simmering ethnic problems of the French overseas territory of New Caledonia troubled not only that island but in late 1984 and early 1985 also entered into French domestic politics.

Annexed by France in 1853, New Caledonia had been first a penal colony, then a major source of nickel ore. The high price of nickel in the 1970s attracted new immigrants, who came to be a sixth of the total population of 150,000. Approximately half the population were autochthonous Melanesians, granted the right to vote in this French overseas territory only in 1952. A radicalized independence movement, the Front de Libération Nationale Kanak Socialiste (FLNKS) pitted the natives (*Kanaks*) against the European *caldoches*. Until 1981, government policy had been to increase autonomy under the aegis of the "national" parties, particularly the Rally for New Caledonia in the Republic (RPCR), which was close to the RPR and included some Melanesians. In 1981, the Socialist government had attempted a new policy of balancing the claims of independence-minded *kanaks* and loyalist *caldoches*. The plan was to increase self-determination (on a regional basis) and explore an autonomy that might lead to independence inside the French *Communauté*. The ambiguity of this scheme led the more militant FLNKS to call for independence immediately, while the *caldoches* feared the Socialist government planned to abandon them. In January 1985 several armed FLNKS militants were killed by French gendarmes. One was a top leader of the movement. The government sent out Edgard Pisani, a former Gaullist minister who had joined the PS in the 1970s, to represent it in New Caledonia and propose rapid measures for self-determination. His stay was troubled by much disorder, including murders of both Europeans and Melanesians. Pisani presented a plan calling for independence in association with France, with a special status for the Europeans. More violence caused Pisani to declare a state of emergency after *caldoche* demonstrations in the capital city of Nouméa.

A violent debate in France accompanied the events in New Caledonia. The opposition attempted to take maximum advantage of the government for actions described as dilatory, lax, and equivocal. The RPR leader in the Senate, Charles Pasqua, even threatened the president with an accusation of treason for illegal acts.[45] All ex-prime ministers and ex-president Giscard joined in a declaration against the government's policy, and the New Caledonian imbroglio seemed for a moment to open a new abyss of unpopularity for the Socialists.

In late April 1985 Fabius decided to defuse the situation by delaying the referendum until after the 1986 legislative elections. He calmed the situation by proposing the division of the island into four regions, each with an elected council, plus a territorial congress made up of all council members. Three of the regions would give the FLNKS a majority. Pisani, who had lost the confidence of the European population, was recalled and given the consolation post of minister for New Caledonia. In the September 1985 regional elections anti-independence forces won sixty percent of the vote with eighty percent of the voters participating.[46]

More trouble arrived for the government in July 1985, when an explosion in distant New Zealand sank the *Rainbow Warrior*, a ship belonging to the ecologist movement Greenpeace. The *Rainbow Warrior* had been anchored in Auckland harbor, preparing to lead an ecologist demonstration against French nuclear testing in the South Pacific. Two bombs timed to explode at intervals sank but did not destroy the ship. The second bomb killed a crew member, a Portuguese photographer of Dutch citizenship. Two days later the New Zealand police arrested two persons posing as Swiss tourists, who were rapidly uncovered as Dominique Prieur and Alain Mafart, officers of the French external intelligence service, the Direction Générale de Sécurité Extérieure (DGSE). Implicated in the sabotage action, they were charged with murder.

High officials of French intelligence had convinced themselves that the Greenpeace expedition was a major menace to their nuclear testing and heavily penetrated by agents of Soviet espionage.[47] Their operation involved bombs that would first frighten the crew from the boat, then sink it; no one was supposed to be killed. French intelligence had however thought very little about the dangers of an action unavoidably stamped with French fingerprints, conducted in a harbor of a foreign country whose government was already on record as anxious to gain domestic credit by protesting nuclear weapons in the Pacific.

The French press, and particularly *Le Monde*, showed more initiative in investigative journalism than had been customary in such affairs. It pointed out that an expensive operation of this type had to be approved at high levels, and identified General Jean Saulnier, chief of the president's military staff, as the man who had approved the funding. Defense Minister Charles Hernu, who had final responsibility for the DGSE, clearly had to know about the operation. The roles of the president and the prime minister in all this were unclear.

An embarrassed French government attempted to stonewall, denying any knowledge of the affair. Nearly a month went by before Mitterrand ordered the prime minister to order "a rigorous investigation." Mitterrand then demonstratively reiterated an order to the armed forces to halt any incursion into the waters of the testing site at Mururoa island, if necessary by force. He followed this up by a lightning trip to Mururoa on September 12, declaring on his return that France would continue nuclear testing as long as it thought tests necessary to its defense. He had already, on August 1, promoted General Saulnier to chief of the army general staff.

Fabius commissioned a report of inquiry from a distinguished Gaullist, Bernard Tricot, a former secretary general of the Elysée. Tricot's report, published in late August, was based on information provided by the DGSE and Hernu. It admitted the presence of French agents in New Zealand, but asserted that their action had been limited to reconnaissance. Since this amounted to saying yes, we had intelligence agents in the area, but the sabotage of the Greenpeace ship was an inexplicable coincidence that has nothing to do with France, it is hardly surprising that only seventeen percent of the public claimed to believe the report. Tricot himself admitted that his sources might have sought to deceive him.

Finally, on September 17, *Le Monde* disclosed that the actual sabotage had been conducted by a team of French frogmen which had swiftly been removed from the scene. All these revelations weakened the determination of the president and his men not to know anything about the affair and not to inquire into it. Mitterrand was reluctant to part with Hernu, a very old friend and companion, who was also popular with the armed forces. But he finally had to let him resign, and on the same day dismissed the head of the DGSE.

A protracted scandal had cost Mitterrand prestige and a minister. Exactly how much he or Fabius had known of the operation in advance is unclear. After the scandal broke, Mitterrand was conspicuously uninterested in clarifying the matter, very much interested in displaying his concern for national security. Hernu however was not a scapegoat—the responsibility for approving an operation foolish in conception and bungled in execution was clearly his. The French remained unexcited about the affair, and the damage to the government's reputation arose mainly from its clumsiness at cover-up and denial. Hernu remained popular, Mitterrand's and Fabius' poll ratings did not sink, and the opposition studiously refrained from attacking the government on a security question. The overall view of the uninformed man in the street was summed up in a quote from a taxi driver: "Terrific, that Hernu! He was damn well right to sink that Russian boat!"[48]

Fabius' relative popularity did not rub off on the Socialist party. In the March 1985 cantonal elections it lost seven more presidencies of departmental *conseils généraux*. The Left now controlled only twenty-eight of the hundred councils. Together with the collapse of the PCF vote in the June 1984 European elections and the PCF withdrawal from the governing coalition, the 1985 cantonal elections again demonstrated that there was no hope of recreating a workable Left majority in 1986. The president was obliged to face instead the prospect of a heavy Right majority in 1986, one so large and intransigent that he would be forced to resign.

In these circumstances, Mitterrand looked again at his 1981 campaign promise to introduce electoral reform using proportional representation. (The election laws in France have been changed ten times since 1871; this would be the fourth change since 1945.) In April 1985 the government announced that it would bring in a proportional representation bill, and it was duly passed by the National Assembly in June. The new law was drawn up to protect a PS standing alone and reduced in strength against a landslide that would throw its leaders out of national office. Voters had to choose from inflexible party lists, and the department became the basic voting unit instead of the smaller electoral districts. There was to be only one round instead of two, and departmental lists winning less than five percent of the vote would be disqualified. The new law did include much needed redistricting, in which the Parisian representation dropped from thirty-one deputies to twenty-one, while Paris suburban departments became more fairly represented. Glaring inequalities disappeared, such as the discrepancy between the two deputies returned by the 57,000 registered voters of the Lozère and the four deputies accorded the 600,000 voters of the suburban Paris department of the Essonne. The Lozère kept its two deputies (as did all the other small departments), while the Essonne got ten. Other Paris suburban departments, as well as the Bouches-du-Rhône (Marseilles), the Alpes-Maritimes (Nice, Côte d'Azur), and the Var (Toulon) all gained several new seats, while only Paris actually lost any. The new total of deputies in the National Assembly rose to 577 instead of 485, counting departments and territories outside metropolitan France. (This increased total was maintained in 1986 when the new conservative majority dropped Mitterrand's proportional representation, restoring single-seat constituencies and the winner-take-all system.)

The first result of the proposal to change the election laws was the resignation of Agriculture Minister Rocard. He based his resignation on opposition to proportional representation, but he had clearly chosen the opportunity to take his distance from a government which was doing little for his image, and too much for that of Laurent Fabius. He planned to try another run for the presidency in 1988, and announced his candidacy in June 1985.

The summer of 1985 saw a quarrel between Fabius and PS first secretary Jospin about which of them should have the principal responsibility for the conduct of the 1986 National Assembly election campaign. Fabius was attempting to de-emphasize socialism, talking of a *Front républicain* designed to bring in sympathizers who did not wish to call themselves Socialists. Jospin was wary of slogans that were not explicitly socialist. He also saw Fabius as a rival to his own position and future ambitions. The Rocard faction might become his ally. There was also a real danger that factional maneuvers too clearly aimed at boosting Fabius might even push the Rocardians out of the party. Mitterrand decided that Jospin should work out a compromise in this quarrel between his two lieutenants. Although he attempted not to favor either one, the advantage went to Jospin.

Fabius had moved upward too fast to please many of his fellow Socialists. Pierre Mauroy's friends had little love for him, nor did the party left wing. By the fall of 1985 the Socialists were concerned with the preparation of a legislative election they knew they could not win, in order to secure Mitterrand's position for the final two years of his term. If the years 1986-1988 did not go too badly, the Socialists might hope to win another presidential election. But with the president's record considered negative by sixty to fifty-five percent of the electorate, another Mitterrand candidacy then seemed unlikely. The most plausible Socialist replacement for him appeared to be not Fabius, but Rocard.[49]

Rocard spent most of 1985 after his resignation from the government in reorganizing his own faction in the party. Elections for departmental delegates to the Socialist party congress scheduled for October in Toulouse showed that his followers now represented some twenty-eight percent of the party, with special strength in the west and fairly good overall representation. Always quick to say "I told you so," Rocard had never been a team player, but the Mitterrandists had never wanted him on the team either. Now it looked as if they must prepare for that possibility. Rocard's main programmatic point was to insist that the PS fully accept the identity created by its party's record in office and not backslide into the left-wing ideologizing of the 1970s. Since his followers had reproached him for not doing enough for them in 1981, he also had to demand as many places as possible for them on the party slates being prepared for the legislative elections. He settled for eighteen percent of Assembly candidacies, with a larger proportion on lists for the regional council elections to be held concurrently with elections for the National Assembly.

Rocard spoke on the first day of the PS Congress to an audience prepared to hear and perhaps be impressed by him. Inexplicably, he had not prepared a crowd-pleasing speech. Droning on endlessly and obscurely, talking away from the microphone, Rocard delivered a speech that might have been suited to a technical meeting. Once again he raised doubts about his talent as a political tactician. The next day, Laurent Fabius filled the congress' emotional needs by attacking the opposition leadership as a "mediocre wax museum" and hailing the liberating action of democratic leaders in South America and South Africa. Fabius succeeded in making the assembled Socialists forget that many of them did not love him very much. His listing of economic achievements won only polite applause, but the congress loved the red meat.

On the ideological front, the congress demonstrated that the PS accepted Rocard's positions, less because they were his than because there could be no turning back from the president's and party's record of 1983-1985. The final resolution of the congress stated: "There are constraints which no power can shake off in a democratic and open society. Clarity about the facts implies that one analyze them as they are." It continued:

> The crisis has put this brutal truth in sharp light: the only revenue that can be distributed is the counterpart of that which can be produced and sold. The Socialists have taken better account of the necessity to remain competitive, to make profits in order to invest, to contain the costs of production.[50]

Fabius thus seemed to emerge from the Toulouse congress as the charismatic leader of a party newly united around the idea of modernization. Three weeks later, he appeared on television in a debate with Chirac meant to build him up as the new leader of the Left. Attempting with short sharp questions to provoke the conservative leader, he fell victim to his own tactics when Chirac told him, "Please let me speak and stop interrupting constantly, a bit like a yapping little dog." To this insult the younger man replied to the older ex-prime minister with hauteur and a scornful gesture: "Listen, you are talking to the prime minister of France."

Fabius had blundered; his arrogant rejoinder seemed to sum up a chilly and dismissive aspect of his personality which was already troubling the public. In early December he made another error. When Mitterrand unexpectedly received the visiting Polish leader Jaruzelski, giving no explanation, Fabius told the National Assembly that he was "troubled" by the president's action. Although the Socialists were also disturbed, they were more upset at Fabius' attempt to take his distance from his chief.

Fabius' poll ratings went into a steep decline. Jospin could lead the campaign, but who was able to carry the banner for the PS? The result was the president's return to the political arena. In October 1985 it had seemed to many Socialists that even if he were not swept away by the tides of 1986 he would depart two years later. By early 1986 it was clear that only François Mitterrand could save PS fortunes, and his own.

NOTES

1. *Le Monde*, July 4, 1984.

2. See the extensive biographical article on Fabius in *Le Monde*, October 26, 1985, and an interview in which he provided some biographical information, "Le Socialisme et la dynamique de la démocratie, entretien avec Laurent Fabius," *Le Débat* 49, March-April 1988.

3. *Le Monde*, July 19, 1984.

4. Cf. "Le programme Fabius," *Regards sur l'actualité* 104, September 1984, pp.11-14 summarizing Fabius' Assembly speech of July 24, 1984; also see *Journal officiel* no. 78, July 25, 1984 for National Assembly discussion.

5. Thierry Pfister, *La Vie quotidienne à Matignon au temps de l'Union de la Gauche*, p. 358.

6. Direction générale des douanes, cited in *Quid 1987* (Paris: Robert Laffont, 1986), p. 1452.

7. *Le Monde, dossiers et documents* no. 118, January 1985.

8. Christian Stoffaes, *La Politique industrielle*, p. 289.

9. Ibid., p. 177ff.

10. See the detailed analysis of deindexation in Alain Fonteneau and Pierre-Alain Muet, *La Gauche face à la crise*, chapter 5.

11. SOFRES, *L'Etat de l'opinon publique-clés pour 1987*, pp. 136-137, 236.

12. Jacques Julliard, "Réflexions d'après le prochain congrès," *Intervention* 5-6, September-October 1983, p. 5.

13. Marie-Noëlle Lienemann and Patrice Finel, "Pour un libéralisme de gauche," *Nouvelle revue socialiste*, September-October 1984, pp. 17-18; Jean-Louis Andréani, "Peut-on être socialiste aujourd'hui?", *Le Monde*, December 6, 1984.

14. *Libération*, May 10, 1984.

15. *Le Monde*, July 12, 1984.

16. Cf. Denis Jeambar, *Le P.C. dans la maison*, for a rather alarmist view of the question.

17. Pfister, *La Vie quotidienne*, p. 156.

18. Ibid., pp. 155-157.

19. Cf. *Le Monde, dossiers et documents: Les Élections législatives de 1986*.

20. Jacques Chirac, *La Lueur de l'espérance* (Paris: La Table Ronde, 1978), quoted in Franz-Olivier Giesbert, *Jacques Chirac*, pp. 306-307.

21. Jean Boissonat interview with Raymond Barre, *L'Expansion*, September, 1978.

22. Giesbert, *Jacques Chirac*, p. 335.

23. René Rémond, *Les Droites en France*, p. 317.

24. Pierre Bréchon, Jacques Derville, and Patrick Lecomte, "L'Univers idéologique des cadres RPR," *Revue française de science politique* 37, pp. 677-678.

25. Suzanne Berger, "Liberalism Reborn," in *Contemporary France; a Review of Interdisciplinary Studies, 1987*, eds. Jolyon Howorth and George Ross.

26. Friedrich Hayek, *Scientisme et sciences sociales*, translated by Raymond Barre (Paris, Editions Plon, 1953).

27. Bréchon et al., *L'Univers idéologique*, pp. 690-694.

28. Cf. Giesbert, *Jacques Chirac*, p. 359.

29. These statistics are drawn from *Quid* 1987, p. 698, and from "L'Insécurité," *Le Monde, dossiers et documents* no. 122, May 1985.

30. SOFRES, *Clés pour* 1987, p. 222.

31. *Le Monde,* June 21, 1983.

32. Quoted from Jean-Marie Le Pen, *Les Français d'abord* (Paris: Editions Carrère, 1984), in *Le Monde, dossiers et documents* no. 122, May 1985.

33. Jean-Claude Casanova, "Après trois ans," *Commentaire* 7, Autumn 1984, pp. 453-454.

34. For the crime figures and other considerations on Le Pen, see Edwy Plenel and Alain Rollat, eds., *L'Effet Le Pen*; here p. 209.

35. Cf. the discussion of statistics on immigration in "Les Immigrés en France," *Le Monde, dossiers et documents* no. 115, October 1984.

36. Louis Pauwels, "Les Sarrasins en Corrèze," *Figaro Magazine*, May 18, 1985.

37. SOFRES, *L'Etat de l'opinion — clés pour 1988*, p. 134.

38. *Le Nouvel Observateur,* 7-13 February 1986.

39. SOFRES, *Clés pour 1988*, pp. 131-132. Presidential figures for 1988 are cited from an exit poll made by Bull-BVA, in *L'Election présidentielle*, supplement to *Le Monde, dossiers et documents*, May 1988, p. 41.

40. Anne Tristan, *Au Front*, p. 255.

41. Plenel and Rollat, *L'Effet Le Pen*, p. 24.

42. *Le Monde, L'Election presidentielle 1988*, p. 41, and SOFRES, *Clés pour 1988*, p. 138.

43. Cf. Jérôme Jaffré, "Front National: la relève protestataire," in *Mars 1986: la drôle de défaite de la gauche*, eds., Elisabeth Dupoirier and Gérard Grunberg, pp. 212-213.

44. On the National Front, see Plenel and Rollat, *L'Effet Le Pen*; Martin Schain, "The National Front and the Construction of Political Legitimacy," *West European Politics*, no. 2 (April, 1987); Jérôme Jaffré, "Front National: la relève protestataire," SOFRES, *Clés pour 1988*, pp. 138-142, and Nonna Mayer, "L'Usure de 'l'effet Le Pen?,'" *French Politics and Society* 6 (April 1988).

45. *Le Monde,* December 22, 1984.

46. *Le Monde,* May 23, 1985, and *Le Monde, dossiers et documents: L'Histoire au jour le jour 1974-1985*, pp. 216-217; *Le Point,* April 29, 1985.

47. See the accounts of the *Rainbow Warrior* affair in *Le Monde, dossiers et documents: L'Histoire au jour le jour 1974-1985*, pp. 214-215, and *Le Monde*, March 19, 1988. The latter reconfirms the military obsession with security.

48. Quoted in J. W. Friend, "A Rose in Any Other Fist Would Smell as Sweet," *French Politics and Society* 12. For an account of the affair, see Jacques Derogy and Jean-Marie Pontaut, *Enquête sur trois secrets d'Etat*; Eric

Cahm, "From Greenpeace to Cohabitation," in *Contemporary France, a Review of Interdisciplinary Studies*, eds. Jolyon Howorth and George Ross; and Stephen E. Bornstein, "An End to French Exceptionalism? The Lessons of the Greenpeace Affair," ibid. For the Tricot report, see *Le Monde*, August 28, 1985.

49. Cf. Gérard Le Gall, "Sondages, l'état de l'opinion," *Revue politique et parlementaire* 921, p. 7.

50. Quoted in *Le Figaro*, October 14, 1985. Also see J. W. Friend, "A Rose in Any Other Fist Would Smell as Sweet," and Eric Cahm, "From Greenpeace to Cohabitation." pp. 9-11.

4

What the Socialists Accomplished

THE SERENDIP EFFECT

In 1986 the Socialists would ask the country to renew its confidence in them on the basis of the laws they had passed and their record as administrators. The voters' judgment on the administrative record of 1981-1983 was harsh, although their view of much of the legislation enacted in 1981-1986 was favorable.[1] The list of laws passed and administrative actions taken does not, however, sum up all the transformations in France that came about as a direct or indirect result of the Socialist victory in 1981. The Socialists had thought of themselves as the architects of change. With the retrospect of only a few years it is possible to see them instead as its agents, generating change here, eliciting it elsewhere, often without deliberate intent or preconceived plan.

In 1976 the Gaullist politician and writer Alain Peyrefitte described the role of the unexpected and unintentional in the history of France:

In the strange country of Serendip, everything happens backwards. You find what you were not looking for; you never find what you are looking for. . . . The serendip effect is the daily bread of our history. It affects all the regimes that France has given itself — they have all achieved the opposite of what they sought.[2]

The Socialists do not love Peyrefitte the Gaullist politician, but might nevertheless admit some resemblance between the serendip effect and the course of events after 1981.

A striking example of an indirect result of Mitterrand's election is the conversion of the French Right from Gaullist *dirigisme* to free enterprise, provoked to a considerable degree by its need to find a doctrine totally distinguishable from *dirigiste* socialism.

The second great unintentional change of 1981-1986 was that in the Socialists themselves. Their program, combining certain socialist measures and left-Keynesianism, was thrown off balance by bad timing and mistaken estimates. What followed, after 1983, was a general Socialist retreat from ideology. The Socialists of 1981 had seemed more firmly ideological than they really were, in part because they were persuaded that all their ideas were logically interconnected.

Reflation (with socially beneficent effects) would aid a centrally controlled economy to expand, and vanquish unemployment. The link connecting reflation, nationalization, and Socialist ideas in general was shattered when reflation failed and the "commanding heights of the economy" turned out to command only the necessity of assuming new fiscal burdens. The cure for debt and inflation had to be found in an austerity that kept growth low while unemployment rose.

As intoxication with their rhetoric evaporated into a disabused hangover, French Socialists came to realize that new and non-ideological policies were necessary. They had fallen into an error Stanley Hoffmann has described as "typical of Liberals (be they reformist democrats or social democrats): a belief that all good things must come together," a mindset which sees no reason why obtaining social justice by higher corporate taxation might be incompatible with a desired rise in profits and investments.[3]

Once the Socialists fully recognized the incompatibility of economically necessary policies with ideology, they faced the choice of falling back on the interior lines of bunker ideology or advancing into the unexplored country of pragmatism. Under the leadership of the president, most of the party found it possible to understand that some of its goals might be contradicted by others.

Some of their original goals were reached, other results were at least in part unintentional. The impact of the Socialist victory on the conservative legitimism of the Fifth Republic and on French institutions will be described in a later chapter. The results of ambitious Socialist legislation on decentralization, nationalization, labor relations, audio-visual communications, the administration of justice and other areas remain to be considered.

THE PROGRAMMED LEGISLATION

Decentralization, declared *"la grande affaire du septennat"* by François Mitterrand, was a reform carried out by the Socialists, not a socialist reform. Since the early nineteenth century a centralization begun by the monarchy and systematized by the Jacobins and Napoleon had come under regular attack. By the 1960s, centralization was seen as an obstacle both to economic growth and to democratic participation. Shades of opinion from Gaullist technocrats to PSU leftists could agree that local communities should have more voice in their own economies and development. But the *notables* of the provincial establishment were deeply suspicious of changes in a system affording them comfortable arrangements with the central power and had always blocked innovation.

In 1971 Interior Minister Raymond Marcellin tried voluntary fusion to reduce the number of the 36,000 *communes*, the smallest territorial administrations. Only some 2,000 mergers took place. In 1982, half of the French population lived in the 800 *communes* which had towns of 5,000 or more people, while eighty percent of the *communes* had fewer than 2,000 inhabitants. Of the 32,417 mayors of these tiny jurisdictions, sixty-eight percent presided over *communes* of fewer than 500 inhabitants.[4]

Each *commune* had an elected council which in turn elected the mayor. Collectively, they were responsible for basic services such as garbage collection, sanitation, maintenance of tertiary roads, problems of housing, parks, libraries, etc. The mayor was subject to the authority of the prefect, and responsible for making known and enforcing legislation. Mayors of very small towns, often part-time officials quite unable to cope with all the laws, regulations, and circulars streaming out of Paris, inevitably deferred to the prefect and his services. The mayors of medium-sized and larger towns, however, resented the need to ask for government approval on local matters such as zoning and building permits. In the larger towns mayors came to a tacit understanding with cooperative prefects, who did not care to frustrate men who were often also senators or deputies to the National Assembly. By the 1970s, the prefect would customarily guarantee a delay of no more than two weeks on local requests by the mayor.[5] Meanwhile, mayors of small places were frequently grateful to the prefect for taking from them the responsibility to veto popular but costly projects.

The prefects were highly trained and high-powered officials appointed by the minister of interior and usually graduates of the Ecole Nationale d'Administration. They were the executives of the ninety-six *départements* of metropolitan France, and coordinators of all national services emanating from the various central ministries. Prefects also presided over the twenty-two regions created in 1972, which possessed no legal personality and were only public establishments for economic planning.

Restless under Gaullist power, the Left had sought a means to give localities more autonomy in the areas of housing, public transport, and education. The Common Program of 1972 already advocated most of the decentralizing measures enacted into law a decade later.[6] The *Projet Socialiste* of 1980 breathlessly described decentralization as "one of the most powerful levers of the break with capitalism, which will allow citizens to take

direct part in the immense enterprise of social transformation. . . ." Many on
the Right as well desired decentralization, though more soberly. A bill
drafted under Giscard's Interior Minister Christian Bonnet was discussed
in the Senate in 1980-1981 but did not become law.[7]

In the formation of the Socialist government Gaston Defferre made it
plain that he wished to have the portfolios of both interior and decentralization. The latter activity was to be his contribution to the history of the *septennat*, an achievement paralleling his framework law of 1956 which had
prepared the way for decolonization. Defferre was in a hurry—the possibility
that delay might allow opposition both outside the majority and within it to
delay and weaken his bill was only too evident in the prior history of
decentralization. He chose to enact irreversible principles first, and let
details follow. In the lengthy parliamentary debate over decentralization the
opposition introduced over 4,000 amendments, opposed Defferre's
priorities, and warned of financial difficulties to come.

Defferre's first step was meant to be irrevocable. The law of March 2, 1982
suppressed all *tutelles* or controls over local authorities, and replaced them
by partial controls administered by tribunals. The office of prefect was
abolished (but in practice, most prefects immediately became *commissaires
de la République* and were still addressed as *"Monsieur le Préfet"*). The
prefect's executive powers over the department were transferred to the
president of the departmental *conseil général*. In the next step, a more complicated one which took place between 1983 and 1985, some responsibilities
(and resources or financing) were transferred from the state to lower levels.
In all, thirty-three laws and 219 decentralization decrees (and a large number of circulars, many of them very long) were issued between 1982 and 1985.

The Right voted en masse against the early laws, even though it did not
fundamentally oppose decentralization. The Socialists can claim credit for
bringing about this long delayed evolution. As cantonal and then municipal
elections showed a swing away from the Left, however, they rapidly discovered that the Right would profit more from it.

The important questions on decentralization concerned its scope and purpose—what levels of administration would be decentralized, what means
would be used, how drastic would it be. Above all, would it genuinely attack
a widely perceived problem—that of a society too tightly and inefficiently
controlled by a central bureaucracy? Would it advance democratic participation as well as economic growth?

In its 1977 proposals for the revision of the Common Program, the PS had
upheld and praised the existence of all 36,000 communes, while calling for
the abolition of the office of the prefect. By so doing, the Socialists signaled
unwillingness to attack the interests of the local *notables*, an appreciable

percentage of whom were themselves Socialists. In 1981, other potential obstacles were avoided: communes, departments, and regions were all treated as equals, with no level having any power over the others. The question of the *cumul des mandats* — the simultaneous holding of political offices at different levels — was postponed until later.

When discussing decentralization with an American, Frenchmen almost invariably warn him not to confuse it with federalization, rejected as not in the French tradition and "unsuited for a middle-sized country such as ours." (Switzerland, of course, has approximately one-ninth the population of France.) The comment points up the relatively restricted nature of the reform. Decisions on zoning and land use have been transferred to local mayors. But education (under local control even in centralized Britain) remains a state monopoly — except that the localities now have the dubious privilege of school maintenance and transport. The police, as one might expect, remain national.

On the *commune* level, the new dispensation has confirmed and systematized a long-term evolution toward autonomy for big-city mayors, has given more scope to energetic mayors of medium and small towns, and presented both opportunities and problems for mayors of tiny *communes*. The prefects, rebaptized "commissioners of the republic" and re-rebaptized prefects by the Chirac government, retain an important role as coordinators of national services, and especially vis-à-vis the mayors of small *communes*.

The prefect is no longer the executive officer of the department. A president of the *conseil général* is now responsible for presenting its budget and chairing the departmental assembly. The *conseillers généraux* elect the president, who acting together with his *bureau* of four to ten vice-presidents, plus an often sizable staff, has become a real departmental executive. Finally, the region has become a major player, with regional representatives (*conseillers régionaux*) directly elected for the first time, although from a departmental list.

Block grants (*dotations budgetaires*) from the national budget help to pay for the responsibilities the state has transferred to a lower level. Other taxes, such as annual automobile registration fees and drivers licenses, have also been transferred to the *collectivités locales*. An important local levy is the business tax (*taxe professionelle*), introduced by Chirac in his first prime ministership, denounced but retained by both Mitterrand and then Chirac. Since it brings in about forty-five percent of local revenue, it has been difficult to find a replacement for it.

The region is in many ways the most interesting of the newly manumitted *collectivités locales*, but also the most problematic. Many Frenchmen believe that France cannot afford four levels of government — national, communal, departmental, and regional, and that in any case the responsibilities of these various levels overlap confusingly. For example, Orléans mayor Jacques Douffiagues, (a Parti Républicain leader who later served as transport minister under Jacques Chirac) told an interviewer in 1985 that he greatly preferred departments to regions. Douffiagues, president of the *conseil général* of his department, feared that regional "barons" (he named powerful conservative politicians in western France) would be only too happy to create "feudalities" in their regions to widen their power base. Douffiagues' preference lay with a clear distinction of powers for the different territorial levels; he doubted that France needed regions. He saw questions involving roads and schools as problems of restricted geographic areas, with the region as a rather artificial construct not very useful on the economic level. Where the power did not exist on the local level to cope with an economic problem, why, he asked, should one refer it to a medium-level authority, and not the national one? Douffiagues and Jacobins like him also remain suspicious of the pretensions of regions which have or "claim to have" a local language. Here they express the enduring apprehension of French centralizers that the state will be weakened if centralized conformity is relaxed.[8]

While the powers of the regions are equal, some possess an historic identity. Douffiagues' Orléans is situated in a composite region colorlessly named the Center, and no one is geographically a "Centriste." But for two hundred years since the Revolution abolished the old provinces Frenchmen have continued to identify themselves with the names of many of the old provinces which are the new regions—as Auvergnats, Bretons, Bourguignons, Lorrains, Alsatiens, Picards, etc. The Jacobins fear that national unity will suffer from revived particularisms; proponents of the region dismiss this as scare tactics.

The regions are very unequal in population and wealth. The Ile de France, with more than ten million inhabitants, is more populous than all but six American states. Only Rhône-Alpes, with its five million, comes near to matching it, although even little Limousin, the least populous region with 737,000 inhabitants, has more people than six U.S. states.

Whereas the departments are burdened with multiple responsibilities, the regions—still seen as centers for economic development—have greater potential scope. They have relatively little money: the 1988 budget of the Ile de France region is roughly six billion francs, a fifty percent increase since 1984. This is more comparable to the budget of a very rich American county than that of a large state. American and French local expenditures on education are of course not comparable—an American county may spend from a quarter to three-quarters of its revenue on education, while the personnel expenses of the French system are entirely borne by the national government. The Ile de France region, responsible for technical training only, plus construction and maintenance of its secondary schools, budgeted 362 million francs for its *lycées* in 1986.[9] The main expense of a regional budget is investment; sixty-five percent of the Ile de France's expenses go for transportation: the suburban lines (RER), buses, subways, etc. Though Jacobins continue to worry over the danger of an enlarged bureaucracy, this has been successfully avoided so far — the Ile de France in 1987 had only 400 employees.

Regionalists contend that the possibilities of imaginative investment are already creating new visions. Jean-Marie Rausch, formerly president of the Lorraine region, senator and mayor of Metz, told an interviewer in 1986 that with these accumulated offices he could wield an authority at least equal to that of the *Minister President* of neighboring Saarland. The border region of Lorraine has a number of problems in common with the Saar and Luxembourg across the frontier, which were formerly handled by officials of the French state in a trans-border commission. In 1984 Rausch took advantage of the new laws to deal directly with foreign officials of equal level, setting up a Saar-Lor-Lux community which has the advantage of being able to get direct financial aid from the European Community.[10]

The new ability of regional authorities to discuss problems and undertake initiatives with their colleagues across national frontiers is one notable advantage of decentralization. All of France's neighbors — Belgium, West Germany, Switzerland, Italy, and Spain are now themselves either federal or decentralized. The regions may also play an important role in the post-1992 Europe of disappearing frontiers. The Nord-Pas-de-Calais can look to the Walloon region of Belgium and, especially when the cross-channel tunnel is completed, to closer ties with England. Midi-Pyrénées looks to its Spanish neighbor, Provence-Côte-d'Azur to Lombardy and Piedmont. The planned development zones cut across frontiers.

Regions can also look to more distant partners — French regions are cooperating with Bavaria, with its new high tech industries, while the Ile de France was involved in the French-sponsored projects for the Cairo subway and is now interested in a new Beijing subway.

The state has the predominant role in education, but the regions may introduce auxiliary programs. The Nord-Pas-de-Calais region, for instance, pioneered in introducing computers in its schools before the state program took shape. The overall advantage of decentralization lies in the increased scope it gives to initiative. It reduces the red tape involved when local communities wish to repair buildings, conserve natural resources, or increase cultural opportunities. It encourages the regions to invest in infrastructure and seek out new economic opportunities, again without the drag a central bureaucracy puts on initiative, and permits *collectivités* at all levels to seek out and take up small scale initiatives to fill needs the state might not recognize or would disdain.

A necessary corollary to decentralization was limitation on the *cumul des mandats*, the French tradition whereby a politician could, as in the extreme case of Jean Lecanuet, be at once mayor of Rouen, president of the *conseil général* of the Seine-Maritime department, regional councilor (i.e. regional deputy) of the Upper Normandy region, a senator, and a deputy to the European parliament. In 1978 all fifty-two mayors of cities larger than 80,000 inhabitants were members of the National Assembly or Senate, and until March 1986 more than ninety percent of French senators and more than eighty percent of French deputies had at least two offices. The "deputy-and-mayor" or "senator-and-mayor" is able to intercede for his constituents at the national level with an effectiveness mere local officials cannot attain. Deputies and senators are dependent for research and much office work on the joint services provided by the staff of their parliamentary groups. Their office space is exiguous and shared with a single secretary. Their mayor's offices in French town halls give them far more scope to confer with constituents and handle business of many kinds. French politicians continue to hold their jobs as mayors of major cities even when elevated to the highest levels. While serving as prime minister, Jacques Chaban-Delmas, Pierre Mauroy, and Jacques Chirac remained mayors respectively of Bordeaux, Lille, and Paris.

The law on the *cumul* adopted in December 1985 limited this system without abolishing it. A politician may now hold only two important offices. The office of deputy or senator is incompatible with more than one other office — European deputy, regional or departmental councilor, Paris city councilor, or mayor of a town of more than 20,000 inhabitants. (Only 386 mayors are affected.) One man may not be president of both a *conseil général* in his department and of the regional council of his region. However, a politician may run for a third office, and if elected choose which one he wishes to renounce. Most mayors of large cities will prefer to give up their seats in departmental or regional councils rather than their seats in parliament. The result will swell the ranks of younger or local politicians holding office in these councils. (The aftermath of the 1988 legislative elections saw the first big wave of resignations from departmental or regional offices by newly elected or re-elected deputies.)[11]

At least on the communal and departmental levels, French decentralization has not so much created local self-government as it has transferred administrative responsibilities. The French political scientist and decentralization expert Yves Mény writes:

The quintessential characteristic of decentralization . . . is less "democratization" than the generalization of the "authoritarian executive" model which now totally dominates French institutions. The model has two variants — the mayoral and the prefectoral — at the local level. The mayoral variant has now been extended to *départements* and regions, turning their executives into genuine local "bosses."[12]

Thus the "democratization" in this reform lies essentially in the efficiency of having services provided at a level less remote from the people than the central government. Certainly it is likely now that public opinion will be better heard and even listened to on questions of zoning and town planning, cultural services, and the creation of new schools. Local mayors will no longer be able to duck behind the authority of the prefect, using him as an excuse for not taking responsibility. One may, however, legitimately doubt whether much "democratization" is possible in the departmental, rather than the state control of a variety of social and health services (much the largest and most expensive of relocated tasks), or in administration of commercial and fishing ports. Decentralization may facilitate popular discussion on these questions, but much of the debate will unfortunately center on whether and how to increase benefits in an economy that is not getting richer — in other words on a limited set of hard and frequently unpleasant choices. It is undoubtedly healthy for the national state to delegate and so rid itself of many of these responsibilities. The changes are considerable, long-needed, and promising — but something less than revolutionary.[13]

INSTITUTIONAL CHANGE

The constitution of the Fifth Republic had been legitimized not only by the referendum which ratified it, but by its success in providing stable government. At the end of the 1970s the new institutions were generally accepted by a country almost equally divided between Left and Right. Nevertheless, the system still seemed blocked, and endangered by the seeming impossibility of electing a president and a legislature of the Left. The elections of 1981 took care of this problem, and Mitterrand declared at the beginning of his first term that he would "exercise the full powers granted him by the constitution, neither more nor less."[14]

One institution created by the constitution of 1958 posed a special problem for the Socialists. This was the Constitutional Council, a body intended by the founders of the Fifth Republic as an executive instrument to check the powers of a potentially assertive legislature. Its chief purpose was to provide a constitutional body to clarify the distinction between laws and regulations. The constitution defined certain areas where only the parliament could pass statutes, mentioning but not defining other areas with "a regulatory character" (Article 37/2), where the government could rule by decree. The Constitutional Council's task was to determine whether such decrees were in fact "regulatory." The Council was also supposed to review disputed elections and annul them where fraud or other irregularities were discovered, and to watch over the regularity of the presidential election.

The other key text governing the Council's powers (Article 61) allowed it to verify the constitutionality of laws, prior to their promulgation. Originally, however, only the president, prime minister, and the presidents of the National Assembly and Senate possessed the power of referring legislation to the Council — which they used so sparingly that between 1959 and 1974 only twenty-nine cases were sent to it. The original intent of this provision was once again to act as a check on the parliament. The authors of the constitution did not wish to create a court undertaking judicial review, with the extensive scope and powers of the American Supreme Court.[15]

In 1974 President Giscard was searching for liberal social or institutional measures which he hoped would attract moderates on the Left to back his programs. In this spirit, he sponsored a constitutional amendment allowing the Council's examination of a bill to be invoked by a petition signed by sixty deputies or senators. The suspicious Left parties voted against the amendment. Believing that the voters would soon entrust the government to them, they saw in the amendment only the strengthening of a non-legislative power wielded by a body of conservative magistrates.

The idea of judicial control over the legislature was in any case foreign to the national tradition. The Constitutional Council had only the slightest precedent in French constitutional history — a Constitutional Committee instituted by the Fourth Republic. It had little power, and met only once. The German and Austrian Bundesgerichtshöfe and the Italian Corte Costituzionale were little known or regarded in France, while the better known American Supreme Court inspired distrust. Frenchmen spoke of a "government by judges," a concept vaguely recalling the *parlements* of the old regime abolished by the Revolution. The Left opposition nevertheless did make some use of the new constitutional provision, referring sixty laws to the Council in 1974-1981.[16]

When the Left won both the presidency and a National Assembly majority in 1981, conservatives realized that the Council was the only constitutional weapon left in their arsenal. Its nine members had all been appointed by their side: by past presidents of the republic, the National Assembly, and the Senate. Each of these named three members, who sat for a term of nine years.

The Council proved a considerable obstacle to the smooth passage of legislation by the overwhelmingly powerful Left majority. In January 1982 it blocked the nationalization law, on the grounds that while nationalizations were acceptable on principle (they were even mentioned in the constitution) the formula for compensation was not just.

The opposition and the conservative press were overjoyed at this blow to the Left. A redrafted law was presented to the National Assembly ten days after the Council's decision and pushed through to go to the Senate and the Council two days later, but the cost of nationalizations had been increased by thirty percent. The total delay was only one month, and Socialist complaints about the extra cost must be weighed against their own insistence on one hundred percent nationalization. The real Socialist objection concerned the frustration of the popular will by an unelected court.

The Council's decision celebrated the rights of property. It was based on the Declaration of the Rights of Man of 1789, which together with the preamble to the 1946 constitution figured as a preamble to the constitution of 1958. These preambles had been recognized in a 1971 decision as an integral part of the 1958 document. The Council's decision concerning property rights thus had the additional effect of reaffirming the Declaration as a French Bill of Rights, guaranteeing the rights of the individual as well as of property.

Sixty-six laws were appealed during the life of the 1981 legislature, and the Council declared thirty-four to be at least in part unconstitutional. Many of these judgments concerned loosely drafted legislation. Even though the Council had to give a judgment within a month after its opinion had been requested, government procedures were delayed and the government was frequently infuriated by adverse Council decisions forcing redrafting. Given the speed with which the government was presenting legislation, it seems likely that the Council forced the improvement of many texts, and Socialist measures were rarely rejected *in toto*. However, since the Council ruled adversely on twice as many cases referred to it in 1981-1986 as it did during the seven years of Giscard's presidency, its conservative bias remained evident.

The most important government bill which was really frustrated by the Council was the 1984 law limiting the concentration of ownership of the press. Commonly referred to as the Hersant law, the bill (despite theoretical merits) had been pushed by Prime Minister Mauroy and the Socialist party in a highly partisan manner. (See Part II, above.) The Council rendered the Solomonic decision that the law was constitutional but could not be applied retroactively—thus leaving the Hersant press empire intact.

In September 1986 the conservative government of Jacques Chirac brought in a new law replacing the High Authority for Audio-Visual

Communication with a new one, the National Council for Communication and Liberties (see next chapter). The Council demonstrated its concern for plural ownership of the press and audio-visual media by striking down two key articles in the bill which it judged insufficiently protective of pluralism. In other 1986 decisions unwelcome to the Chirac government, the Council placed difficulties in the way of the prime minister's plan to legislate extensively by decrees authorized by general framework laws, *lois d'habilitation*, and demanded that such laws be more specific. (Article 38 of the constitution provides for such *lois d'habilitation*, which specify the area in which decrees — *ordonnances* — are legally valid.) In January 1987 the Council objected to an amendment fixing work hours and inserted into a general law on social affairs, on the grounds that it exceeded the inherent limits of the right to amendment. The conservatives were outraged, in a mirror image of Socialist fury when the Council had found against them. The conservative presidents of the Senate and the National Assembly protested this decision as an arrogation of new power and "an attack on national sovereignty embodied in the parliament."[17]

Thus both Left and Right have found cause for frustration at delays to or blockage of their legislation by nine magistrates not elected by the people. Because or in spite of this, the Constitutional Council emerged from the double alternation in power of 1981-1988 with increased authority and prestige. An August 1986 poll found that fifty-nine percent of respondents thought the powers of the Council a good thing, with higher percentages among Socialists and adherents of the RPR and UDF.[18]

The Council has confirmed its legitimacy and lasting importance — but has not become a "government by judges." (Indeed, its members are not necessarily even jurists like the justices of the U.S. Supreme Court, although a majority of the present council is made up of lawyers or law professors.) The Council has emerged as a check on the power of the legislature, but still more on that of the executive, drafter of the vast majority of bills. The weight of its prestige lies heavily on the clumsy and imprecise drafter, who will not wish to be accused of "manifest error."

Four members of the present Council were nominated by Socialist officials (including its president, Robert Badinter), and with Mitterrand's reelection its political balance will tilt leftward in 1989. Though the Constitutional Council does not much resemble the U.S. Supreme Court, and the Council operates in general as a check on the government in power, it is possible that just as Democratic anger in the 1930s at the "Nine Old Men" was replaced by Republican anger at the Warren Court in the 1960s, the Socialists will increasingly come to be the partisans of the Council and the conservatives its opponents. With this alternation the Council will have proved its non-partisan worth. Here, as in other areas, the arrival in power of the Left did not create change by deliberate intent – but did serve to precipitate it.[19]

THE ELECTRONIC MEDIA: A REAL REVOLUTION

In the early years of the Fifth Republic an American or Briton who watched news programs on French television or listened to the French radio might easily have concluded from their content and tone that the electronic media in France were closer to Soviet than to American or British standards for coverage and freedom. Censorship of the written press was abolished in France in 1881. The electronic media had no such freedom after a government monopoly in radio broadcasting was established in November 1945, and the Radiodiffusion Télévision Française agency (set up in 1959) was placed under the authority of the minister of information, who appointed the directors of radio and television networks. No private radio stations were permitted. The *radios périphériques*, Radio-Télédiffusion Luxembourg (RTL), Europe 1, Radio Monte Carlo – commercial stations with their headquarters outside France – were in turn indirectly controlled by state participation in much of their capitalization.

General de Gaulle in particular paid close attention to the content of TV news, frequently firing off complaints to his information minister. Thus:

> The TV news suggests that nothing is going on in France besides strikes, catastrophes, and conflicts of all sorts. It's a bit much. . . . Must the state radio [sic] serve to do nothing but stir up and extend opposition in contempt of the reality which is, at least in large measure, something else? . . . The TV news is back to its previous style and form. Today it's all about strikes, demands, agitation. . . . Milk has gone up by four centimes, etc. All this set forth by a "journalist" [the general's quotation marks] who obviously has no directive, or if he has one takes no notice of it.[20]

Georges Pompidou, who referred to television journalists as "the voice of France" (i.e. *his* France) approved of the existing system, and Prime Minister Jacques Chaban-Delmas' attempts to relax state control were reversed by his successor Pierre Messmer. In 1974, Giscard reorganized the unitary radio and TV into several agencies: one for each of the three TV channels, TF1, Antenne 2, FR 3; another for Radio France; one for production; one for managing broadcasting installations; and one for training and archives. The government still appointed the heads of all agencies, and the state monopoly remained. Government intervention diminished somewhat, although a TV reporter has related as typical how during the 1978 elections a story he had prepared on quarrels within the conservative camp was killed, while a similar story about the Left was broadcast. Nor was he ever allowed to report on the allegations that the Central African president/emperor Bokassa had presented diamonds to Giscard.[21]

By the early 1980s, there were 20,500,000 television sets in France, and 47,000,000 radios. Television had become the principal source of news and entertainment. Radio, restricted to a few stations, could satisfy neither the demand for a wide variety of musical fare nor for much cultural variety of any sort. Pirate radio stations sprang up, but were immediately repressed by the police.

Mitterrand entered office having promised to remove state controls over radio broadcasting, with the result that a number of local stations sprang up instantly in Paris and other cities. The new Mauroy government decided to create a new High Authority of Audio-Visual Communication, which would guarantee the independence of broadcasting from government interference. The High Authority became effective in July 1982. Its most conspicuous function was to name the heads of radio and television networks. Though modeled in some ways after the American Federal Communications Commission, the High Authority possessed neither the FCC's technical responsibilities of licensing (sharing its responsibility with the state) nor the budget and personnel to monitor the airwaves. The result was immediate confusion, as stations proliferated on the FM band. No transmitter was supposed to exceed 500 watts, but the High Authority found it hard to stop them—some Paris stations tested out at twenty or twenty-five kilowatts. In December 1984, when the High Authority tried to crack down on the popular Paris rock station NRJ for this reason, NRJ was able to bring thousands of young protesters into the streets.

While the Socialist government wished to free the airwaves, its ideological prudery on commercial radio forbade the new stations from selling advertising. This policy of "hang your clothes on a hickory limb, but don't go near the water" was naturally not very effective. Disguised publicity appeared instantly, and again the Authority found it possible to intervene only in the more flagrant cases.[22] Finally, in a press conference in April 1984, Mitterrand conceded that numerous stations needed to accept advertising in order to exist.[23]

Before the High Authority was established, the new government had removed all the directors of the three television channels, the general news editors, and the chief editors of political news desks. All were replaced by loyal Socialists or persons thought close to the government. The nine members of the Authority itself were named in groups: three, including the Authority's president, by the president of the republic, three by the president of the National Assembly, three by the president of the Senate. Six of the nine were thus named by the Socialists.

Michèle Cotta, the able and experienced journalist selected to head the new body, has told how Mitterrand sounded her out on the job, saying that he would not interfere, but did ask one thing, "that the office of president not be attacked. Would your sense of professional ethics keep you from doing this?" She replied that there would doubtless be conflicts, though she would not look for them, but thought that at some point she would come in conflict either with him or his government. "And if I go too far?"[24]

Here was the difficulty: the Socialist government wished to free the media, and at the same time wanted the media to be kind to it. Although Pierre Mauroy won respect from the High Authority for not protesting often critical coverage, this was far from true of other ministers or figures in the Socialist party, who kept the phone lines to the High Authority humming.

In 1984, the much respected and very independent Pierre Desgraupes, head of Antenne 2, was obliged to retire on grounds of age. New prime minister Laurent Fabius told Cotta that he and Mitterrand had "our candidate" to take over A2. Bristling at this direct interference, Cotta asked who Fabius' candidate was, and then blurted, "Bad luck. He's not mine." The government's candidate, Jean-Claude Héberlé, was nevertheless appointed. One account of the affair has Mitterrand telling Cotta, "I created you to resist me, naturally, but only up to a certain point!"[25] The High Authority had been shown vulnerable to government wishes, and its reputation never entirely recovered from the Héberlé affair.

The government's desire to secure more influence in the affairs of television was again apparent in 1984-1985, when new commercial channels were finally licensed. A commercial movie channel, Canal Plus, was authorized and launched in fall 1984, after negotiations where the Elysée played a major role and the High Authority was not consulted.[26] Although the network was nominally independent, nearly half of its stock was held by the large government-owned advertising agency Havas, whose chairman, the president's friend André Rousselot, was also the organizer of Canal Plus. The channel, which used a scrambled signal with decoders, took off slowly. By late 1985, however, it had gained over a million subscribers.[27]

In 1982 the government had considered various plans to satisfy a large public demand for more variety in television, while hoping also to increase the audience for French-produced material. More funding was authorized for both cable television and satellite broadcasting. The cabling plan of 1982 intended to develop the fiber optics industry by providing cable facilities to six million households by 1992. Progress was slow, in part because many towns shied away from the expense of committing funds for part of the costs. Communist-run towns wanted to pay for cabling by taxes; Chirac's Paris and other conservative municipalities preferred the American plan of individual subscription. By 1985, only 200,000 households had cable, and thereafter the Chirac government declined to commit funds for large-scale expansion of the network.[28]

The first French broadcasting satellite, TDF 1, was scheduled for launching in July 1986, with a sister satellite following. Relatively inexpensive small dish antennae of thirty to sixty centimeters in diameter were to permit a Europe-wide service which could theoretically reach 250 million people, while multiple sound channels would solve the language problem. But the program ran into financing problems, the Chirac government gave it low priority, and in May 1988 the first French satellite had yet to be launched.

Multiple ambitions drive the satellite program. The French electronics industry is looking for new outlets. Together with the Dutch Philips group, Thomson hopes to take a world lead in the technologies of satellite reception and transmission techniques. The French producers of television programs (and the defenders of French culture in general) take alarm at the massive importation of American television shows, exported inexpensively because their production costs have already been met in the giant American market. The purely French industry cannot hope to compete if confined to the area of fifty-five million Frenchmen, plus some six and a half million Francophone Belgians and Swiss. Expansion to a European market is thus a necessity if French production is not to be driven back entirely to talk shows, movies, and special programs, the latter two increasingly financed by the state. European television companies are intensely conscious that if they do not create a European network for programs and news, the Americans will do it for them. "The shadow of Ted Turner," said a TV official, "is hovering over the development of communications in Europe."[29]

By 1985 the promise of mass cable hookups had vanished over the horizon. The decision to advance into pay television had already been taken in principle with Canal Plus, and once the radio stations had been allowed to take advertising there was no logical justification for blocking private television. The conservative opposition had never done anything in its twenty-three years of Gaullist power to disestablish state control over television. Now that it had been converted to free enterprise, it would certainly set up and control private networks after its expected victory in 1986. Mitterrand and the French Left had always defended publicly-owned television as superior to the commercial system dominant in the United States, which they found distasteful, or to the chaotic mix of public and low-quality private television in Italy. But political logic outweighed distaste, and Mitterrand decided that he must make a virtue of necessity. He would demonstrate that the Socialists believed in free enterprise – and establish private TV ownership friendly to the PS.

His first step was to commission a report to explore the number of new networks the French advertising market could support. The three existing ones drew revenues from limited advertising and funds from the television tax paid by all set owners. The Bredin report issued in May 1985 recommended establishment of one additional national private network, with a charter limiting the amount of permissible advertising per hour.[30] The problem was that there was just so much money available in France for advertising, and the government was under pressure from the written media not to sop up too much of it. Mitterrand nevertheless decided to create two private networks to cover most of France by late 1986, one with a general program for a mass audience, the other mainly musical, aimed at young people. Less than a year remained for the Socialist government if it wished to be midwife to the birth of private television in France.

The favored candidate to organize the private fifth network, baptized *La Cinq*, was the Compagnie Luxembourgeoise de Télédiffusion (CLT), mother society of RTL, owned in part by Havas, but also by the Luxembourg government and the giant Belgian Banque Lambert. While the CLT was ready in principle to meet the French government's specifications, the Fabius government suspected it of dragging out negotiations until a new conservative government was installed in Paris. Furthermore, Mitterrand's old friend Jean Riboud had ambitions for a company to be organized by his son Christophe and Jérôme Seydoux, another member of the immensely rich but pro-Socialist Seydoux-Schlumberger clan. Suspicious of CLT's political connections, desirous to entrust friends with a television channel that might favor the Socialists after their 1986 defeat, and perhaps wishing to do a last favor for Jean Riboud, who was dying of cancer, Mitterrand decided immediately after Riboud's death in October 1985 to give the contract to Seydoux's Compagnie des Chargeurs Réunis. But since Seydoux had neither sufficient capital nor technical staff to proceed alone, another entrepreneur was brought in, with a forty percent interest, in the person of the Italian television magnate Silvio Berlusconi.

Berlusconi had a bad reputation in French television and cultural circles. He had risen rapidly in the Italian television world after the state monopoly on television was lifted, evading the ban on national networks by organizing the country-wide simultaneous transmission of pre-recorded programs. Most of them were the American situation comedies and shoot-em-ups that French intellectuals deeply deplored. Nicknamed "*Sua Emmittenza*" by the Italian press, Berlusconi had so flooded the Italian entertainment market that the Italian motion picture industry was near death after the loss of half of its public within five years.[31] Fears were immediately expressed for the

French industry, already heavily subsidized by the state in order to keep it alive. But if *La Cinq* was to go into production by early 1986, Berlusconi was the necessary man.

A howl went up in French cultural circles (and particularly those on the Left) when it became known that the contract negotiated by Berlusconi granted very easy conditions for presenting original French productions and in setting minimum quotas for French and European programs (as opposed to American ones). The quantity of permissible advertising spots (restricted to the beginning and the end of programs in French television) was unclear, and many wondered whether private television in France would begin to resemble the chopped-up late night movies on American television. Mitterrand had disappointed his own camp by choosing the politically opportune solution at the expense of Socialist ideas.

Jacques Chirac immediately announced that when the Right returned to power he would rescind the contract for *La Cinq*, and the contracts for both private channels were in fact revoked by decree in August 1986.[32] Exit Seydoux—but not Berlusconi, who became a partner in a new consortium for *La Cinq*, together with French press lord Robert Hersant. Channel Six, now called M6, had begun broadcasting only in February 1986. Its control was awarded to a group organized by the Belgo-Luxembourgeois CLT and the French conglomerate Compagnie Lyonnaise des Eaux.

The victorious Right then pursued plans to privatize one or more of the existing state channels. Hot debate ensued over the question which one (or two) would be selected. Culture and Communications Minister and Parti Républicain leader François Léotard expressed one opinion, the RPR another. Finally it was decided that Channel One, TF 1, was to be put up for sale. Although Jacques Chirac had told High Authority president Michèle Cotta shortly before the 1986 election that the High Authority had proved its value and would be continued, Léotard speedily announced plans to replace it by a new organization, the Conseil National des Communications et des Libertés (CNCL).[33]

The Right had criticized the lack of independence shown by the High Authority, with special reference to the nomination of Héberlé. The CNCL was presented as an improvement of the old institution. Where the High Authority had possessed a very small staff and an annual budget of twelve million francs, the CNCL had 223 employees and a 150 million franc budget. It could authorize frequencies, choose licensees, and designate the heads of the public channels. The idea was to create a jurisdiction on the lines of the American FCC. The CNCL had, however, less authority and a much smaller staff (the FCC has some 1300 employees).

Where the High Authority's nine members had been nominated in groups of three by the presidents of the republic, the National Assembly, and the

Senate, the CNCL's thirteen members were chosen by allotting only two members each to these high officials, with four more elected by the Conseil d'Etat, Cour des Comptes, Cour de Cassation, and the Académie Française. Finally, three other members were co-opted by the first ten, and the whole body elected its president. All members were to serve nine years.

Although the CNCL possessed more extended powers and resources than the High Authority, what had really happened was that an authority with a majority appointed by Mitterrand had been replaced by another one with a conservative majority. (Mitterrand's appointees formed a minority of two on the CNCL.) When presidents of public networks were replaced, with three jobs going to persons close to the RPR, Communications Minister Léotard began uneasily to suspect that the RPR would have too much control over television.

A major question hovering over the new dispensation was concentration of power in the press and electronic media. The leading candidate to take over a privatized TF 1 was not Hersant (who contented himself with a share of *La Cinq*) but big industrialist Jean-Luc Lagardère (Matra) who also controlled Hachette, France's biggest editorial chain, and was the owner of the radio network Europe 1. The CNCL decided instead for a consortium headed by cement and prefabricated housing tycoon Francis Bouygues. New restrictions imposed by the Constitutional Council limited concentration of ownership of TV networks, radio, and the press.[34]

The CNCL nevertheless failed to convince the country that it was accomplishing its mission. After Mitterrand criticized it in a September 1987 interview, a poll found that while nearly half of respondents did not agree with the president, only twenty-four percent believed that the CNCL was doing a good job.[35] Charges by a magistrate that CNCL member and academician Michel Droit had intervened to grant a license to a right-wing radio station in Paris did nothing for the CNCL's reputation.

Mitterrand means to replace the CNCL with a regulatory institution with undisputed and real authority, capable of making itself respected. The current composition of the CNCL will be changed and its powers increased. The statutes of the new organization will be inserted by amendment into the constitution, thereby granting it permanence and status. Mitterrand has said that he is not eager to re-nationalize TF 1, but does not rule out changes in the management of the other two private networks. The new communication commission will probably be called the High Audio-Visual Council. It will undoubtedly have extended powers — and many problems to solve. In her memoirs of her presidency of the High Authority, Michèle Cotta sums up: "Whoever is in power, the audio-visual structure is only the facade of ideological structure. Behind the changes made by politicians is one fact: an irresistible mistrust of audio-visual power, an irresistible desire to 'take things in hand.'"[36] Certainly neither the Socialists, for all their talk about *"espaces de liberté,"* nor the conservatives, with their new talk of *libéralisme,* resisted this desire.

Still, despite early hesitations on financing and a too-evident desire to free the media and still maintain some control, the Socialist government brought a freedom to the electronic media that the press had achieved a hundred years earlier. Under Socialist and conservative governments, TV and radio journalism is now more independent than ever before. The news director of a network can refuse a minister's request for TV time. Stories are broadcast that displease the government, and if it is not yet unthinkable that a network chief, a news bureau head, or a journalist may be fired for *lèse majesté,* it is already much harder to do so and may become impossible. The proliferation of hundreds of small radio stations has been largely positive.

The next few years will present grave financing problems and the question of cable channels and TV satellites, complicating the overall situation. Yet despite the contradictions and uncertainties in its media policy, the Socialist government elected in 1981 can be justly proud of at least one real revolution in French life, one which daily touches the lives of almost all Frenchmen.

THE SOCIALIST ECONOMIC PERFORMANCE

Partisan descriptions of the Socialist record in economic management have concentrated on two different periods. Critics of the Mitterrand administration have been anxious to show that the Socialists not only bungled economic management in 1981-1983, but also that their errors spoiled a promising economic comeback underway in 1981. By their mistakes they had condemned France to high indebtedness and a dangerous lag in the economic race with her competitors.[37]

Socialist apologists have instead pointed out that French growth was higher than West German in 1981-1983, and that the French economy behaved as well as the EC average in 1981-1985. Because of the reflation of 1981-1982, the statistical patterns of the French economy diverge from those of her European partners. Reflation produced growth in 1981-1983, and austerity braked it, while other European countries were in recession early in the decade and recovered later. Selected statistics from 1981-1985 can therefore be used to bolster quite different views.

"While some variation in the timing and intensity of devaluation and the macroeconomic stance might have improved the overall level of France's economic performance in 1981-1985," writes the Harvard political economist Peter Hall, "the room for maneuver was not great. French levels of growth, unemployment, and inflation were close to the European averages, and there are few grounds for thinking that macroeconomic policy could have been substantially different given prevailing international and domestic constraints."[38]

There is no argument whether the Socialists made mistakes in 1981-1983 (they admit they did) and there is room for argument on what statistics may prove. A larger question is the severity of the structural problems in the economy the Socialists inherited. In the 1970s the Socialists had blamed the crisis almost entirely on the policies of Raymond Barre and denied its structural and international nature. Once in office, the Socialists were obliged to face these factors, which the Right in its turn happily overlooked when damning them. The condition of the industries nationalized in 1982 (and of many that remained private) was too serious to be the result of instant Socialist mismanagement. French industrial problems arose in large part from underinvestment throughout the 1970s, higher raw material costs, and increased international competition (as well as from the social costs increased in 1981 by Socialist legislation). The French balance of trade, briefly positive in 1978, was again dangerously negative in 1980 (nearly sixty-two billion francs) and only slightly better in 1981 before plunging disastrously to ninety-three billion francs in 1982. Redressed in the following years of austerity, it became positive (barely) in 1986.[39] It was negative again in 1987.

The nationalized industries were nursed back to health by the injection of sixty billion francs of capital and guaranteed loans.[40] By 1984 all but two of the conglomerates taken over in 1982 were in the black, and the electronics manufacturer Thomson and computer firm Bull turned a small profit in 1986. In 1987 Renault was again profitable, and even a slimmed down steel industry has hopes of emerging from the red.

The rehabilitation of the nationalized giants still does not answer the question of whether Socialist industrial policy was a success. As noted earlier, exhortations to invest addressed to small and medium-sized entrepreneurs were not very successful, and French industries continued to lose market share to their competitors. French exports are spread out over a number of fields, with no sector where France is dominant. France fights for markets today in Europe against other European countries, Japan, and new Third World exporters. Sixty-seven percent of French imports came from Western Europe in 1986; 66.7 percent of her non-military exports went to Western Europe.[41] The big export markets France has tried to develop in the Near East are disappearing, except for armaments. Even in this profitable field France's export possibilities are shrinking, as French production becomes more high-tech and expensive and cheaper producers like Brazil bite into the market with less expensive weapons and equipment. Modest gains were made in high technology, but France could not even dominate her home market in computers.

These were enduring problems which faced the new Chirac government in 1986, and remain as serious challenges for the Rocard ministry under a re-elected Mitterrand.[42] What the Socialists did achieve between 1983 and early 1986 was a reputation for *bonne gestion* — efficient administration. In the 1970s they would have scorned the honor; in 1986 the electorate was only partly aware of their successes. And like some of the social reforms directly aimed at the Left electorate, much of their work won little applause.

The deindexation of industrial wages in 1983 was a major victory in the battle against inflation, which fell from fourteen percent for 1981 to 4.7 in 1985. However, it meant that living standards for salaried workers declined, while the loss in buying power was even greater for the middle-middle class and well-paid salaried employees. New measures against youth unemployment in 1984 introduced contracts for work useful to the community (*travail d'utilité collective*-TUC). These contracts at first affected unemployed persons from sixteen to twenty-one, and after August 1985 also those aged twenty-one to twenty-five on the unemployment rolls for more than a year. In 1985, 330,000 people benefited from the TUC program.[43]

INSEE statistics demonstrate that unemployment in France is heavily concentrated among young men and young women and the middle-aged. The table below shows the patterns in the increase in unemployment between 1977, when it stood at 1,100,000, and the 2,500,000 rate in 1986.

TABLE: Unemployment Rate by Sex and Age Group

	1977		1986	
Age	M	W	M	W
15-19	74.3	78.4	83.5	87.9
20-24	28.5	31.4	33.7	34.5
25-49	3.4	39.1	3.4	28.0
50-54	6.6	47.5	9.2	40.9
55-59	16.1	53.6	30.6	56.9

Source: INSEE, *Annuaire statistique 1987*, p. 97.

These statistics configure France's social problem: late entry into the work force for a third of the young population, with obviously greater worries for the poorly educated and non-Europeans, and the inability of underskilled older men (and to a greater degree, women) to find jobs once they have lost them. Gloomy predictions speak of four million unemployed in the 1990s.

The inability of the Socialist government to keep its rash promise of reducing unemployment from its 1,750,000 figure in 1981 weighed heavily against it in the March 1986 elections. Exit polls showed that all voters listed job creation as the most important priority for France. All voters but those of the National Front cited unemployment as the most important motivating factor in their vote. National Front voters cited immigration and crime as even greater problems, but the unemployed and those seeking a first job voted for the National Front in 1986 and 1988 at a rate well above that party's national average.[44]

Another of the main themes of the Socialists in 1981 was the reduction of social inequalities in a country where these were generally reckoned the highest among developed countries. The Socialists had spoken in the 1970s of reducing discrepancies in wages and moving toward equal pay for equal work among men and women. These goals were not met, as the need to combat the crisis and restore the health of the French economy clashed with social goals. The relation between the average salary of an executive (*cadre supérieur*) and a worker, calculated at 4.5 to one in 1970, had been reduced to 3.6 in 1980, and though it diminished slightly in 1983, by 1984 it was back at 3.6. Average executive salaries in relation to average employee salaries remained at their 1980 level of 3.1. Unskilled workers saw their buying power rise slightly in 1981-1983 and fall again in 1984, and the average net buying power of all salaried workers in the private and semi-public sectors rose by only 1.4 percent in 1981-1984. Better paid workers did not do this well: middle-level executives lost 3.7 percent of their buying power in these years.[45]

The Socialists were thus not able to meet the most important social goals they had proclaimed as their priorities. But their non-success did not come from lack of trying, and the least-favored workers benefited most from their efforts. Although a notable percentage of the poor and unemployed drifted away from the Left (both Communist and Socialist voters) and sought political solace in the quack nostrums of the National Front, the Socialists did not suffer greatly from the loss of worker votes in 1986, and recouped in 1988.[46]

SUCCESSES AND FAILURES

Decentralization and the liberation of the audio-visual media must be reckoned the two great reforms of 1981-1986. Another much-discussed reform was the Auroux laws of 1982 on labor rights. Bitterly attacked by the

Right when first presented in the National Assembly, they too have turned out to be less than revolutionary. These laws provided for obligatory firm-level bargaining, systematized the arrangements for committees dealing with health, safety, and working conditions; defined workers' rights and provided in particular for new shop-level "rights of expression." ("Collectivism," said the RPR leader Bernard Pons.)

The overall intent was to strengthen workers' rights and provide stronger incentives to collective bargaining at the lower levels rather than on an industry-wide level. Continuing dissension among the three main union confederations and the decline in French union strength in a period of industrial restructuring contributed to altering the effect expected of these laws. They did not strengthen the union movement; they simplified the task of management in dealing locally with its workers.

Profound changes took place in the structure of employment in the 1980s. Mining, synthetic textiles, and steel production declined steeply. A million industrial jobs disappeared in 1973-1984, while between 1967 and 1984 2.7 million jobs were created in the tertiary sector. The number of salaried workers in enterprises employing 500 or more workers (those most likely to be unionized) dropped between 1972-1984, and increased in the smallest enterprises employing fewer than fifty workers. One plausible estimate of the rate of unionization in late 1985 put it at fifteen percent of the work force (counting teachers' unions, independent and autonomous unions), down from some twenty percent ten years earlier.[47] Thus if the Socialist party hoped both to increase the rights of workers and the power of trade unions it succeeded in the former but not the latter task. By 1988 it had become apparent that the traditional tripartite labor scene had not changed, but the union confederations were weaker. Many Socialists had believed that their party must develop a new and deeper relation to the labor movement, on the model of the social democratic parties of most other European countries. These hopes (most of which attached themselves to the CFDT, but some to the CGT) had not altogether vanished by 1988, but were definitely on the wane.[48]

One of the surprises in Socialist economic management was modernization of French financial institutions. A second stock market for new companies appeared in 1983, and in 1985 a financial futures market, innovations one might have expected from conservatives. Ways were found to bring private capital into some of the nationalized industries even before the victorious Right began to privatize them. The ideological approach that had insisted on 100 percent nationalization in 1981 gave way to a mild preference for nationalization, which mixed with near indifference to privatization when it came. (The terms of privatization, however, left much room for the partisan temper.) To everyone's amazement, the Paris Bourse had never been so prosperous as under the Socialists in 1985, and Economics Minister Bérégovoy basked in the approval of the financial community. After the 1988 presidential elections, when he was reappointed to the same post in the Rocard government, *Le Monde's* cartoonist Plantu could wickedly portray brokers downing celebratory champagne on the stock market steps while muttering, "Just suppose Chirac had been elected. . . . "

STRONG ON CIVIL LIBERTIES

The Socialist record on civil liberties was one of the brightest pages of their record, for which they were not given sufficient credit in popular opinion (and indeed suffered some harm). Abolition of the death penalty and the *"anti-casseurs"* law aimed at persons suspected of damaging property during demonstrations were early priorities. Justice Minister Badinter's intent here as elsewhere was to check the arbitrary exercise of police power and overly swift court action that might deprive suspects of their rights. More controversial was the attempted repeal of former Justice Minister Peyrefitte's law on security and liberty, which provided for minimum sentences for violent crimes, reduced judicial discretion, and gave the police the right to ask for identity documents without a warrant or reason. Objections to outright repeal came from Interior Minister Defferre, who was trying to restore his control over a restive police, and the law was not repealed in its entirety.

In 1984 Badinter brought in another important legal innovation, a habeas corpus act providing that no one could be placed in temporary detention without being informed of his right to counsel or without the accused's right to challenge his arrest. In principle, custody was limited to twenty-four hours for minor infractions unless an examining magistrate issued a warrant, when it could be extended to forty-eight hours.

Returning to power with a tough law and order program, the Right introduced minimum sentences for crimes of violence and gave judges discretionary power to impose a thirty-year minimum sentence. Police verification of documents was also reintroduced.[49]

SOFT ON CRIME?

The reputation for good management that the Socialists had cultivated in 1983-1986 was still insufficient in the minds of voters in 1986 to obliterate the memory of 1981-1983. Yet the same voters wondered whether the new free enterprise doctrines of the Right would bring much change. A major factor in swinging voter sentiment to the Right was the continuing belief that emphasis on civil liberties really meant that the Socialists were soft on crime.

The rise of the National Front registered in the 1984 European elections demonstrated that a considerable part of the electorate had been convinced by the charge (initiated by the RPR and UDF) that the Socialists lacked the will and even the intent to proceed against rising criminality.

Pierre Joxe, who replaced old Gaston Defferre as interior minister in July 1984, worked hard to win over the police and carry out a stern law and order policy. The ranks of the police had actually been enlarged in 1982-1983, but Joxe pursued a well-publicized plan of police modernization adopted in 1985, which aimed at more efficient repression of minor crime, more effective and scientific criminal investigation, and better police protection. With these general objectives went specific action against drugs, improved police intelligence work and coordination, and anti-terrorist measures that included better international coordination. Nearly a billion francs for new internal safety programs were added to the budget for 1986.[50]

TERRORISM

Terrorism had causes quite separate from crime, but a continuing wave of bombings in Paris, other major cities, and on trains contributed to the general sense that the streets, public places, and the citizen's home were increasingly less and less safe.

Terrorism had two separate tracks — native and international. The movement calling itself *Action Directe* resembled some of the far larger Italian terrorist movements of the 1970s. It was vaguely anarchist, and determinedly violent. Two of its leaders had been pardoned in the presidential amnesty of 1981 and used their liberty to reorganize their terrorist band — as Chirac did not fail to remind Mitterrand in their presidential debates of 1988. Before most or all of its members were arrested in 1987, *Action Directe* had wounded numerous people in bomb explosions, and murdered three prominent persons, including an army general and the president of Renault, Georges Besse.

Terrorism of Near Eastern origin was still more troublesome. In 1982 it killed at least seventeen persons; ninety persons were wounded. In 1983 the Armenian terrorist group Asala killed eight persons and wounded sixty in a shoot-out at Orly airport; in 1985 bombs were set off at the crowded department store Au Printemps and the popular university bookstore Gibert Jeune, while in 1986 the ultra-modern Paris-Lyons TGV train was bombed and another bomb devastated one of the crowded FNAC discount stores. Immediately after the 1986 elections a bomb went off in a shopping mall on the Champs-Elysées, another unexploded one was discovered on a suburban electric train, and in September 1986 five bomb explosions terrorized Paris, killing eleven people and injuring 160 others.

The latter attacks demonstrated that Near Eastern terrorism would continue under conservative government, but the cumulative effect of the terrorism of the mid-1980s was nevertheless a burden for the Socialist government. A SOFRES poll taken in April 1986 showed that next to discontent over Mitterrand's failure to tame unemployment, more people registered unhappiness with his record in the area of public security than in any other, sixty-six percent considering it negative.[51]

THE BALANCE SHEET

The Socialists in power thus had many accomplishments to their credit, and many failures. They had thought that power would allow them to change France. They changed much, but the experience of government altered them also. By 1986 they understood better that legislation is not the only engine of reform, and that duration in power serves not only to permit continuing innovation but also to insure that reforms once introduced can slowly take root in practice. Gradualism, a word not earlier in high Socialist favor, was now admitted to their vocabulary. The Socialists and the left intelligentsia had discovered the importance of production—not in the sense of Soviet Stakhanovite mythology—but in the conditions of enlightened capitalism. The mandarins of the university had become less reluctant to work together with industry to develop new products. The entrepreneur—O paradox—had become a hero in a France ruled by Socialists.

In 1986 the Socialists faced the imminent surrender of power. Mitterrand would presumably remain in office, under conditions still unclear. The twenty-six months before the presidential elections were to determine whether the Left (now incarnate almost entirely in the PS) could return to power, or whether the years between May 1981 and March 1986 would appear as an anomaly in the political history of France.

NOTES

1. Cf. Jean-Luc Parodi, "Tout s'est joué trois ans plus tôt," in *Mars 1986: la drôle de défaite de la gauche*, eds. Elisabeth Dupoirier and Gérard Grunberg; and Pascal Perrineau, "Glissements progressifs de l'idéologie," ibid.
2. Alain Peyrefitte, *Le Mal français*, pp. 429-430.
3. Stanley Hoffmann, "Conclusion: Paradoxes and Discontinuities," in *The Mitterrand Experiment*, eds. George Ross, Stanley Hoffmann, and Sylvia Malzacher, p. 345.
4. Cf. *Quid* 1987, p. 656c.
5. Author's interview with Yves Guéna, mayor of Perigueux, October 1985.

6. *Le Programme commun de gouvernement de la gauche—propositions socialistes pour l'actualisation* (Paris: Flammarion, 1978), pp. 101-103.

7. I have drawn here on the article by Catherine Grémion, "Decentralization in France, a Historical Perspective," in *The Mitterrand Experiment*, eds. Ross, Hoffmann, and Malzacher.

8. Author's interview with Jacques Douffiagues, October 1985.

9. *The Washington Post*, May 18, 1986; Author's interview with Ile de France regional officials, October 1987.

10. Jean-Marie Rausch, "Réalités régionales, un président de région s'explique," *Projet* no. 185-186 (May-June 1984), p. 578, and author's interview with Jean-Marie Rausch, March 1986. With the new law on the *cumul* Rausch would have had to drop one of these three jobs. He became minister for foreign trade in the second Rocard government.

11. I am heavily indebted for this account to the article by Yves Mény, "Le Cumul des Mandats," *The Tocqueville Review* 8.

12. Yves Mény, "The Socialist Decentralization," in *The Mitterrand Experiment*, eds. Ross, Hoffmann, and Malzacher, p. 260.

13. On decentralization, see especially the articles by Yves Mény "The Socialist Decentralization" in *The Mitterrand Experiment* and "Le Cumul des Mandats," cited above; Vivien A. Schmidt, "Decentralization, a Revolutionary Reform," in *The French Socialists in Power*, ed. Patrick McCarthy; *La Décentralisation en marche, Cahiers français*, special issue 220 (March-April 1985); Mark Kesselman, "The Tranquil Revolution at Clochemerle: Socialist Decentralization in France," in *Socialism, the State, and Public Policy in France*, eds. Philip Cerny and Martin Schain; Nicolas Tenzer, *La Région en quête d'avenir*; the special number of *Projet* devoted to the subject, entitled "Décentraliser vraiment?"; and *Collectivités locales*, eds. Francis Paul Benoit et al. I have also benefited greatly from interviews with Yves Mény and Jean-Pierre Worms, and with a number of French mayors and other local and regional officials.

14. Interview with *Le Monde*, July 2, 1981.

15. See John T.S. Keeler and Alec Stone, "The Emergence of the Constitutional Council as a Major Actor in the Policy-making Process" in *The Mitterrand Experiment*, eds. Ross, Hoffmann, and Malzacher, pp. 162-163.

16. Keeler and Stone, "The Emergence of the Constitutional Council," p. 164. There are now constitutional courts in nine of the twelve EC countries. See Louis Favoreu, *Les Cours constitutionnelles* (Paris: Presses Universitaires de France, 1986).

17. *Le Monde*, January 25-26, 1987. See also Guy Carcassonne, "A propos du droit d'amendement: les errements du Conseil constitutionnel," *Pouvoirs* 41 (1987). The author, an expert on constitutional law (now on the staff of Prime Minister Rocard), subjects the Council's decisions of late December

1986 and January 1987 to a severe procedural examination. In a paper given at a NYU-Columbia University conference in October, 1987, he remarked, however, that the criticisms of both Left and Right tend to validate the Council's activities.

18. SOFRES, *L'Etat de l'opinion publique – Clés pour 1987*, p. 215.

19. I have drawn for this section on the article about the Council by Keeler and Stone in *The Mitterrand Experiment*, cited above, as well as on Louis Favoreu, "Conseil constitutionnel: mythes et réalités," *Regards sur l'actualité*, no. 132 (June 1987). See also Louis Favoreu et Loïc Philip, eds., *Les Grandes décisions du Conseil constitutionnel*, 4th edition, (Paris: Sirey, 1984).

20. See Michèle Cotta, *Les Miroirs de Jupiter*, pp. 32-33.

21. *Le Nouvel Observateur*, January 23, 1987.

22. *Le Monde, dossiers et documents*, "La Révolution des médias," October 1984, p. 74.

23. *Le Monde*, April 5, 1984.

24. Cotta, *Les Miroirs*, pp. 16-17.

25. Jean-Marie Colombani, *Portrait du Président*, p. 123.

26. Cf. Jean-Michel Quatrepoint, *Histoire secrète des dossiers noirs de la gauche*, p. 43.

27. Cf. *Le Monde, dossiers et documents*, "La Révolution des médias," p. 42; Roland Cayrol, "L'Audiovisuel dans les années socialistes," *The Tocqueville Review* 8, p. 298.

28. Cf. Jean-Marie Guéhenno, "France and the Electronic Media," in *The Mitterrand Experiment*, eds. Ross, Hoffmann, and Malzacher, p. 283, and Cayrol, "L'Audiovisuel," p. 293.

29. Cited from an interview in *Le Monde* with Jacques Pomonti, president of the Institut National de la Communication Audiovisuelle, May 10, 1985.

30. *Le Monde*, May 21 and May 22, 1985.

31. Cf. Cayrol, "L'Audiovisuel," pp. 303-307.

32. Cf. *Le Journal Officiel*, August 2, 1986, and *Le Monde*, August 5, 1986.

33. Cf. Cotta, *Les Miroirs*, p. 197.

34. See Olga Blanc-Uchan, "Communications: les nouvelles lois," *Regards sur l'actualité*, no. 127 (January 1987), especially p. 11 on media concentration.

35. *Le Monde*, September 25, 1987.

36. Cotta, *Les Miroirs*, p. 29.

37. Cf. the annual reports on French economic and social conditions published by Raymond Barre in *L'Express*, especially the 1986 report "L'Etat économique et social de la France en mars 1986," *L'Express*, 26 February-6 March 1986.

38. Peter Hall, "The Difficult Economics of French Socialism," in *The Mitterrand Experiment*, eds. Ross, Hoffmann, and Malzacher, pp. 63-64.

39. INSEE, *Annuaire Statistique de la France, 1987*, p. 821.

40. Calculated from a table in ADA, *Bilan de la France 1986*, p. 161.

41. INSEE *Annuaire Statistique*, p. 823.

42. OECD, *Etudes economiques, France 1986/87*, pp. 19-23.

43. Antoine Artois and Natacha Wolinski, eds. *L'Etat de la France et ses habitants* (Paris: Editions La Découverte, 1987), p. 68.

44. SOFRES, *Clés pour 1987*, pp. 107; 111; 114, and *Le Monde, dossiers et documents*, "L'Election présidentielle 1988," p. 41.

45. INSEE figures, from ADA, *Bilan de la France 1986*, pp. 278-283.

46. See, on these topics, besides the sources cited in notes above, "Pauvreté et revenu minimum garanti," *Regards sur l'actualité*, no. 123 (July-August 1986); various articles on the economy in the special issue of the *Revue Politique et Parlementaire* entitled "Les Reformes de la Gauche 1981-1984," no. 916/917 (May-June 1985); Bela Balassa, "Five Years of Socialist Economic Policy in France: a Balance Sheet," *The Tocqueville Review* 7 (1985-1986).

47. *Le Monde*, March 17, 1986, and November 7, 1985.

48. For more detailed accounts of this, see George Ross, "From One Left to Another, *Le Social* in Mitterrand's France," in *The Mitterrand Experiment*, eds. Ross, Hoffmann, and Malzacher, and George Ross, "Labor and the Left in Power," in *The French Socialists in Power*, ed. Patrick McCarthy. For an account of CGT/CFDT relations in the 1970s, see George Ross, *Workers and Communists in France*. Also see the special number of *CFDT Aujourd'hui*, September 1987, devoted to the topic of unionism and innovations.

49. Cf. William Safran, "Rights and Liberties under the Mitterrand Presidency: Socialist Innovations and Post-Socialist Revisions," *Contemporary French Civilization* 12 (Winter-Spring 1988).

50. Cf. "La Modernisation de la police," *Regards sur l'actualité*, no. 118 (February 1986) and ADA, *Bilan de la France 1986*, pp. 335-340.

51. SOFRES, *L'Etat de l'opinion — clés pour 1988*, p. 23.

5

From Confrontation to Cohabitation

THE ELECTION OF 1986

By early 1986 the stringent economic policies launched in 1982 and 1983 had begun to bear fruit. Inflation was down and expected to sink further, the wave of mass lay-offs in industry seemed to have ended, and the national-ized industries were beginning to show a profit. Citizens were, if not optimis-tic, at least less pessimistic about the future. A poll taken in December 1985 showed only thirty-eight percent of respondents who characterized 1985 as a bad year for themselves and their families. In earlier year-end polls forty-four percent of respondents had thought 1983 a bad year, and fifty-four per-cent viewed 1984 in the same way.[1]

Nevertheless, the polls of early 1986 clearly indicated that after swinging toward the right in 1982, the country had not again altered course. The themes dear to the Right — the importance of industry, profit, admiration for business success — had gained an approving audience among a majority of the French. The Socialists (without the Right's evangelistic enthusiasm) had emulated the conservatives in praise of the entrepreneurial spirit. While the country had taken note of this change, it was not sure what to make of it. A confident opposition found it advisable to campaign against the errors of 1981-1982, suggesting that they would be repeated should the PS continue in power.

The RPR program for the 1986 elections, entitled "The Renewal," proclaimed that the Socialists had failed in everything they had attempted. It nevertheless took care to emphasize that the thirty-nine hour week, the fifth week of paid vacations and retirement at sixty were not threatened. Neo-liberalism was heavily stressed. "Renewal," proclaimed the program, "turns its back uncompromisingly on socialism, but turns its back also on the inter-ventionism sprung from our Jacobin tradition." And under the rubric "Give the economy back the means of development," appeared the message, "What has characterized French society for nearly twenty years is the result of Frenchmen's labor, confiscated by the state. This spoliation went on quietly in the past, and became triumphant in 1981. . . . "

Chirac's RPR, the largest party on the Right, was thus asserting its agreement with a Parti Républicain that under François Léotard had now gone over completely to free enterprise and Reaganian principles. And it was openly admitting that it had turned its back on methods of controlling the economy held valid by Chirac's great patron Georges Pompidou.

The Socialists were well aware that they had no chance of winning the elections. (The president's proportional representation law was a purely defensive measure designed to hold onto a maximum number of seats in the Assembly. The Socialists could not have won a majority under its provisions even in the flood tide of 1981.) At the very most they might hope for a legislature with no clear majority that would give Mitterrand a freer hand. But this assumed that National Front deputies would not be accepted into a coalition, and was a recipe for dissension, muddle, and drift. The Socialists' best hope was to rally as much of their 1981 electorate as they could. To do this they had to admit some of the errors of 1981, while trumpeting the virtues of a courageous and effective administration since 1983.

Both the PS and the RPR thus confessed past errors and presented themselves in a new light for the future. Each attacked the other, however, as basically unchanged. The RPR and UDF claimed the Socialists would resume their old ways if they could; the Socialists sought to present the Right as partisan, selfish, and interested in the welfare only of the rich. The first PS election poster showed a frightened woman calling out, "Help!!! The Right is coming back!" This was deemed too defeatist, and was replaced by a Disneyoid Big Bad Wolf addressed by Red Riding Hood *La France*: "Tell me, pretty Right, why do you have such big teeth?"

Under the new proportional representation law, fifty of the ninety-six departments had only two to four seats, a total of 149. In almost all departments the first choice candidates of the three large parties were assured of victory. To guarantee that a system favoring larger parties would help them, the RPR and UDF concluded a pact for joint candidacies in two-thirds of the departments. The smaller parties — the PCF and National Front — could win only where they had strong local support, or in very large departments where even five or six percent of the vote might suffice to gain a seat. The system was so predictable that the *Nouvel Observateur* could come out on February 14 with a (largely accurate) feature article entitled "The 448 deputies already elected." That left only a presumptive 129 seats in doubt.

The only question left to the voters was whether they wanted a greater or lesser disavowal of Mitterrand. In either case his proportional representation law would hold off a landslide favoring the Right. Mitterrand presumably would not have to resign, but if the vote went heavily against the

PS his position would be seriously weakened. Voters were unsure how a conservative majority and a conservative prime minister would contrive to coexist (or, as a new expression had it, cohabit) with a Socialist president whose seven year term did not end until May 1988.

Tradition holds that the French have little or no ability to allow their institutions to evolve gradually, that they remain rigidly the same until abrupt change brings new institutions and a new number for the republic. It would be more correct to say that the frequency of abrupt change in French history has produced a general apprehension that institutions can stand few shocks. The prospect of cohabitation engendered considerable anxiety, enhanced by constant discussion in the press, radio, and television.

Although the framers of the 1958 constitution had not expected perpetual parliamentary majorities, all elections since 1958 had returned National Assemblies in which conservative forces dominated. In 1973, Georges Pompidou had declared in the face of the new Union de la Gauche that if his government lost its majority he would resign. Taken as a warning to the electorate, even a threat, the statement played its intended part in a comfortable conservative victory. In 1978, when a Left victory seemed overwhelmingly probable, Giscard had told the nation that he would not resign—but warned that he would then have no powers to block the programs of the Left. In 1986, Mitterrand had no temptation to resign or power to warn. His aim was to hold thirty percent of the electorate, hang on and fight another day.

In 1984 the noisier members of the opposition had declared that there could be no question of living together with François Mitterrand, who would be disavowed by the electorate and must be driven from the Elysée if he persisted in holding on to his office. Someone even suggested that Mitterrand could be evicted by cutting off the electricity in the presidential palace. Gambetta's famous demand that President MacMahon must submit to legislative will or resign, "*se soumettre ou se démettre*," was extensively quoted by the journals and orators of the Right.

Presidential hopeful Raymond Barre announced that no good could come out of cohabitation, which would bring in two years of confusion and drift, meanwhile eroding the strong presidential institutions of the Fifth Republic. As polls showed Barre far more popular than Chirac at this time, he appeared to be hoping that a rapid showdown between a conservative majority and an intransigent president would force Mitterrand's resignation and a new presidential election.

In taking this stand Barre made what proved to be a serious strategic error. He had no party behind him that could enforce such a decision. His announcement that he personally would vote no confidence in any government intending cohabitation might influence his friends but could not bind them.

In April 1985 only forty-one percent of UDF voters and thirty-nine percent of RPR voters approved Barre's position.[2]

Jacques Chirac saw in cohabitation a means to refashion an image still overshadowed by a reputation for impetuosity and inconstancy. Edouard Balladur, secretary general of the Elysée in Pompidou's administration, who became one of Chirac's principal counselors in 1983, publicly argued the necessity of cohabitation as early as September of that year in a *Le Monde* article approved by Chirac.[3] Balladur argued that the constitution was sufficiently flexible to fit a situation in which the president's party no longer had a majority. The equilibrium between the two offices and the two personalities would be delicate, conflicts would be possible and government might lose some of its efficiency. But this would be the result of a popular decision that must be taken into account.

Chirac was long uncertain whether he should head a government of cohabitation, often repeating when asked if he would become prime minister, "I've done that already." In May 1985 he told a radio interviewer that he had no intention of taking the job, and no vocation for it.[4] Apparently Chirac feared that he might be bogged down in an association with the Machiavellian Mitterrand, with Barre sniping from the sidelines and dividing the governing majority. However, since Barre was well ahead of him in the popularity polls as a future presidential candidate he needed the prime minister's office to renew his reputation. After the October 1985 television debate between Chirac and Fabius, when the young Socialist leader torpedoed his own prestige and advanced the cause of Jacques Chirac, little doubt remained that Chirac would demand the prime ministry.

With Fabius among the walking wounded, it became more necessary than ever for Mitterrand to take an active role in the campaign. There was no clear precedent for a president taking an active role campaigning for his party. Mitterrand's predecessors had often pretended to stand above the party melee. De Gaulle believed that winning legislative elections was the job of the prime minister. Pompidou was more the chief of the Gaullist party than his patron had been, but still kept to this tradition. Giscard, who had not had a political prime minister in Barre, had offended against public opinion by his engagement in the 1978 elections.

As observers have pointed out, it is somewhat contradictory to affirm that one's presidential legitimacy is not affected by a legislative election and simultaneously to take part in it. However, by 1986 the French were relatively accustomed to the process. Mitterrand began with a television interview in mid-December 1985 in which he stated his hopes for a Socialist victory. He followed this up with mass rallies in the home constituencies of his two prime ministers, in January in the Rouen suburb of Grand-Quevilly and in February in Lille. Polls showed that by the end of the campaign two-thirds of the electorate felt that the president had not exceeded his constitutional role in campaigning for his party.[5]

Mitterrand's main theme was "do not turn back." He picked up on an idea suggested by one of the better Socialist campaign posters, showing a pretty girl with a sheaf of wheat and the slogan, "I want to harvest what I sowed on the Left." Great efforts had been been made, said the president, and should not be abandoned. The Socialist campaign also dwelt on the divisions of the Right – its disagreements on cohabitation, and its temptation to compromise with the National Front. Some leaders of the UDF and RPR seemed open to a deal with Le Pen. Others, particularly Chirac, were not. The issue was complicated by the simultaneity of legislative and regional council elections; a politician might oppose opening the ranks of the parliamentary majority to Le Pen and company and still admit the possibility of forming regional alliances with them.

In a very real sense the 1986 election was the first round of the 1988 presidential race. No one knew whether the period of cohabitation would last for the twenty-five months officially separating the two contests, but it was clear to all that to remain united and combat-ready the Socialists needed to win at least thirty percent of the vote. For Chirac the 1986 election was a rung on the ladder he must climb to reach the presidency. For Barre, the election would test his prophecy that cohabitation was a mischievous policy and bound to fail – its success or failure affecting his own presidential candidacy.

Those whose fortunes were not immediately involved in the next presidential election saw the legislative elections as more important. The new young leaders of the Republican party knew that victory meant their emergence into full public life as ministers, promotion of their several careers and of their free enterprise ideology. Jean-Marie Le Pen sought to confirm and enlarge the successes of 1984, thus forcing the other parties to recognize him as a legitimate and major player. The Communists desired to win back their losses of 1981, and hoped that a Socialist defeat would bring disunity to the PS and allow the PCF to emerge again as the dominant force on the Left.

Opinion was uncertain whether cohabitation would or would not weaken the presidential office. Many argued that with the president in the Elysée warring with the prime minister in the Hotel Matignon across the Seine, France would become ungovernable, and return to the piteous state of the Fourth Republic.[6]

In mid-January 1986 the RPR and UDF produced a joint campaign platform which backed away slightly from some of the extreme neo-liberalism of the earlier years. (In 1984 a neo-liberal economist had even proposed to sell off the national forests.) The nationalized sector would be privatized – but the process would be spread out over the five year term of the legislature.

The allies promised a return to the old election procedure with single-member constituencies, the removal of price controls, changes in state control of broadcasting, firm measures on law and order, tax cuts, and much more.[7]

There was much overlap here with the real program of the Socialists in the last twenty months of power: the Fabius government had moved toward removal of price controls, improved relations with the police and taken a tougher line on crime and terrorism. It had even moved one step toward denationalization by selling shares in the subsidiaries of nationalized firms.

The electorate, however, still mistrusted the Socialists. No one in the campaign was talking much about reducing unemployment. (The Socialists were acutely conscious that their 1981 promises to reduce it now looked ridiculous, while the Right knew itself powerless to bring rapid improvement.) The voters, however, consistently listed this as their highest national priority, and the Socialists' record weighed heavily against them. Other issues hurting the Socialists were crime and the immigration question. Though the voters of the National Front placed these higher on their lists than did others, they ranked high in all lists of concerns.[8]

The campaign itself was slickly Madison Avenue, evidence of an Americanization of French manners that marked an immense change since the distant days when Frenchmen feared that if they drank a dubious brew called Coca-Cola they would cease to be the heirs of Descartes, Racine, and Corneille. The principal PS slogan, "A France that's winning," was balanced by the RPR slogan "On to tomorrow!" A campaign that took place during an exceedingly cold winter was illustrated by RPR billboard posters of politicians in shirtsleeves, the head of the party list in each department photographed with Chirac, all grinning inanely in the best American manner, their neckties blowing in a studio wind.

The trend of polls appeared to show that while the electorate had focused in early January on the disappointments brought them by five years of Socialist rule, many (though not a majority) had concluded by election day, March 16, that the total Socialist record was not so bad—that Mitterrand and his prime ministers had shown courage and the ability to learn from their mistakes. This change was reflected in the final election results.

The Socialist politicians and observers gathered at party headquarters on election night to await the results were still apprehensive. A few days earlier terrorists in Lebanon had kidnaped four members of an Antenne 2 news crew the day after their arrival in Beirut, and PS leaders feared this fresh humiliation would renew old grievances on the delicate crime-terrorism question. Polls indicated that the PCF would do badly, but no one knew who might benefit from a further drop in the Communist vote. The day before, Robert Hersant's *Figaro* had infringed against the rule forbidding publication of polls in the week before the election with a "prediction" that gave the RPR/UDF a crushing majority of 334 seats. The Socialists' own polls told them they would do better — but how much better? Win or lose, the PS had laid in an ample supply of champagne to comfort or soothe its leaders and their guests. By eight o'clock, corks began to pop. Computer projections digested the mixed results of late polling and post-election exit polls and showed the PS vote exceeding the crucial barrier of thirty percent, rising toward thirty-two. A mile away the conservative guests of *Le Figaro* found less savor in their champagne. Long faces on the Right, excitement among the Socialists might have confused an observer unsure of the identity of the winner.

The conservatives had won, but not triumphed. The "breakwater" of proportional representation had deprived the RPR/UDF alliance of the big majority it would have won under the old election law: the National Front had thirty-five seats for its 9.82 percent of the vote where it would have had none before. The total vote on the Right was 54.6 percent, but the respectable Right with its 44.68 percent had only 291 seats, for a majority of two.[9] On the Left, the Socialists had shored up their position, but the Communists were no longer even arithmetically a possible coalition partner, and the total of votes on the Left was one of the worst scores of the Fifth Republic — forty-four percent.

There could however be no talk of a triumphant Right hounding a disavowed Socialist president out of the Elysée. The Socialists and small allies had won 32.6 percent of the vote and with 216 deputies were the strongest single party in the new National Assembly. Cohabitation was a political necessity. And the man who had decried it, Raymond Barre, had disappointed his supporters by demonstrating short coattails in his home department of the Rhône, distanced by a Socialist ticket led by Charles Hernu.

Barre had proclaimed that he would not vote confidence in a cohabitation government. But the Right's exiguous majority gave him and his friends no choice on voting confidence, even as it removed any possible doubt in the conservative ranks that Chirac was their necessary choice for prime minister. Rumors abounded that Mitterrand would try to appoint former premier Jacques Chaban-Delmas, the popular ex-health minister Simone Veil, or even ex-president Giscard. Mitterrand made a tentative effort to enlist Chaban, but the game was already played out — the Right wanted Chirac and Chirac had long since decided that he wanted the job.[10]

On the Tuesday after the election Elysée secretary general Jean-Louis Bianco announced that the president had asked Chirac to see whether he could form a government. On the following day, Chirac's nomination was formally announced. The five years of Socialist power had ended, and a coexistence of uncertain duration had begun.

CHIRAC RETURNS

Energy and ambition were the most striking characteristics of the new prime minister, whose rapid career had been marked both by ability and unpredictability. Born in Paris in 1932, Jacques Chirac descended from two grandfathers who were both Radical Socialist schoolmasters in their native south-central department of the Corrèze. His father had abandoned teaching for banking, rising to be a bank director and financial adviser to the airplane builder Marcel Bloch-Dassault.[11]

Chirac's education was formed by the Institut d'Etudes Politiques (*Sciences Po*), by military service in Algeria commanding a platoon on the Algerian-Moroccan border, and by the Ecole Nationale d'Administration. He spent one summer in the United States, where he went to Harvard Business Summer School, and rose from dishwasher to counter-man at a Howard Johnson's. The experience of combat and command in Algeria were formative experiences in his life; he discovered the pleasures of action.

The Chirac who returned to Paris from Algeria in 1957 to enter ENA was not yet a Gaullist, although the inability of the Fourth Republic to master the Algerian problem was now plain to him. In 1959 he graduated sixteenth in his class — good enough to be assigned to the prestigious Cour des Comptes. In 1956 he married Bernadette Chodron de Courcel, daughter of a distinguished aristocratic family, whom he had met at *Sciences Po*. The keys to success — slow or rapid — were in his hands.

Success was rapid. In 1962 he became a junior member of the staff of the new prime minister, Georges Pompidou. The young *chargé de mission* for questions of transport and civil aviation rapidly discovered that in his position he could deal as an equal with government ministers. His energy and authority were remarked by his elders, including Pierre Juillet, the mysterious, irascible political brains of the Pompidou period. Pompidou was not long in taking notice of this rarity among young bureaucrats, who never explained why something could not be done, but instead went out and did it. He called him affectionately "my bulldozer." In 1967, Chirac was encouraged to run for the National Assembly in the Corrèze. After a narrow victory over a Communist in this left-wing territory, he remained tireless in the service of his increasingly devoted constituents, even after he was elected mayor of Paris.

In the next seven years the young civil servant turned deputy became successively state secretary for employment, budget minister under Economy Minister Valéry Giscard d'Estaing (one of the few people who have ever intimidated him), minister for parliamentary relations, agriculture minister (a very popular one), and briefly, just before Pompidou's death, interior minister.

Under Pompidou, Chirac was powerfully influenced by Pierre Juillet and his coadjutor Marie-France Garaud. Secretive, power-hungry, right-wing, they hated Pompidou's first prime minister Jacques Chaban-Delmas. On Pompidou's death, Chaban declared his candidacy for the Elysée. Chirac had neither love for nor faith in Chaban, and could expect nothing from him. Chirac first tried to block Chaban by inciting Prime Minister Pierre Messmer to declare his own candidacy. When this failed, he prevailed on a number of Gaullist deputies to sign a letter which cast doubt on Chaban's chances. Without openly opting for Giscard, the other conservative candidate, Chirac torpedoed a Chaban candidacy already listing to port. In the first round, Giscard had over twice Chaban's percentage of the vote, and went on to win narrowly over Mitterrand.

Giscard rewarded Chirac by making him prime minister. Chirac was apparently not certain he wanted the job – not because he lacked ambition, but because his real design was to take over a Gaullist party in disarray. Giscard mistakenly thought that his young prime minister would tame the Gaullist party for him; instead, Chirac began to reorganize it in his own image. Within two years, the two men had fallen out, and in August 1976 Chirac resigned. In 1977 he ran for mayor of Paris against Giscard's candidate and made the city his fief. Strengthened by this victory, he thought that the RPR plurality won in the 1978 parliamentary elections should give the RPR a major voice in the cabinet and the government's decisions. Giscard did not see it that way.

In late 1978, preparing for the first European elections to be held by popular vote, Chirac once more let himself be influenced by his familiar demons Pierre Juillet and Marie-France Garaud. Their hold on him was the despair of the rest of his entourage. In them a Gaullist nationalism bordering on caricature mixed with deep contempt for modern society and reformist temptations, all blended together with a tactical sense capable both of amazing coups and incredible blunders. Scornfully domineering, they had maneuvered Chirac since his days as a young state secretary. Once when he expressed his gratitude for their aid, Juillet remarked, "This is the first time a horse has praised its jockey."

The RPR appeal for the European elections, drafted by Juillet but signed by Chirac and issued in his name said yes to Europe, but no to "a vassal France in an empire of merchants. . . . As always when France is about to abase herself, the party supporting foreigners is at work with its calm and reassuring voice. Frenchmen, do not heed it. . . . " This mixture of Napoleonic war propaganda and bombastic Gaullism of the worst period struck an entirely false note. The RPR was criticizing the economic policy and European vision of a government it claimed to support, and alienating public opinion where it thought to attract it. The proof was its score in the

June 1979 European elections: 16.25 percent, last behind the PCF (in its last hurrah at 20.57 percent), the PS (23.57 percent) and the UDF ticket (27.55 percent).

Breaking with Juillet-Garaud after the disaster of 1979, Chirac began to explore non-Gaullist free enterprise ideas. But the shadow of the "infernal couple" still hung over him. Who was this man, wondered an uneasy public, this leader so energetically decisive and so undecided, so prompt to charge in an uncertain direction, so charismatic (for his own flock) and so easily manipulated by his counselors? Did he have any fixed ideas, or only fixed ambitions?

Chirac ran for president against Giscard in part to demonstrate that he existed, knowing he had little chance to win. Apparently he did hope to control a new legislature after Mitterrand dissolved it. Yet his record of miscalculations did not damage him badly — Giscard's errors (and loss of power) hurt the ex-president far more. Chirac remained the unquestioned leader of the biggest and best organized party on the Right, and could look forward to fulfilling his presidential ambitions in 1988.

Chirac's problem in March 1986 was thus the double dilemma of time and program. He had a maximum of twenty-five months before him to establish a record that would banish abiding doubts on his constancy and character. His government faced not only the unknowns of cohabitation with a Socialist president determined to maintain his prerogatives, but also the problems of a coalition in which his RPR had 145 deputies and the UDF 129. Together with some other conservative deputies, they had a slim majority of two. The coalition was in fact soldered together by this slight majority. The rivalries between the leaders of the RPR and the young Turks of the UDF, most vociferous champions of the new *libéralisme*, were however barely hidden.

THE DYNAMICS OF COHABITATION

Cohabitation had always been understood as a transition, an interval before the next presidential election. Still there was much debate about the length of the interval, and fear that the strong presidential institutions of the Fifth Republic might be permanently affected by a period in which the president would take a back seat to the prime minister. The drafters of the constitution of 1958 had provided for a strong president able to reinforce the powers of his nominee the prime minister, on the assumption that the National Assembly would continue to be dominated by the multiple and shifting party alliances of the Third and Fourth Republics. In fact, de Gaulle had enjoyed a de facto majority in 1958-1962, and thereafter all presidents had controlled an Assembly majority and had increased their powers.

Now the question was whether practice could elucidate a potential problem left unmentioned in the constitution: would the president be able to block the new majority, and if so, would he have to be forced from office, incurring a dangerous precedent like that with MacMahon in 1877-1879? Or would the prime minister so whittle down a presidential power more customary than statutory that the office would be permanently altered?[12]

Although these were serious and important questions, events conspired to make them less relevant than they seemed to observers in 1986. Cohabitation did go to term, presidential powers suffered no lasting damage, and Mitterrand's re-election in 1988 revived the familiar pattern of a strong president who can dissolve an inconvenient Assembly to seek a better one. If either Chirac or Barre had won he would have dissolved the Assembly for much the same reasons. Yet the institutions of the Fifth Republic might have suffered some of the damage needlessly feared if Mitterrand, the master of maneuver, had not protected both his political fortunes and his office so well. In retrospect, the struggles of cohabitation appear as a shadow play, where no blood is sought or drawn, but where the most skillful actor wins the prize.

One major uncertainty soon disappeared, as it became evident that neither the president nor the prime minister had any interest in hastening the presidential election. The country liked the idea of cohabitation — at least for a while — and might punish the author of a sudden and partisan rupture. As Balladur put it: "It's the opposite of a western — the one who draws first is dead." Chirac needed to establish a record. Mitterrand, meanwhile, was intent on reworking his image to become a father figure who would smile on what was done well, meanwhile reproving mistakes. Cohabitation was defined by their several needs, reciprocal yet antagonistic. It was less a struggle for power — the constitution clearly gave that to the prime minister — than for the semblance of power. Mitterrand could not permit himself to be humiliated, must continue to be conspicuous in the determination of foreign policy even though its diplomatic and economic machinery was controlled by Chirac. Above all, Mitterrand needed to embody the supreme political-moral authority in France. If he lost this, he would be seen only as an aging man, feebly remonstrating from his gilded palace against the actions of his vigorous and decisive juniors.

Mitterrand's interest was thus to let the country believe that it was governed by a dyarchy, sometimes concordant, sometimes discordant, where one power could check the other. Chirac stood to lose at this game, but lacking sufficient popularity to win an immediate presidential election was obliged to go on playing it to the end.

In this curious period Chirac's UDF allies, the Socialist party and indeed the National Assembly itself were pushed to the sidelines. Chirac's small majority, need for discipline, and lack of time obliged him to enact his program as rapidly as possible — by decree where he could, or often by legislative choke-off. (The notorious article 49/3 clause of the constitution permits a government to force the Assembly to choose between a negative confidence vote and automatic passage of a bill.) In 1981-1986 the deputies had found themselves merely the *godillots* (footsoldiers) of their commander in the Elysée, as so often before in the Fifth Republic. In 1986-1988 the National Assembly did not regain stature, as some had thought it might. Instead it was commanded by a different executive, the prime minister. Meanwhile, Mitterrand's Socialist party was upstaged by the president. It had to support him, and it could not get far ahead of him on pain of damaging its leader. In this waiting role its first priority was to maintain its unity and hope that as the new majority committed inevitable mistakes the Socialists would look better.

The tone for mutual forbearance between president and prime minister was set in the first meeting after Mitterrand asked Chirac to try to form a government. The two men knew each other only slightly and disliked each other; each was convinced the other was an unprincipled opportunist. Mitterrand had already made clear in a television interview in early March that he would resign rather than yield his essential functions. But Mitterrand knew that whatever was still Gaullist about Chirac forbade him to strip the president of his powers in defense and foreign affairs, and he could surmise that Chirac had no interest in a speedy election. In their first conversation, Mitterrand posed three conditions: that the new government not seek to humiliate the president, that it not seek to re-establish the death penalty, and that the president's right to participate in decisions on defense and foreign affairs be respected. In return he agreed to sign the laws passed by the new majority in the National Assembly (which he had no authority to veto, although he was supposed to sign them) and to sign decrees (which he was not obliged to do), "if they are in conformity with republican legality."[13]

Mitterrand also made it clear that he wanted a veto power on the designation of the foreign and defense ministers, so that those chosen would be persons he could work with in confidence. This led to a comedy act in which Mitterrand vetoed his old rival Jean Lecanuet, president of the UDF, as a potential foreign minister and the ambitious young PR chief François Léotard, who aspired to be defense minister. It is unlikely that Chirac much wanted either — both were UDF leaders who might cross him.

The government which was announced four days after the election was a nearly even balance of RPR and UDF personalities. As foreign minister Chirac chose Jean-Bernard Raimond, previously Mitterrand's ambassador to Moscow. He thereby continued the tradition (not always honored) of choosing as foreign minister a career diplomat who would manage his old department but not play too large a personal role. Defense Minister André

Giraud, a senior technician who had been industry minister under Giscard, was also uncontroversial. The most important minister (the only one with the honorific title of *ministre d'Etat*) was Chirac's gray eminence Edouard Balladur. A counselor of Georges Pompidou when he was prime minister, secretary general of the Elysée after his chief became president, the fifty-seven year old Balladur had moved into relative obscurity in private business after Pompidou's death. He re-entered Chirac's inner circle just after the RPR leader broke with the Mephistophelean Pierre Juillet. Having advised against Chirac's presidential candidacy in 1981, in 1983 he became the theoretician of cohabitation as the best road to the presidency in 1988.

Another important figure in the new government was Interior Minister Charles Pasqua. Born in 1927, the son of a Corsican policeman, Pasqua was a teen-aged member of the Resistance in his native Alpes-Maritimes. From this experience he drew a taste for action and clandestinity and an unshakable loyalty to Gaullism. He had an important role in the *Services d'action civique* (SAC), the Gaullist security squads of dubious memory, dissolved in 1981 after one group murdered a renegade and his whole family. Pasqua was a prime organizer of the June 1968 march up the Champs Elysées opposing the May disorders, which drew half a million people into the streets in support of de Gaulle; he proudly displays a painting of it on his office wall. Twice in the cohabitation period Pasqua would urge a repetition of this populist rallying technique. Together with his junior minister for public security Robert Pandraud, a civil servant with years of experience directing the police, Pasqua intended to reassure a nervous France (and the voters of the National Front) by playing the tough cop.

The justice minister was Albin Chalandon, civil servant, banker, ex-minister, ex-head of the oil firm Elf-Aquitaine. René Monory, another ex-minister, received the education portfolio. The young Turks of *"la Chiraquie"* entered the government: Philippe Séguin, an able, ambitious young left-Gaullist had the difficult ministry for social affairs and employment. As junior ministers, Alain Juppé, with the budget, Michel Noir, foreign trade, and Camille Cabanna, privatization, were supervised and sometimes smothered by their chief Edouard Balladur.

The UDF leaders, with François Léotard's friends (*la bande à Léo*), had lesser jobs. Léotard had to content himself with the ministry for culture and communication, his friend Alain Madelin was industry minister, and their associates Jacques Douffiagues and Gérard Longuet junior ministers for public works and transport, and the post office and telecommunications. These men, mostly in their early forties, were the most enthusiastic and noisy advocates of free-enterprise *libéralisme* in the government, as opposed to Balladur or even Chirac, graduates of the school of Pompidolian *dirigisme*. The most prominent Barre supporter in the cabinet was Pierre Méhaignerie, president of the Centre des Démocrates Sociaux, who consented to take the technical ministry of public works, housing, and regional development. There were no women among the senior ministers, but Michèle Barzach would make a name for herself as junior minister for health. Three women served as state secretaries. Valéry Giscard d'Estaing would have been willing to return to his old post as minister of the economy but was not offered the job, and Chirac looked past him to patch up a quarrel with another old enemy, Chaban-Delmas, by backing him as president of the new National Assembly. Raymond Barre remained ostentatiously out of the government of cohabitation that he had denounced as a mistake.

The government's program was to free the economy by privatizing nationalized industry—both that taken over in 1982 and also those industries nationalized in 1945 by General de Gaulle's government. It would bring back the old system of majority voting, free prices, and lower taxes; attempt to cut unemployment and balance the social security system. Tougher measures against crir e and terrorism were promised, as well as a law to make it harder for young foreigners born in France (i.e. mostly North Africans) to become citizens automatically.

Before the new government was a week old, Mitterrand declared that he would not sign a decree abolishing restrictions on firing workers. He followed this with a message to the new Assembly on April 8 declaring that he would not automatically sign decrees (*ordonnances*) set before him; they must be few in number and their purpose so clearly explained by enabling legislation that the parliament and Constitutional Council could judge them. A government in a hurry needed decrees to save both time and potential stress within its small majority. While Chirac needed to impress the country with the verve and rhythm of his new government, the president intended to stand as the champion of measured procedure against rashness, haste, and retrograde legislation. To emphasize that he was a guardian, not a participant in the new government, he forbade his own staff to sit in on interministerial meetings (where Chirac did not want them anyway) with the exception of defense and foreign affairs.

The question of just how much authority the president would retain in foreign affairs arose immediately. When in early April 1986 the United States government requested permission to overfly France to bomb Tripoli, Chirac claimed that the president had concurred with his decision to refuse. The decision appears to have been the result of common consultation and agreement. Mitterrand was furious, however, because the prime minister presented himself as the principal personage in this joint decision. (See the chapter on foreign policy, below.)[14]

Chirac's decision to show who was boss of French foreign policy by accompanying Mitterrand to the Tokyo economic summit in early May 1986 completely upset the protocol-sensitive Japanese. Unused to roosters with two heads, Gallic or otherwise, they could find no way to seat Chirac at the opening banquet for chiefs of delegations. The efforts of Chirac's staff to exert influence on a meeting already almost completely prepared merely confused diplomatic contacts, while Chirac's explanation to Prime Minister Nakasone that the French president henceforth had a merely ceremonial role in foreign affairs was promptly leaked to the press and had to be denied.[15]

This preliminary skirmishing on the domestic and diplomatic fronts set the tone for the months to follow. Mitterrand declared on May 18 that his duty was "to permit the majority elected by the people to govern," but also "to intervene each time that a decision might harm the unity of Frenchmen, appear unjust or exclude ... part of the French people." Following this logic, the president refused to sign *ordonnances* on the privatization of sixty-five industries, banks, and insurance companies, on a new electoral law, and on new regulations on working hours, forcing Chirac to push bills for these measures through the National Assembly. The government thus did not save time on these and other matters which Mitterrand refused to approve and risked seeming to move more rapidly than carefully. The president also did not hesitate to make plain his disapproval of some ordinary bills presented to the National Assembly, such as the law on dismissals and a new statute for New Caledonia.

In other legislation, the government repealed the surtax on large fortunes and enacted an amnesty to repatriate funds that had illegally left the country in the days when the Socialo-Communist menace had panicked some of the rich. Both of these measures were unpopular; they also gave the new Socialist opposition an opportunity to cry that the Right was repaying its paymasters.

The government's privatization law of August 6, 1986 provided for changes over a five-year period in the status of eleven industrial groups, three giant insurance companies and fifty-one banks. After the partial conversion of the oil company Elf-Aquitaine to the private sector, a campaign designed to create a popular mass capitalism on the Thatcher model opened in late November 1986 with the privatization of the glass and plastics giant Saint-Gobain. This operation was heavily over-subscribed. Economy and Finance Minister Balladur was encouraged to move rapidly toward twelve other privatizations in 1987, involving six million stockholders — until the stock market crash of October 1987 brought a temporary halt. In this process the government privatized two giant investment banks taken over in 1982, Paribas and Suez, and a major deposit bank, the Société Générale, which had been in the public sector since 1945. After the first tremors of the crash had passed, the government also privatized the munitions firm Matra in January 1988, but then paused to await the elections. Six of the major in-

dustrial groups taken over in 1982 (Roussel UCLAF, Péchiney, Rhône-
Poulenc, Thomson, Bull, and Avions Marcel Dassault) remained in the
public sector at the time of Mitterrand's re-election.

As a means of defending major industries or banks against raiders, Balladur built a regulation into the privatization scheme stipulating that
selected purchasers would in exchange for a fixed price for stocks obligate
themselves to keep the stock purchased for two years, and sell in the three
following years only with the approval of the board of directors. These so-
called stable blocs of holdings, or *noyaux durs*, made up twenty-five to thirty percent of the total capital. Balladur selected the core shareholders,
composed of companies and individuals who were in many cases close to the
RPR. This operation was severely criticized, not only by the Socialists but
also by Raymond Barre. The controversy over them, and the relative loss of
confidence in popular capitalism consequent on the 1987 market crash considerably dampened the political usefulness of Balladur's privatizations.[16]

The president had refused to sign a privatization decree, but the Socialists
were unwilling to defend their nationalizations to the last trench. Pierre
Bérégovoy (who returned to his old post as minister of economy and finance
in May 1988) told an interviewer in October 1987 that it was not the state's
job to finance industry. In April 1988 Mitterrand declared on television that
he would proceed to no new privatizations before 1992, and suggested that
he would do nothing to re-nationalize companies. Bérégovoy's preference
lies with a state sector able to raise capital by issuing blocks of non-voting
stock, the tactic he used with some small companies in 1985. In his view, the
state should be able to create new companies, if its intervention is needed,
but also be free to sell off companies.[17]

Although the first privatizations went off well, unemployment continued
to rise and in August 1986 Social Affairs Minister Séguin frankly admitted
that France would have to accustom itself to at least two and a half million
unemployed for a long time.[18] The need to alleviate an unemployment
characterized by long duration and less and less softened by insurance, became plain to all. But as all parties realized that no measures would shrink
unemployment quickly, politicians became more and more wary of talking
about it; the 1988 presidential campaign heard none of the promises to cure
joblessness that resounded in 1981 and even (to a lesser extent) in 1986.

Chirac and his interior minister Charles Pasqua intended to show they
could do much better than the Socialists (and win over voters from the National Front) by showing themselves the determined enemies of illegal immigration, crime, and terrorism. Bombs had continued to go off in Paris as
elsewhere—beginning in March just as Chirac was named prime minister.
In the first two weeks of September 1986 after terrorist bombs bloodied
Paris, the government imposed visas for all foreigners except nationals of

the European Community and Switzerland, and ordered soldiers to patrol the frontier. The police were again authorized to check identity documents at will, and multiplied their efforts. One hundred and one illegal Malian immigrants were demonstratively flown home on a government chartered aircraft. Despite the terrorist carnage, the government continued to benefit from greater approval on the topic of internal security than on any other question.[19]

The Chirac government's first serious setback came from an unexpected but familiar quarter: lycée and university students. Junior Minister for University Affairs Alain Devaquet had worked out what seemed a moderate reform for a pressing problem. The French university system is obliged to accept all students who pass the baccalaureate examination, a number enormously swollen in the past thirty-five years. The establishment of new universities in the past generation (there are now seventy-four universities in thirty-eight cities) has not sufficed to control this problem; classes are overcrowded and the prestige of a university education has fallen. Devaquet's law would have permitted each university to set its own admission quotas for the different faculties. In addition, each university would have handed out its own diploma and not a uniform document issued by the state. Registration fees (French universities are free) would have been set at 450 to 900 francs.

The government thought that opposition to the bill might come from its own right wing in parliament but not from the students. It was therefore taken by surprise in late November when, after the Fédération d'Education Nationale and the PS called for a demonstration against the project, over a hundred thousand students gathered at the Place de la Bastille to denounce the law. Four days later, after coordination committees had sprung up at most universities and many provincial lycées, another sea of students took to the streets—two hundred thousand in Paris, three hundred thousand in the provincial cities—far more than the mostly amateur organizers had expected.

The students were neither violent nor particularly angry. They were however frightened by a badly explained education bill which they feared would limit their access to universities, force them into undesired career choices, and devalue diplomas issued by the less prestigious universities. Some also feared that the registration fees, minor in themselves, were the thin edge of the wedge for tuition charges.

Unrest continued, with another monster rally on December 4 that saw more than half a million students in the streets. The government wavered, and the younger UDF and RPR ministers, horrified at the idea of losing a young generation hitherto rather favorable to *libéralisme*, demanded that Chirac withdraw the bill. Chirac did not want to disclaim Education

Minister Monory (the only major CDS politician who backed him rather than Barre for president) and Monory stubbornly refused to retreat. Chirac, remembering May 1968, feared that if he withdrew the bill he would seem to be taking orders from the street. Interior Minister Pasqua was at first flexible, then shifted to toughness and advocated a counter-march of RPR partisans, à la 1968. On the night of December 5, after disorders of unclear origin, Pasqua's police took their truncheons to a young Algerian-French student with weak kidneys who died of the beating. The government had to back down in disarray, while Mitterrand hastened to visit the dead boy's family.

The student troubles at the end of 1986 broke the momentum of the Chirac government. The prime minister had shown himself imperceptive and irresolute while the dissension within his government was widely reported, then brutally resolute, and finally compelled to give in. Mitterrand, meanwhile, had appeared as the high guarantor of calm and measure. A whole age class had been soured on Chirac and the RPR.[20]

Troubles did not come singly. In December there were wildcat strikes by railroadmen and by personnel of the Paris metro and suburban railroad. France was briefly paralyzed, in a winter of extreme cold. Chirac felt obliged to cancel a special January session of the National Assembly and postpone controversial measures. A bill on restriction of automatic naturalization (principally aimed at young North Africans) was deferred until a blue-ribbon commission could mull it over and finally postponed until after the next election. Unemployment continued to increase, and the government's handling of social affairs was judged ineffective.

Generally approved by a bare majority of the people when it took office, the Chirac government's popularity had risen, with momentary dips, until the disaster of the November crisis and the strikes. Thereafter it skidded, diminishing throughout 1987.[21] However, the departure of the Socialists was still not much regretted, and in February 1987, after the student troubles, only thirty-one percent of SOFRES respondents wanted the Socialists to return to power as rapidly as possible.[22] The voters thus seemed to be in the process of withdrawing the credit they had tentatively advanced to the Right, yet unready to give it again to the Left. In this state of indecision and disillusion, a majority of the people and even half of Socialist supporters thought there were few basic differences between the PS and the parties of the Right.[23] Ideologies were at a discount, and the weight of the personalities of rival candidates for the presidency became increasingly decisive.

TOWARD THE PRESIDENTIAL ELECTION

Jacques Chirac had hoped that his record as prime minister would efface the doubts about his character and judgment disturbing many of his compatriots. He had known from the beginning that Mitterrand would be spared the unpopularity that accompanies responsibility, and would seek to rebuild his own prestige at his prime minister's expense. But the president had turned seventy in 1986. He might or might not seek re-election, and if he did not the Socialist party had no single and popular choice to succeed him. In the meantime, Chirac had to worry about Raymond Barre, the rival in his own camp.

Barre's standing in the polls suffered during most of 1986 from his opposition to cohabitation. But by early 1987 both supporters of the RPR-UDF and voters at large consistently began telling pollsters that they thought Barre the best candidate of the Right in 1988.[24] Barre's strength lay in his air of assurance and popular confidence in him as the best man to assure economic growth. Against the energetic but erratic Chirac, he was Mr. "Slow and steady wins the race," and he dubbed himself "the tortoise."

Barre was a deputy from the Rhône department and a member of the UDF, but he had always disdained organizational politics and the little world of politicians, which he scornfully termed "the microcosm." His friends had, however, built up a network of *Barriste* committees all over France. He enjoyed the particular support of the CDS leaders, while the young leaders of the Parti Républicain eyed him with mistrust but admitted that they would have to back him. His relations with his original patron, ex-president Giscard, were correct but distinctly cool. But Giscard remained unpopular and had lost his grip on the levers of party machinery in his old Parti Républicain.

Would Mitterrand again be a candidate in 1988? His popularity had plunged to its nadir in late 1984-1985; in January 1985 only a third of poll respondents considered the balance sheet of his administration to be positive, and his unpopularity diminished very slowly in the course of 1985.[25] At the PS congress in Toulouse in October 1985 the general tone was defensive—few thought the president could do more than hold out through the hard times of cohabitation to come. If the PS could eke out a respectable score in 1986, Mitterrand would not be forced from office, and the PS could avoid the round of recriminations and the bitter power struggle that would almost certainly accompany total defeat. The most plausible PS candidate in 1988 was thought to be Rocard or perhaps Fabius.[26]

Mitterrand's performance in rallying his party in the 1986 elections and his consistently skillful conduct of cohabitation changed all that. As early as June 1986 a poll showed that forty-seven percent of voters and seventy-four percent of Socialist voters wanted him to run again in 1988.[27] When a Socialist party congress met in Lille in April 1987 to prepare the 1988 elections there was no discussion of Mitterrand's candidacy, precisely because almost all the Socialist leaders were convinced that he would run again. The congress passed a final resolution formally settling all internal differences and elected a secretariat in which all factions were represented. Michel Rocard continued to insist that he too would run for president, but he was now felt to be more an alternative than a real rival to Mitterrand.[28]

The president's popularity as the great cohabiter held steady throughout 1987, reaching the heights attained in early 1982 before disappointment had set in. His opponents took comfort, however, from polls reflecting doubts about his earlier record and on the wisdom of choosing him for another seven years. Nevertheless, polls after June 1986 consistently showed that Mitterrand would defeat either Chirac or Barre in the second round in 1988. Chirac and Barre partisans could only hope that the popularity of the president-arbiter would not transfer itself to the president-candidate, once he finally declared himself.

Mitterrand was in no hurry to declare himself. Lesser candidates like the soporific André Lajoinie of the PCF or the able demagogue Jean-Marie Le Pen needed a head start, announcing their candidacies in 1987. (A battered Georges Marchais grimly held on to power in the PCF, but had no wish to head a ticket almost certain to see the worst score the party had ever had.) There were the usual minor candidacies, including an ecologist, Antoine Waechter, and a dissident Communist slate headed by former Politburo member Pierre Juquin — now backed by one of the Trotskyite groups. Chirac formally declared his candidacy in January, Barre in early February. Mitterrand delayed until March 22.

By this time all doubt about his decision had disappeared, but instead of anti-climax he had achieved an effect of welcome confirmation. Mitterrand had no laundry list of new proposals to submit to the French this time. He ran as a candidate in whom the people could have confidence, and a poll in late March suggested that the frequent reproach of inconstancy had for a large majority yielded to admiration for his ability to adapt to changing situations.[29] While not renouncing his past as a Socialist, Mitterrand laid his major emphasis on reunifying the French and imbuing them with a sober determination to face the economic challenges of the 1990s and beyond, building a strong France in a more unified Europe.

Confidence was also Barre's stock in trade, and in some mysterious way as confidence in Mitterrand was confirmed confidence in Barre ebbed away.

A steady decline in his ratings set in after the New Year, unchecked by his formal declaration of candidacy and accentuated by his wooden and uninspiring performance. By March he was clearly far behind Chirac, whose ratings were rising. Without the formidable party machinery Chirac possessed in the RPR, and given only perfunctory support by the young leaders of the Parti Républicain who were already calculating the terms of an alliance with Chirac, Barre had no hope of emerging successfully from the first round.

The first round of the elections on April 24 confirmed Barre's collapse — a poor showing of only 16.53 percent. But Chirac had done badly as well. Generally credited in the polls until the end with some twenty-three percent, he ended with 19.95 percent. The major surprise of the first round was Jean-Marie Le Pen's unexpected 14.38 percent — polls had credited him with twelve percent at the most. Mitterrand, with 34.11 percent, had run slightly behind polling predictions. The Communist party had its worst score in history: 6.76 percent.

Le Pen had clearly taken votes from all sides — many from the RPR, certainly, but also from voters reckoned in the Mitterrand column, and National Front strength was impressive in towns and industrial suburbs which the PCF had formerly dominated. Le Pen's strength increased in the cities of the Mediterranean littoral where he had already shown himself strong. He now had 28.34 percent in Marseilles, 25.92 percent in Nice, 27.04 percent in Toulon. His average vote in the ten biggest cities in France was 17.52 percent. He had made inroads into small towns, where there were few or no immigrants, and in the countryside. For once, Le Pen was taken at his self-estimate when he called his results "an earthquake."

Chirac knew that he could not expect to win in the second round unless all the Le Pen voters backed him, and he could not realistically hope to garner them all, or even all of Barre's. His campaign in the next two weeks was directed to narrowing the gap with Mitterrand — hoping perhaps for a miracle, but really attempting to maintain his position as leader of the Right after the election.

He evidently hoped that headline-grabbing actions overseas would help him. Pasqua's emissaries had been negotiating with Iran to free the remaining French hostages held in Lebanon well before the elections, and after several hitches they were released early in the week before the second round. Immediately thereafter, French gendarmes in New Caledonia stormed a cave on an outlying island where a commando of Kanak guerrillas were holding French hostages — the hostages were rescued, but two gendarmes and nineteen guerrillas were killed. The next day, Paris announced that Captain Dominique Prieur — one of the two French intelligence officers caught by New Zealand in the *Rainbow Warrior* affair and sentenced to ten years imprisonment—would be flown back to Paris. Chirac had negotiated an agreement with New Zealand to commute the sentence of the two officers to three years on a remote French Pacific island. Prieur's partner Major Mafart had already been brought back to France because of illness (not severe enough to keep him from following a course at the Ecole de Guerre); and Captain Prieur (whose husband had joined her on the island) was pregnant—though not expecting until January.

The release of the hostages was popular, but Chirac (or Pasqua) had probably overdone the sensational action. Desire among swing voters to vote against an RPR apparently ready to make deals with Le Pen played a large role in second round reactions (especially after Pasqua was quoted as saying that the values of the National Front did not differ from those of the RPR). In any event, Chirac's score in the second round on May 8 was only 45.98 percent against a triumphant 54.02 percent for Mitterrand. Exit polls showed that the president had won almost all of the Communist and other extreme leftist vote, four-fifths of the ecologists, twenty-two percent of Le Pen voters, and thirteen percent of Barre's.[30]

Mitterrand's victory had been expected. What Mitterrand might do with that victory remained unclear. He had been elected as a unifier, preferred to Chirac because the traditional Left electorate retained confidence in him and a significant portion of the center-right voters preferred him to Chirac, a man of many contradictory policies and no clear core identity. But Mitterrand's policy of *ouverture*—opening—was deliberately vague. At a minimum, it meant a rejection of the exclusive Left policies of 1981-1983. Mitterrand now had to fill in the content and the political tactics of *ouverture*.

His first step was to name a new prime minister. The Right still had a majority in the National Assembly, but Chirac had declared that he would resign if defeated. Mitterrand chose the Socialist most popular in the country at large (but not in the Socialist party), his perennial rival Rocard. Having insisted in 1987 that he was a serious candidate for the presidency, Rocard had slackened his efforts by the winter of 1988 and had come to a tacit understanding with Mitterrand.

The president's choice of prime ministers was in fact limited. He needed someone who shared his general outlook, a Socialist who could symbolize the idea of *ouverture*. Rocard and Pierre Bérégovoy (now well seen by the business community) were the only immediate candidates, but Rocard was more popular and a better politician, while Bérégovoy would be seen as too close to the president to provide the shielding effect traditionally attached to the prime ministerial office. Anointed as prime minister, Rocard might take a place among the *dauphins* for Mitterrand's succession, but he would aspire to that in any case. His success would reflect well on Mitterrand, while lack of it would at least open the way for other possible successors personally closer to Mitterrand — Fabius or Jospin.

Rocard's nomination was well received (with some grumbling from the left wing of the PS), but the cabinet appointments led to a controversy that immediately laid bare the ambiguities attached to *ouverture*. The Rocard government would be seventy-five votes short of a majority in the National Assembly. To pass laws it would need more than half the votes of an UDF uncertainly poised between tactical and total opposition. Did opening to the Center (and just what was the Center?) mean a programmatic alliance? On what program, and whose? Few spoke up for an alliance, although polls appeared to show that the country vaguely wanted some such arrangement. A somewhat more plausible scheme was a day-to-day understanding that a part of the Right would function as an obliging Center, not overthrowing the government and supporting it on selected issues.

Valéry Giscard d'Estaing, visibly pleased by the defeat of his two former prime ministers and rivals, smoothly argued for this kind of "constructive opposition." Mitterrand instead tried to sign up leading non-Socialist politicians to enter the government on an individual basis, and three former ministers under Giscard who were not personalities of the first rank did accept portfolios in the new government. So did a non-party leading industrialist and a senior magistrate, who became ministers of industry and justice. But the nomination of nine ministers from the Fabius government (including Bérégovoy, Dumas, Joxe, Lang, Delebarre in their old ministries and Chevènement at Defense), delineated a government dominated by Socialists. Although forty percent of the members of the new government were not PS members, the opposition immediately charged that Mitterrand (who by all accounts had the major hand in drafting the list of ministers) had produced a false opening and a real Socialist hegemony, using the same old people.

This accusation was hardly disinterested. Giscard desired to retake the leadership of the Center, and he needed to hold on to the largely Catholic CDS. The CDS in turn was restless under the UDF tent in close proximity to a domineering and insistently free enterprise Parti Républicain, and tempted by the notion of a real center party that might exercise the pivot role played by the Free Democratic party in West Germany. Raymond Barre, little damaged by defeat because Chirac had also done poorly, looked on benevolently, and did not discourage centrists who consulted him about entering the Rocard government. Meanwhile Giscard discouraged his party friends (notably Simone Veil) from entering the new government.

Mitterrand was not attracted to the idea of depending on a coy and easily hostile UDF for a majority and leaving unexploited the chance to seek a better one. Centrist Senator Michel Durafour, one of the new ministers, remarked: "Mitterrand could not give Giscard a dagger, saying to him 'kill me when you wish.'"[31]

Exit polls suggesting that the Socialists might win a large majority furnished another argument for rapid dissolution. Wooing an irresolute and possibly hostile Center while the decisive moment for a Socialist majority slipped away seemed a risky course. On May 14 the president announced that he was dissolving the Assembly and called for elections to take place on June 5 and 12. Believing that it would have a large majority, the Socialist party, on presidential instructions, offered to support ministers who were non-Socialists as well as other prominent non-Socialists, in a number of constituencies. The maneuver did not sit well among PS militants, as always unhappy at the idea of leaving cherished jobs to outsiders who had been political opponents.

The campaign was fought by the Socialists on the theme of "support the president," using the question of alliances with the National Front as a bugaboo. The Right campaigned largely on local themes. The result was to emphasize the strength of local notables both of the Left and Right. Abstention was at record highs in both rounds – 34.26 percent in the first round and 30.05 in the second. After the first round it was clear that the pink wave predicted by pollsters had failed to materialize, but fresh polls predicted a small but comfortable Socialist majority.

In the first round a number of non-Socialist ministers and even PS figures (including two close collaborators of the president) were defeated. "Parachuted" into unfamiliar constituencies, none of them had much opportunity to court their new voters. Some were outpolled in the first round by Communists. A PCF taken for dead after the disaster of Lajoinie's 6.76 percent showed that it still had drawing power in selected constituencies, polling 11.32 percent. In contrast, the National Front ticket had not done nearly as well as Le Pen's presidential candidacy – 9.65 percent against 14.43 on April 24. In a much denounced bargain, Le Pen withdrew some of his candidates in the Bouches-du-Rhône department (where he himself was a candidate in Marseilles) while local leader Jean-Claude Gaudin agreed not to oppose certain Front candidates.

A week later an extraordinarily close second round produced more surprises. The PS did not achieve its expected majority. It needed 289 seats for a bare majority. With 276 it had what in Italian politics is always referred to as a "relative majority." The Right had fewer seats, the National Front had won only one, and the Communists (backed by the PS in the second round) had an unexpected twenty-seven seats.

Exit polls did not explain the unprecedentedly high level of abstentions, but one poll did indicate the mixed motivation of an electorate which had produced this result. It found fifty-six percent of respondents saying that they did not wish to see a PS majority, and fifty-nine percent who did not want an RPR/UDF majority. (Nevertheless, sixty-three percent had wanted to see a majority of some kind emerge from the vote.)[32]

In the ultimate irony of a presidential-legislative campaign billed as a move toward the center, the voters had produced a Socialist-Communist majority like the one feared in 1981. But nothing in the political landscape resembled 1981 — Georges Marchais instantly announced that his party would not cooperate with the Socialists, and for Rocard and Mitterrand *ouverture* forbade all but small tactical deals with the PCF.

Confirming that Rocard would continue as prime minister, Mitterrand told the country that the constitution provided for just such contingencies as the present one and noted that a number of stable Western European democracies operated with coalition majorities. There was however to be no rapid coalition-building. The second Rocard ministry formed in late June brought in a few more centrist personalities formerly close to Giscard, now closer to Barre, but remained essentially a Socialist government with non-Socialist participation.

NOTES

1. SOFRES, *L'Etat de l'opinion publique — clés pour 1987*, p. 136.

2. SOFRES, *Clés pour 1987*, p. 52.

3. Franz-Olivier Giesbert, *Jacques Chirac*, p. 358. The *Le Monde* article appeared on September 16, 1983.

4. Giesbert, *Jacques Chirac*, p.361.

5. See Olivier Duhamel and Jérôme Jaffré, "La Découverte de la cohabitation," in SOFRES, *Clés pour 1987*, p. 51, and Jean-Louis Quermonne, "La présidence de la République et le système des partis," *Pouvoirs* 41 (1987), pp. 99-104.

6. For one such alarmist version, written immediately after the elections, see the article by Denis Jeambar, "La France sera-t-elle gouvernable?," *Le Point,* March 17, 1986.

7. RPR/UDF pamphlet, *Plateforme pour gouverner ensemble*, January 16, 1986.

8. Cf. SOFRES, *Clés pour 1987* for polls taken in January and March 1986, pp. 107 and 111.

9. Cf. Alain Lancelot, "Le Brise-lame: les élections du 16 mars 1986," *Projet* 199 (May-June 1986), and Georges Lavau, "The Incomplete Victory of the Right," in *Contemporary France; a Review of Interdisciplinary Studies, 1987,* eds. Jolyon Howorth and George Ross.

10. On the Chaban initiative, see Thierry Pfister, *Dans les coulisses du pouvoir*, pp. 371-372.

11. The following account of Chirac's career draws largely on Franz-Olivier Giesbert, *Jacques Chirac*, much the best book on the RPR leader.

12. Cf. Stanley Hoffmann, "The Odd Couple," *New York Review of Books*, September 25, 1986.

13. Giesbert, *Jacques Chirac*, p. 374.

14. Cf. Jean-Marie Colombani and Jean-Yves Lhomeau, *Le Mariage blanc*, pp. 141-145 and Giesbert, *Jacques Chirac*, pp. 403-404.

15. Cf. Thierry Pfister, *Dans les coulisses du pouvoir*, pp. 236-240.

16. Cf. "Privatisations: un premier bilan," *Problèmes économiques*, no. 2037, August 26, 1987, and *Le Monde* supplement *Affaires*, May 28, 1988.

17. Author's interview with Pierre Bérégovoy, October 1987; *Le Nouvel Observateur*, April 8-14, 1988.

18. *Le Monde*, August 21, 1986.

19. SOFRES, *L'Etat de l'opinion — clés pour 1988*, p. 147.

20. Cf. Giesbert, *Jacques Chirac*, pp. 419-428; *Le Point*, December 1, 1986 and December 15, 1986.

21. SOFRES, *Clés pour 1988*, p. 145.

22. Ibid., pp. 161-163.

23. SOFRES poll of March 20-26, 1987, in SOFRES, *Clés pour 1988*, p. 158.

24. SOFRES, *Clés pour 1988*, p. 122.

25. "La Popularité des présidents," chart of IFOP results in *Pouvoirs* 41 (1987), p. 162.

26. Cf. J.W. Friend, "A Rose in any Other Fist Would Smell as Sweet," *French Politics and Society,* no. 12 (December 1985).

27. SOFRES, *Clés pour 1987*, p. 232.

28. Cf. J. W. Friend, "Counting Down to '88: The PS Congress," *French Politics and Society* 5, no. 3 (June 1987).

29. SOFRES poll in *Le Monde*, March 24, 1988. Sixty percent of respondents admired Mitterrand's adaptability.

30. On indications of last-minute voter sentiment and on exit polling, see Roland Cayrol, "Ce qui a changé dans le paysage politique," *Le Journal des élections*, no. 2 (May 1988), pp. 9-10.

31. See *Le Monde, dossiers et documents* supplement, *Les Elections législatives*, June 1988, pp. 18-19.

32. I am grateful to Professor Stéphane Courtois of CEVIPOF for the complete results of a Louis Harris post-electoral poll conducted for *Le Figaro*, dated June 11, 1988. Its results indicated that a majority in all age groups opposed the idea of an RPR/UDF majority, as did a majority in all occupational groups except farmers and artisans. A plurality of the two last groups opposed it. A majority of all age groups and in all occupational groups except workers did not want the PS to have a majority.

6

Foreign Policy in the Septennat

THE SHAPING OF MITTERRAND'S FOREIGN POLICY

When François Mitterrand took office in 1981 his views on foreign policy and those of his party had undergone a number of changes from their pacifist and anti-nuclear positions of a decade earlier. A convinced European since the days of the Fourth Republic, Mitterrand was obliged to repel several left-ist attempts to influence PS foreign policy in the early days of 1971-1973. He kept the PS in a Socialist International thought by leftist militants to be hope-lessly reformist and pro-NATO, and fought off proposals to take France out of the Atlantic alliance and the European Community.[1] In order to ac-complish these ends Mitterrand made other gestures pleasing to left-wing sentiment in the PS. He tried in vain to organize a French-led group of Mediterranean Socialist parties within the Socialist International which would approve alliances with Communist parties. At every opportunity, he denounced the iniquities of multinational business.

In those years, some Socialists appeared to fear the United States more than the Soviet Union; Mitterrand worried in 1974 that if he were elected the U.S. might try to destabilize him in the way Henry Kissinger had tried to destabilize Salvador Allende. At the same time he had no love for the Soviets, who in turn missed opportunities to cultivate him. His pride was offended when immediately after Pompidou's death the Soviets abruptly canceled a scheduled trip to Moscow already twice put off, without offering to re-schedule it. Their ostentatious preference for Giscard (repeated in the 1981 election) was a constant affront.[2]

From 1975 on, neutralist and anti-NATO tendencies in the PS diminished, and after their 1977 break with the Communists the Socialists were more open to the winds of anti-Communism that were beginning to sweep over the intellectual Left. On the urging of then international affairs secretary Robert Pontillon and Mitterrand's friend Charles Hernu, the party expert on defense, the PS drafted a statement in November 1977 singling out the Soviet

Union as the only power to use military force in Europe (against its own allies) since World War II. After the Communists had preceded the Socialists in accepting the French nuclear deterrent, the PS finally decided in January 1978 to support maintenance of French nuclear forces—though with some reservations.[3] Mitterrand, still profoundly uneasy about nuclear weapons, led from behind in proselytizing for them, telling Hernu, "Go ahead—convince the party and then I will support you."[4]

American power seemed on the wane after the Vietnam disaster, while Soviet power became more assertive in Africa and in the missile build-up. Mitterrand's thinking on the Soviet threat began to change. His ideas on this question in 1977-1979 were not influenced by parallel ideas developed by Helmut Schmidt. The PS leader resented Schmidt's obvious preference for Giscard; their relations were chilly, although Mitterrand became friendly with Willy Brandt. Mitterrand's first statement favoring the NATO decision to deploy Pershing II's and cruise missiles came during a parliamentary debate in December 1979.[5]

In these years of changing military balance the foreign policy of Charles de Gaulle was showing its age. Its military aspects had been accepted (with considerable variation in interpretation and sincerity) by all French parties. All agreed that France should preserve its independent nuclear deterrent, remaining within the Atlantic alliance but outside the NATO military structure. Beneath this general agreement, however, lay differences of approach that posed many questions. Late into the Giscard years orthodox Gaullists were still very influential in the foreign affairs bureaucracy, and treated "as heresy any rapprochement with the United States, any attempt to warm up relations with Israel, any overly systematic cooperation in Europe, any strategic vocabulary that questioned the postulates of dissuasion 'tous azimuts.'" President Giscard, no foreign affairs expert, had innovative ideas in Western European affairs but never rethought the whole complex of Gaullist foreign and security policy. He retained in particular a fascination with the Gaullist legacy of France's "special relation" with the Soviet Union.[6]

In its most ambitious form, the special relation had suggested that an independent France which had escaped from the force field of bipolar East-West tension could play a unique role as arbiter between the USSR and both West and East Europe. When Soviet troops entered Prague in August 1968 de Gaulle immediately realized that his hopes of melting the frozen blocs of the Cold War had ended.[7] Eight months after the blighting of the Prague Spring de Gaulle left office, and Gaullist foreign policy, often flexible in the hands of its creator, was passed on to over-reverent adepts. They were willing to make adjustments— arrangements with NATO softening the harshness of the 1966 break (already begun under de Gaulle with the Lemnitzer-Ailleret agreements), and even the admission of Great Britain into the European Community. Nevertheless, the spirit of Gaullism stalked the corridors of the Quai d'Orsay during the next two administrations, and its precepts continued to be recited in Giscard's Elysée.

The high priests of Gaullist doctrine had also discerned a domestic advantage in the special relation with the Soviet Union. The powerful French Communist party continued to oppose the domestic policies of the Fifth Republic, but in its loyalty to the USSR was compelled to admit that Gaullist foreign policy was sound. Since the PCF appeared totally obedient to the Soviet Communist party, Gaullists concluded that the special relation created a so-called triangular situation, by virtue of which the Soviets might oblige the PCF to emasculate its electoral potency.[8]

In the 1970s this theory argued that while the PCF would keep up its noisy opposition to the conservative government, it would ultimately break its alliance with a Socialist party the Soviets thought unreliable, rather than aid in defeating a conservative regime friendly to the USSR. The theory seemed revalidated by Soviet support for Giscard's candidacy against Mitterrand in 1974, and by the bitter quarrel the PCF picked with Mitterrand later that year. In 1977, when a supposedly Eurocommunist PCF sabotaged the Union of the Left and paved the way for a conservative victory in the 1978 parliamentary elections, PCF action was regarded by many (both on the Right and in the PS) as additional proof that the French Communists had obeyed orders handed down from Moscow.

Clearly the Soviets disapproved of the PCF's alliance with Mitterrand from beginning to end. It is less clear how far the Soviet writ ran in PCF inner councils during the confusing period between 1972 and 1978, when domestic ambitions and resentment of Soviet demands warred with the old instincts of obedience. Soviet pressure was certainly exerted to urge a PCF break with the Socialists, but the leadership's decision was also affected by its own realization that its domestic strategy had gone wrong.[9] In any event, PCF policy after 1978 clearly demanded that the party quietly aid Giscard's reelection, thereby triggering frustration and disorganization in the PS that would aid the PCF.

In 1980 Giscard could thus believe he had good reason to maintain the special relation with the Soviet Union. When in late December 1979 Soviet troops moved into Afghanistan the United States reacted strongly, and requested support from its allies. Giscard refused to join in imposing economic sanctions. Leonid Brezhnev sent him word that the invasion had been forced on him by hard-liners in the Kremlin and asked for help in reinforcing his position and lessening international tension. Giscard rose to the bait, believing that he alone among western leaders could resolve the Afghan situation. Without consulting his foreign minister or other advisers, Giscard dispatched his friend and counselor Michel Poniatowski to Warsaw to arrange a meeting for him there with Brezhnev. To keep the trip secret from the French government, Poniatowski flew in a private plane belonging to the "red millionaire" Jean-Baptiste Doumeng, the PCF's chief money-man. Once Giscard's advisors learned of his plans they tried unsuccessfully to dissuade him. Still the optimist, he flew off to Warsaw in mid-May.

The Warsaw trip ended badly. Giscard was gulled by Brezhnev into announcing to his colleagues at the June economic summit in Venice the good news of a Soviet promise to pull troops out of Afghanistan – a movement which turned out to be a rotation and ultimately an increase in forces.[10]

François Mitterrand described Giscard bearing Brezhnev's message to the other European leaders as "a little telegraph boy." Mitterrand is a master of the biting phrase, but this particular sarcasm had a lasting echo, proving that he had touched a new sentiment in the French people – one unsuspected by Giscard. By the late 1970s faith in the special relation had worn thin, and suspicion of the Soviet Union had grown steadily in the late 1970s, both on the Right and on the Left. (See Part II, above.)

Mitterrand's election thus coincided with a change in French attitudes toward the Soviet Union. A lately converted president and Socialist party arrived in office convinced that a France really menaced by the Soviet Union needed both its own nuclear deterrent and a closer tie with its western allies. When Ronald Reagan sent him an unexpectedly warm letter of congratulation on his election, Mitterrand replied in the same tone. The relation was solidified by a visit from Reagan's friend Senator Paul Laxalt, soon after the election. Mitterrand invited him to his country home at Latché. Laxalt's impression was favorable. Passing through Paris on his way home he told American Embassy *chargé d'affaires* Christian Chapman that he would advise Reagan that despite divergent political ideas he and Mitterrand had in common a sure sense of their identities and of the meaning of their roots, that he was a man one might work with.[11] In June, Vice-President Bush came to Paris. The echo of his cordial talks with Mitterrand was disturbed by the almost simultaneous release of a State Department statement announcing the distress of the U.S. government at the entry of four Communist ministers into the government of an allied power. (This appears to have been the knee-jerk reaction of a government more concerned about a possible precedent for Italy than about problems in France.) Mitterrand had already been briefed by Ambassador Arthur Hartmann on the closely held details of U.S.-French military arrangements and confirmed both to Hartmann and Bush his intention to maintain harmonious relations furthering the common goal of European defense. He told the vice-president that French relations with the Soviet Union would be cooler than under his predecessors – not only because the objective situation called for it, but also because a Left government with Communist participation had a point to prove to its domestic opposition and its allies.[12]

Once elected, Mitterrand met Helmut Schmidt as an equal and realized that he would get on very well with him. Willy Brandt, now head of the SPD, was embittered to find Mitterrand preferring Schmidt to him. Their falling out brought about a failure of communications between the PS and the German Socialist party, at a time when the German Socialists were moving away from NATO orthodoxy and the French closer to Atlantic loyalty. French Socialist foreign policy experts (along with the rest of the French foreign policy establishment) had, since the collapse of de Gaulle's efforts to move West Germany away from its American ties, taken it for granted that German loyalty to NATO was absolute and unalterable. The idea that the West Germans might be drifting from their Atlantic moorings came only slowly to them and alarmed them deeply.[13]

Gaullist foreign policy since the mid-1960s had operated on the unspoken premise that since West Germany was utterly loyal to the United States, France could afford to dance out of line, remaining loyal to the Atlantic alliance but in its own independent and idiosyncratic way. In the early 1980s a distant prospect of a possibly neutralist West Germany appeared as a new nightmare to the French. Voices both on the Left and the Right cried out in alarm — every indication that Germany might be "drifting toward neutralism" was scrutinized.

When Schmidt was forced out of office in October 1982 by a change in domestic alliances, Mitterrand rapidly found it possible to get on well with the new conservative chancellor, Helmut Kohl. The best demonstration of French alarm and determination to hold West Germany in the tight embrace of the alliance was Mitterrand's trip to Bonn in January 1983, shortly before West German elections, to address the Bundestag. A French Socialist president whose own country took an independent stance in the alliance was ignoring the views of German Socialists, and urging German conservatives to accept the stationing of Pershing II and cruise missiles.

Mitterrand's basically pro-American line can thus be explained by the major changes in the international situation since the Cuban missile crisis of October 1962, when Gaullist principles were formulated. Gaullist thinking had thereafter made light of the Soviet threat — until it appeared in the late 1970s as a renewed menace. By 1981 France's special relation with the Soviets was clearly recognized as a myth — which should have been evident since the Czech crisis in 1968. *Ostpolitik* (paradoxically made possible by Soviet self-confidence after the Czech crisis) had encouraged many Germans to doubt the continued value of the Atlantic alliance. Mitterrand also needed to show to his opposition and the world that Communist ministers would have no influence on foreign policy. All these factors combined to move a man who had never been fundamentally anti-American to rethink the importance of a close and warm relation with the United States on most important questions.

The new policies took careful account of the German problem. Mitterrand's Bundestag speech made explicit French support for German dependence on American nuclear firepower (hitherto well cloaked in Gaullist rhetoric), but it also demonstrated his conviction that France should draw closer to Germany, both politically and militarily.

The political rapprochement was relatively simple. Giscard's relation with Schmidt had already been the best between French and German leaders since the de Gaulle-Adenauer partnership, and had lasted longer. Its crown jewel was the European Monetary System – and Mitterrand's decision in March 1983 that France could not afford to leave the EMS was as much political as economic. The semiannual summits between French and German leaders and ministers, and meetings among high officials stipulated in the Franco-German treaty of 1963 had kept Franco-German relations alive even in periods of chilly relations. Now they became an engine to improve bilateral relations. Mitterrand also multiplied the occasions for symbolic rapprochement, such as the ceremony in Verdun in September 1984, when he and Helmut Kohl were photographed hand in hand, together commemorating the horrible bloodletting on that battleground.

Rapprochement in security policy was more complicated. France could not furnish more than a supplementary nuclear guarantee to the Federal Republic. If the U.S. declined to risk Chicago to protect Hamburg, would the French risk Paris, and if so would their forces – even if firmly committed – suffice to deter? Quarterly meetings of the Franco-German defense commission instituted in 1982 encountered two basic obstacles. The West Germans were not really interested in a French nuclear guarantee (never actually offered), but in an increase in French conventional commitment to the defense of Europe. The French did not intend to increase their conventional forces and gave priority to their nuclear forces, the factor distinguishing them from other West European continental powers. Neither were they ready to share their nuclear trigger with the Germans, nor, despite much talk, would they declare officially that France's defense frontier lay on the Elbe rather than on the Rhine.

Nevertheless both French and West Germans wanted to show progress, if only by small symbolic steps – especially after the Reykjavik summit of October 1986 alarmed statesmen in both countries by America's apparent willingness to make agreements with the Soviets without first consulting with its allies. One early step was the creation of the *Force d'action rapide* (FAR) in

1983, intended in part to reinforce French capabilities for prompt action in a European crisis. With its 47,000 men, five divisions, and 220 helicopters, the FAR was also a force which could be dispatched overseas. Critics of the FAR noted, however, that much of the force it would use was already deployed in West Germany, so that it did not add new forces but redeployed (and possibly split up) old ones.[14]

Programs for joint production of armaments have had an uneven record. France decided not to participate in production of a European fighter plane, the Germans have shown no great interest in a military observation satellite, and the two countries could not agree on joint tank production. However, there have been agreements on manufacture of anti-tank and anti-aircraft missiles, and on an anti-tank helicopter.

In June 1987 France and the Federal Republic announced plans for a joint brigade to be commanded in succession by a French and a German officer. Because the West German army is entirely committed to NATO and France intends to remain outside the integrated command, a unit of this sort is an institutional anomaly — and symbolic rather than effective. The brigade will be stationed in southern Germany, and its German contingent composed of territorial troops (i.e. not specifically committed to NATO). Its importance is thus as much political as military, like that of the much-publicized *Moineau hardi/Kecker Spatz* joint maneuvers of September 1987.

The Franco-German summit meeting in Karlsruhe of November 1987 also decided on the creation of a Franco-German defense council, to meet twice a year to work out ideas for the common defense and security, especially on problems such as weapons interoperability.

MILITARY CONSIDERATIONS

France continues to spend more on her armed forces than any OECD country other than the United States — 3.9 percent. (Great Britain spends a larger percent of a GDP which is twenty-six percent smaller than that of France.)[15] The 1987-1991 military procurement law, passed in April 1987 with support from all major parties, provided for an expenditure of 474 billion francs (in constant 1986 francs) on military equipment.[16] The program foresaw the continued refitting of four of the five French nuclear submarines that did not have MIRVed missiles — two now have the capability of firing ninety-six warheads. Three nuclear submarines will be kept constantly at sea. A new generation of nuclear submarines will be developed, the first to be operational in 1994. The existing capability of nuclear submarines makes France a credible nuclear power; the submarine-launched missiles, targeted on Soviet cities, constitute a very real ancillary deterrence to any Soviet aggression. The eighteen intermediate-range missiles based at the Plateau d'Albion in southeastern France and nuclear weapons carried by eighteen Mirage IV airplanes will officially be obsolescent in 1996. To replace them, France plans an air-ground missile with extended range.

The French also plan to modernize other naval forces, build a new battle tank and new attack submarines, a nuclear aircraft carrier and a spy satellite. To do all this, and maintain forces both in Europe and in Africa may be beyond France's budgetary means.

The large question for the 1990s and beyond remains the role of France as a power in Europe. President Reagan's Strategic Defense Initiative dismayed the French both because it appeared to threaten the future viability of French nuclear deterrence and because he denounced the concept of mutual assured destruction (MAD). The French nuclear doctrine on the deterrent force exercised by a weaker nuclear power over a stronger one (*réplique du faible au fort*) enjoys general domestic support – even among French bishops. Denunciation of MAD as immoral undermines that consensus. Development by one (and inevitably the other) superpower of space-based defense would make French nuclear forces obsolete and demote France into the ranks of ordinary conventional powers.

Mitterrand was hostile to SDI, but did not attempt to keep French subcontractors from participation. Chirac cheered for SDI when in opposition, but then subsided when in office. By the end of the 1980s the question seems less urgent than when it was first raised. Research on space-based defense systems will probably not produce results until sometime after the year 2000. Although technological planning for contingencies fifteen or twenty years distant is normal, the political, diplomatic, and economic landscape of that time is exceedingly difficult to predict.

The French accepted the INF treaty initialed in December 1987, though with some misgivings. French policy is exceedingly wary of any agreement that would get rid of all battlefield nuclear weapons, which might presage another agreement on nuclear-capable aircraft. The argument is that such agreements favor the concentration of Warsaw Pact conventional forces and create a special denuclearized zone, essentially in Germany, that would shift the risk of nuclear attack to France, the United Kingdom and the United States.[17]

The French policy consensus calls for continual strengthening of their nuclear force. Alongside this, they will try to cement relations with West Germany by incremental steps, draw other European countries into consortia to develop high technology both military and industrial – and promote the unity of Europe. As a counter-idea to SDI Mitterrand launched the EUREKA program, which rapidly turned into a fund for the encouragement of high technology of all descriptions. Despite initial reticence by European Community officials who feared EUREKA would conflict with similar EC projects like ESPRIT and RACE (on information and communications technologies), EUREKA by 1988 had evolved into a complementary program for the research efforts of nineteen countries (the EC twelve, the EFTA six, plus Turkey). The principal research fields for its 214 projects are robotics, lasers, biotechnology, and energy. France is contributing twenty-five to thirty percent of the 26.5 billion francs involved in this research.[18]

In EUREKA as in bilateral Franco-German defense programs, French policy reflects the belief that in high technology and defense France's future can only be assured by European cooperation. The same idea is reflected in French enthusiasm for the European Single Act. Adopted by the EC countries in December 1985 after a year of discouraging wrangling, ratified by the parliaments of the Twelve in the next year, it was soon regarded by French leaders in all major parties as a challenge that opens the way to a more united and prosperous Europe.

The Europe without tariff walls to be inaugurated by the end of 1992 will feature freer competition in services and little national variation in value added or excise taxes. The usually nationalistic RPR has cheered for this new Europe as loudly as the formerly more European UDF and PS.[19]

A more united Europe may find itself in competition with a U.S. concerned about its own economic problems. French interest in the Atlantic alliance, however, remains strong, amid growing fear that the U.S. will withdraw large numbers of troops from Europe. France is also intensely conscious that the eyes of its West German partner are turned toward the severed portion of the German nation cemented into Eastern Europe. Nervousness over "German drift" mingles with hope that Soviet problems in their East European empire will bring further relaxation, in an area which increasingly looks to the West. German reunification nevertheless worries the French — but it is a prospect distant in the twenty-first century and well over today's horizon. The changes in the East bloc that are now conceivable may create acceptable conditions for moves toward reunification, while advances in the Europe of the Twelve would determine the kind of Europe in which any united Germany would be situated.

In all this there is little room for any resumption of a special French relation with the Soviets. In 1981-1986 Franco-Soviet relations remained mostly chilly. In January 1982, soon after the Polish crackdown on Solidarity, a contract for Soviet natural gas negotiated by Gaz de France technicians without careful attention in the Elysée led to much criticism. Later in the year, American pressure on France, Britain, West Germany, and Italy to disavow contracts for a pipeline to bring in Soviet natural gas strained French and other European relations with the United States. Although French firms were directly involved, the French had the pleasure of letting Ronald Reagan's friend Margaret Thatcher lead the European countries' protest against what they regarded as highly arbitrary procedures – and win their point.

Mitterrand had declared in 1981 that he would not change the tenor of French relations with the Soviet Union until progress had been achieved over Afghanistan. Nevertheless, he flew to Moscow in June 1984 to meet the already moribund Konstantin Chernenko – but also to raise the question of Andrei Sakharov with the masters of the Kremlin. In the following year, Mitterrand received a return visit in Paris from Chernenko's successor Mikhail Gorbachev. Gorbachev's charm has not, however, conquered the French to the apparent degree of its ravages in Britain, Germany, or even the United States. Having come late to anti-Sovietism, the French remain unwilling to switch back – particularly since the warmth of the secretary general's charm is directed primarily at the United States and at West Germany. Paris can accept reduction of super-power tensions as an excellent thing – unless that means agreements made over the heads of the Europeans. And while the French believe in the assurances of European solidarity constantly expressed by the West Germans, and comprehend West German interest in East Germany, they cannot help but remain suspicious of every complicit smile exchanged between Bonn and Moscow.

TIERS MONDISME: FRUSTRATIONS
IN CENTRAL AMERICA AND AFRICA

The general rapprochement of Mitterrand's France with the United States saw one important exception – French Socialist policy on Central America. Socialist Third World ideology (*tiers mondisme*) combined with Gaullist momentum to encourage interest in a French role in the affairs of this region. In August 1981 France issued a joint declaration with Mexico on El Salvador, proclaiming "a state of belligerency" in the area and recognizing the FDR/FLMN insurgents as a "representative political force" ready to assume power. The foreign ministers of nine Latin-American countries protested the Franco-Mexican declaration of 1981 as interference in Salvadorian internal affairs.[20]

In Nicaragua French policy saw in the Reagan administration's ardor against the Sandinistas "the intolerable domination of a superpower over a small country, but also a policy likely to make a bad situation worse and cause upheaval in the entire region."[21] In December 1981 France contracted to supply Nicaragua circa sixteen million dollars in arms useful for counter-insurgency, notably two used Alouette III helicopters and several thousand air-to-ground rockets. The Reagan administration reacted indignantly, dispatching presidential aide Michael Deaver to Paris to protest. During

Mitterrand's March 1982 trip to Washington he agreed not to go beyond the existing contract, and in July the French government announced that no new arms sales were contemplated.[22]

Tiers mondisme met another test in 1982, when Argentine forces took over the Falkland Islands and a British government preparing to retake them looked for diplomatic support. Third Worlders at the Quai d'Orsay (including Cheysson) and on Mauroy's staff were hostile to Britain's plans and wished to display their feelings with an ostentatious neutrality. Mitterrand overruled them; for him European considerations took precedence over solidarity with a Third World nation (in any case an unsavory dictatorship). The British victory justified his position by bringing about the collapse of military rule in Argentina.

Growing recognition that France could not afford either economically or diplomatically to involve herself deeply in Central America blunted the force of French *tiers mondisme*. American displeasure at arms sales to the Sandinista government — and the Socialists' increasingly disabused views on Sandinista democracy — brought an end to remaining arms deliveries to Nicaragua by mid-summer 1983, although some economic aid continued. By September 1984 Foreign Minister Cheysson was telling the San Jose conference of European Community, Central American, and Contadora states that if any French action were requested by the Central Americans, "We will examine it to see if it is possible, but would only act alongside the countries in the region and ordinarily in an international framework."[23]

In naming as foreign minister this outspoken ex-cavalry officer, diplomat, and veteran of the European Community Commission, Mitterrand had not intended to renounce any of his presidential prerogatives. Both were strong believers in the role of France in the Third World. But their incompatibility of temperament outweighed their general accord on principles. Cheysson believed in action, often precipitate; Mitterrand delighted in meditating whether, how, and when action should be taken. The foreign minister was moreover considerably more pro-Arab than his president, who wished to improve relations with Israel. On a visit to Morocco in August 1981 Cheysson compared Yasser Arafat to de Gaulle and the PLO to the Free French. A few days after Anwar-el-Sadat's assassination in October 1981 Cheysson told a radio interviewer: "Horrible in itself, it nevertheless removes an obstacle to rapprochement inside the Arab nation."[24] Cheysson went on to make other gaffes, to push his ideas even when they did not coincide with those of the president, and finally to lose his job after the bungled negotiations with Kadhafi over Chad in 1984 (see below).

Minister for Cooperation and Development Jean-Pierre Cot, responsible for French foreign aid policy, was another believer in a more vigorous French policy toward the Third World and particularly on human rights in Africa.

Cot proclaimed that he wanted to "decolonize" and "deafricanize" his ministry, ideas unwelcome to the Francophone African chiefs of state, France's traditional friends and clients. French foreign aid had largely been directed in the past to their countries in sub-Saharan Africa. Now it was supposed to be enlarged and in part redirected.

By mid-1982 it was clear that a France in economic difficulty did not possess the resources for large increases in its public foreign aid, certainly not to the seven-tenths of one percent of GNP by 1988 which Mitterrand had pledged in 1981. (It was however boosted by 1985 to a level forty-four percent higher than in 1980.)[25] Cot's insistent human rights discourse had also proved a problem with the African presidents, several of whom were running repressive one-party states.

Their complaints led Mitterrand to offer another post to Cot, who chose instead to resign in December 1982.[26] African affairs now came increasingly under the eye of the Elysée, in the person of the president's friend and counselor for African affairs Guy Penne. This shift marked a return to the old system as practiced under de Gaulle and his immediate successors, in which a close aide to the president maintained confidential liaison with the African presidents. Marie-Claude Smouts, one of the best analysts of French Third World policy, remarks that a Socialist policy designed to be different from that practiced under Giscard had here confronted the old realities, with little room for maneuver: the dilemma of dealing with authoritarian regimes where stability often took higher priority than human rights. The Socialists confronted a disastrous economic situation at home. In Africa, foreign aid was entangled in a network of trade, financial, and cultural relations that linked business interests, personal friendships, and the intrigues of French Intelligence. All these factors hindered the application of any grand design.[27]

By 1988 French Third World policy had reduced its ambitions. One of Mitterrand's first actions in his second term was to forgive the debt owed by African countries to France (and encourage others to forgive Third World debts). Here was another admission that France intended to concentrate, not on the Third World as a whole, but on certain regions in the Third World.

France's one military engagement in Africa under Mitterrand took place in Chad, where French power had reluctantly been engaged in the 1970s. French interest in this former colony was almost entirely strategic: if Libyan intervention succeeded in dominating Chad the sub-Saharan states would stand open to Kadhafi's persuasion and subversion. Former president Giscard tells in his memoirs that when Libyan forces aiding the troops of Chadian Toubou leader Goukouni pushed forward in 1978, the African presidents telephoned him to insist that France must intervene. "If we let the Libyans advance in Chad without reacting, it will be a signal to the

Francophone African chiefs of state that security exists only in one camp. And they gave me to understand that some of them were already preparing to draw the consequences."[28]

After more vicissitudes in the Chadian civil war, the Libyans occupied the capital of N'Djamena as allies of Goukouni, and in January 1981 Goukouni visited Tripoli and announced the "fusion" of Chad and Libya. Twelve African chiefs of state protested at the Lomé Organization of African Unity (OAU) meeting. After Mitterrand's entry into office French diplomacy was able to negotiate a Libyan evacuation of N'Djamena, and an inter-African force led by Zaire troops moved in. In June 1982, however, troops commanded by Goukouni's former ally and rival Hissène Habré took control of the capital, and Goukouni fled. Although a number of French military and diplomatic officials were opposed to working with Habré, who had kidnaped a French ethnologist in the 1970s and murdered an officer sent to negotiate her release, Mitterrand concluded that Habré was in control of the country, and agreed to meet him at the October 1982 Franco-African summit. In 1983, after earlier disagreement on which Chadian leader to recognize, the OAU recognized the Habré government.

In June 1983 Goukouni's forces, with Libyan aid, retook the northern Chad town of Faya Largeau. Habré appealed for help, and France sent supplies. In August, when Kadhafi committed his air force and more troops, a French government which had counted on Libyan moderation was forced to take new measures. The Socialist government was very reluctant to intervene again in Chad. Cheysson declared: "We are not going to act like the U.S. in Honduras and Nicaragua." But as Goukouni was now heavily obligated to the Libyans, Paris concluded that the Chad "domino" must not fall totally into the Libyan sphere of influence, with serious consequences in French Africa. Mitterrand decided to send out several hundred instructors for Habré's army and in Operation *Manta* deployed 3,000 French troops on the fifteenth parallel to mark French determination to prevent the Libyans from occupying N'Djamena.

In the summer of 1983 the Mauroy government had just surmounted the March economic crisis and was becoming increasingly unpopular. It rejected any major military action such as an attempt to take out the Libyan air force, which might bring high losses. The *Manta* operation was meant to hold the line, to reassure Habré and the African presidents, and defend Chad south of the fifteenth parallel. No French ground troops went into action against the Libyans, but expensive planes were lost and troops killed in accidents. Mitterrand sought a diplomatic solution, believing that France could negotiate with Kadhafi on the basis that "no one could win." In September 1984, after months of secret diplomacy, Paris and Tripoli announced an agreement on "total and simultaneous evacuation" over a forty-five day period. Habré was unhappy. He had been left in the dark until the deal had been agreed on, as were the African presidents, who were similarly displeased. Habré rushed up to Paris, where the government assured him of continuing French support.

As the weeks wore on the French began to depart, but some indication suggested that the Libyans intended to stay. The United States publicized satellite photos proving that the Libyans were still there, while Cheysson pretended to have no information and denied the American reports. Embarrassed, French intelligence leaked its own proof that the Libyans still had 3,000 men in Chad. In the meantime, Mitterrand had agreed to meet Kadhafi in Crete on November 15, and despite the reports of deceit decided to go through with the meeting. He has said that he used the meeting to tell the Libyan leader that relations between their two countries would remain difficult until Libya respected its promises.[29]

Mitterrand had been made to look foolish; his emissaries – Cheysson, the president's close friend (and Cheysson's successor) Roland Dumas, Arabist diplomat Guy Georgy – had deluded themselves and him by wishful thinking. The Libyans remained in Chad; the French withdrew. But in February 1986 when Goukouni's men and the Libyans attacked across the sixteenth parallel, the French bombed the Libyan air base at Ouadi Doum and then introduced a new force code-named *Epervier*, with a large contingent of airplanes and some 1200 troops. Their purpose was to guarantee Chad south of the sixteenth parallel (and allow Habré's men to operate north of that line). Mitterrand had thus been obliged to renew the French military commitment to aid Habré. However, he took care as before to keep French soldiers out of the line of fire.

Goukouni then fell out with Kadhafi and his forces rallied to Habré. The Libyans attacked them and the French parachuted in weapons and supplies. Kadhafi now had few pro-Libyan Chadians left to legitimate his expedition. In the course of 1987 *Epervier* was reinforced, more anti-tank missiles were supplied to Habré's forces, and between January and April 1987 the Chadian forces had defeated the Libyans in several battles. They captured an enormous booty of tanks, helicopters, airplanes, and missiles, and forced a Libyan retreat up to the Aouzou strip along the Libyan frontier, which had been occupied by Libya in 1973 and afterward annexed.

The rich and powerful Libyans had been defeated by one of the poorest peoples in Africa, although French aid to Habré had of course been decisive in these victories. The vehicles, Milan anti-tank missiles, fuel, and other supplies which Habré received amounted to 400 million francs in the first six months of 1987 alone. French economic aid to Chad rose from 300 million francs in 1984 to 500 million in 1986. French tactical intelligence (and perhaps, according to some reports, the covert involvement of a French parachute regiment associated with the French intelligence service) were also highly useful to Habré's army. But Paris had avoided direct and overt involvement in the Chadian fighting and had even been seen to restrain Habré in his quest for the reconquest of the northern strip of territory held by Libya. The Chadian involvement could, despite the vicissitudes of *Manta* and the botched meeting with Kadhafi, be regarded as a decisive victory. Little French blood had been shed and French policy had triumphed, without France having to make more than a carefully limited military commitment. The African leaders had been reassured, and Habré reinserted as a prestigious leader.

None of this meant an end to problems in Chad, where Habré, who is almost entirely surrounded by members of his own northern tribe, may have future difficulties with the south. Libya is unlikely to accept humiliation and defeat easily in an area where Senoussi territorial ambitions greatly antedate Kadhafi. In 1988, however, the Chadian situation appears better than it has been for over fifteen years.[30]

THE MIDDLE EAST

French policy in the Middle East was marked by tension between the pro-Arab sentiment of Cheysson and the Quai and Mitterrand's desire to improve relations with Israel. The president's desire to mark rapprochement by a visit there was initially frustrated by the Israeli attack on an Iraqi nuclear facility installed by the French that killed a French technician. Mitterrand finally paid his state visit in March 1982. In a Knesset speech Mitterrand proclaimed Israel's right to live – but also that of the people surrounding Israel. The Israeli attack into Lebanon in the following June had the effect of balancing the views of president and foreign minister. Mitterrand refused to receive Arafat in Paris; Cheysson continued to meet him outside France. France told itself that it was declaring the same truths to both sides.

A French contingent dispatched in August 1982 to the international force in Beirut to help evacuate PLO fighters was kept there (like U.S. and other international forces) after the Sabra and Shatila massacres, in which Lebanese Christian militia had killed over a thousand Palestinian civilians. When Shiite militia artillery batteries fired on French troops, French planes attacked them. In October 1983 the explosion of an Islamic Jihad suicide truck killed fifty-eight French soldiers minutes after a similar attack cost 239 American lives. Mitterrand flew immediately to Beirut, and on his return proclaimed that France would remain faithful to her history and her agreements. French planes bombed a Shiite militia camp in mid-November. In late February 1984 Ronald Reagan cut his losses and withdrew the American force. A month later, Lebanese president Gemayel officially ended the international mission Lebanon had requested in 1982, and French troops withdrew in somewhat better order than had the Americans. But the retreat from Lebanon was for both countries a sign that they could not afford to exert direct influence on the ground in a part of the world gone mad.

To what degree did French involvement in Lebanon in 1983-1984 bring on the terrorist problems of 1985-1987? The kidnaping of French (or other) hostages by various terrorist groups seems to have been motivated by the desire to free other terrorists held in Kuwait, or in France. The terrorist actions of Near Eastern origin in Paris in 1985-1986 were similarly intended to pressure the French into releasing prisoners. Nevertheless, the overall context of persistent attacks on the French presence in Lebanon (as with those on the American presence) was the desire of radical, usually Shiite groups to uproot Western influence in Lebanon and the Near East in general. The French intend to resist this threat to their cultural influence in an area where they have long been close to the Maronite community.[31]

THE OVERALL FOREIGN POLICY PICTURE

France under Mitterrand in 1981-1988 thus continued to play the role of the most active of non-superpowers. Mitterrand traveled to every part of the globe in these years (although he left Australia to Fabius). A new consensus on cooperation with the United States took the place of the more chilly relations inaugurated by de Gaulle after 1966. The limits of the new relationship were demonstrated in April 1986 when the U.S. requested permission to overfly France on the way to bomb Libya, and Mitterrand and Chirac concurred in refusal. Nevertheless, there was a new and general tone of pro-Americanism in cultural and economic thinking and in foreign policy—contradicted of course by a number of single events and individual pronouncements.

The counterpart to pro-Americanism was an anti-Sovietism taking its origins in the mid-1970s, and aggravated by Soviet policy in Afghanistan and Poland. When France expelled forty-seven Soviet diplomats and other personnel for espionage in April 1983, the government was giving clamorous and unprecedented publicity to the kind of action which had always before been carried out quietly (and on a much smaller scale.)

As we have seen, the thrust of an assertive Third World ideology was blunted by the resistance of existing responsibilities and old relationships, and well before the end of the *septennat* French relations with her African allies had returned to the clientelism installed by de Gaulle's semi-decolonization.

The major changes in challenges and responses had come in Europe, but by the beginning of Mitterrand's second term only the outlines of possible new policy were discernible. The relation of the French nuclear role to overall European defense is still far from clear. If France's real future lies in an enlarged and empowered Europe, is this entirely consonant with the continuing French desire to be an almost-superpower maintaining extensive interests outside Europe? French aspirations will not always fit the needs of her neighbors, or theirs French needs. Realization of a post-1992 Europe may encounter delays or national antagonisms. So much of Mitterrand's discourse about France's future depends on the success of this new Europe that the risk involved in its failure is high.

Other factors enter the European equation. The relation between the superpowers, the development of Gorbachev's USSR, and the degree to which the United States hearkens to or rejects the sirens of neo-isolationism will evoke French reactions, but are largely beyond the reach of French influence. In his second term Mitterrand will become the senior statesman of Europe. He will have much to occupy him.

NOTES

1. Cf. Jacques Huntzinger, "The French Socialist Party and Western Relations," in *The Foreign Policies of West European Socialist Parties*, ed. Werner Feld (New York: Praeger, 1978), p. 68.

2. Author's interview with PS International Affairs secretary Jacques Huntzinger, June 1984. On Mitterrand and Allende see Franz-Olivier Giesbert, *François Mitterrand*, pp. 312-313.

3. Michael Harrison, "The Socialist Party, the Union of the Left, and French National Security," in *The Foreign Policies of the French Left*, ed. Simon Serfaty, pp. 24-39.

4. Author's interview with former defense minister Charles Hernu, March 1986.

5. Interview with Jacques Huntzinger, June 1984.

6. See Samy Cohen, *La Monarchie nucléaire*, pp. 92 and 114-115.

7. Cf. Jean Lacouture, *De Gaulle 3: Le Souverain, 1959-1970* (Paris: Editions du Seuil, 1986), p. 547. Lacouture writes: "Si peu d'illusion qu'ait entretenu le chef de l'Etat français sur l'issue de l'entreprise, il réagit durement — contrairement à ce qui a été souvent écrit — à une opération qui ruine, plus cruellement que le véto discrètement formulé un an plus tôt à Varsovie, ses perspectives de dislocation des blocs par la détente."

8. Cf. Cohen, *La Monarchie nucléaire*, pp. 127-128.

9. See Julius W. Friend, "Soviet Behavior and National Responses: the Puzzling Case of the French Communist Party," *Studies in Comparative*

Communism 15, no. 3 (Autumn 1982), pp. 221-231. For a statement on Gis-cardian belief in the "triangular" relationship see the quote from an aide to Jean François-Poncet in Cohen, *Monarchie nucléaire*, p. 127-128.

10. See Cohen, *la Monarchie nucléaire*, pp. 128-134.

11. Author's interview with Christian Chapman, former deputy chief of mission, U.S. Embassy Paris, May 1988.

12. Author's interview with Ambassador Arthur Hartmann, May 1988. 13. Interview with Jacques Huntzinger, March 1985.

14. For a summary on the FAR, see "La Force d'action rapide," *Regards sur l'actualité*, no. 105 (November 1984).

15. U.S. Department of Defense figures, *New York Times*, May 20, 1988.

16. Cf. "La Loi de programmation militaire 1987-1991," *Regards sur l'actualité*, no. 137 (January 1988).

17. See François Heisbourg, "Après le traité. Aggiornamento pour une alliance," *Politique étrangère*, no. 1 (1988).

18. See *Le Monde*, June 18, 1988.

19. On this, see François Saint-Ouen, "Le R.P.R. est-il devenu européen? " *Revue politique et parlementaire* 993 (January-February 1988), and the other articles in this issue devoted to France's stake in the Europe of 1992, as well as Jean-Pierre Moussy, "Le Grand marché intérieur européen à l'horizon 1992," *Regards sur l'actualité*, no. 138 (February 1988).

20. *Washington Post*, September 3, 1981. *Le Monde*, August 30, 1981. The author wishes to thank Professor Eusebio Mujal-León for permission to draw on the manuscript of his forthcoming *European Socialism and the Crisis in Central America* for this section on Central America.

21. Quoted in Marie-Claude Smouts, "La France et le Tiers-Monde, ou comment gagner le sud sans perdre le nord," *Politique étrangère*, no. 2 (1985), p. 350.

22. See *Le Monde*, February 1, 1982 and July 14, 1982.

23. For PS views by mid-decade on the Sandinistas, my source is an inter-view with PS international affairs secretary Jacques Huntzinger, March 1986. On Mitterrand's assurances to the Reagan administration on arms sales, see Evan Galbraith, *Ambassador in Paris: The Reagan Years* (Washington, D.C.: Regnery Gateway, 1987), pp. 13-14. On Cheysson's San Jose speech, see Smouts, "La France et le Tiers-Monde," p. 351.

24. See Cohen, *La Monarchie nucléaire*, pp. 137-143.

25. Seven-tenths of one percent was also the unfulfilled official goal of the 1970s. The 1980 figure, slightly down from the mid- 1970s, was .36 percent of GNP, excluding aid to French overseas departments and territories. See Smouts, "La France et le Tiers-Monde," pp. 346-347, and Ronald Tiersky, "The French Left and the Third World," in *The Foreign Policies of the French Left*, ed. Simon Serfaty, p. 56.

26. *Le Monde, Bilan du Septennat*, p. 88, and author's interview with Mitterrand's former African affairs advisor Guy Penne, April 1988.

27. Smouts, "La France et le Tiers-Monde," pp. 339-340.

28. Valéry Giscard d'Estaing, *Le Pouvoir et la vie* (Paris: Compagnie 12, 1988), pp. 229-230.

29. Cohen, *La Monarchie nucléaire*, p. 156-158.

30. See Thierry de Montbrial et al., *RAMSES — Rapport annuel mondiale sur le système economique et les stratégies* (Paris: Editions Atlas-Economica, 1987), pp. 71-76. On reports of French intelligence support for the Chadians, military or otherwise, see *Le Monde*, April 7, 1987.

31. For former prime minister Chirac's thinking on the Middle East, see his "off the record" interview with Arnaud de Borchgrave, *The Washington Times*, November 10, 1986.

7

Mitterrand II

THE NEW PARTY SPECTRUM

The fortunes of the Rocard government and Mitterrand's second term are intimately connected with the process of change in French party configurations and political attitudes. The first two decades of the Fifth Republic saw such change – a gradual reshaping of parties from the multi-party system inherited from the Fourth Republic to the quadripartite system (RPR, UDF, PS, PCF) that emerged from the 1978 elections. This system expressed the logic of the polarized Left-Right opposition implicit in the "Communists or us" spirit of the Fifth Republic, with its winner-take-all elections. But no sooner had the quadripartite system been brought to perfection than it began to fall apart.

Polarization in the Gaullist synthesis rejected alternation in power because that would mean rule by Communists. By substituting Socialist domination of the Left for that of the Communists, Mitterrand began the disarming of polarization. The deflation of Socialist ideology in 1983-1986 moved another step in this direction. French politics are, however, still heavily imprinted with the tone of 1958-1978, and just as it took twenty years to fulfill the logic of the Gaullist synthesis, so reconfiguration is likely to proceed slowly.

The present line-up on the Right and Center is highly unstable. The UDF is an umbrella party, designed to bring together Giscard's Republicans, the Atlanticist and mostly Catholic CDS, and a remnant of the old Radicals. When Giscard referred to the UDF as the Center, the Left referred to it as the Right, and its members (and voters) have always been of two or three minds on the correctness of these designations. Polls show roughly a fourth of UDF voters situating themselves in the center, a third on the center-right, another fourth on the right – but it is never clear just what respondents understand by these designations. (By contrast, however, four-fifths of RPR voters think of themselves as center-right or right.)[1]

By 1988 the polls showed consistently that a number of conservative voters would support Mitterrand on the second round, and it became increasingly clear to the leaders of both the RPR and the Parti Républicain that by presenting two candidates for the presidency they were diminishing their chances. Well before the elections Chirac's lieutenant Edouard Balladur proposed a federation of the RPR and UDF which looked forward to a closer union in government if Chirac were elected and tighter and more effective alliances for legislative elections in any case. The conservative forces did campaign together in the legislative elections of June 1988 on a joint ticket called the Union du Rassemblement et du Centre (URC). (There were only some fifty competitive first round RPR/UDF contests.)

Thus electoral arithmetic would have encouraged consolidation on the Right if Chirac had won, while Barre had made no secret of his intent to re-federate the conservatives should he win. The extent of Chirac's defeat (and the size of Le Pen's vote) complicated plans for federation. By winning slightly less than one-fifth of the first round vote in the presidential elections, and scoring not quite forty-six percent on the second round, Chirac had damaged his prestige as a future leader and federator.

Any realignment on the Right must face the problem of the National Front, which has bitten deeply into the strength of the conventional Right. Viewed regionally, its vote in the first round of the presidential elections constituted between twenty-five and twenty-nine percent of the total Right in six regions, and from thirty to forty-three percent in eight more. (There are twenty-two regions.)[2] Le Pen had an average vote of 17.52 percent in the ten largest French cities.

The RPR and UDF still must decide how best to handle the National Front push expected in the key municipal elections of March 1989. The Front dropped to 9.7 percent in the first round of the legislative elections and Le Pen and his closest lieutenants failed to win election in the second round. If the National Front vote in the presidential elections is regarded as an aberration (and it is hard to say whether this is probable, or merely wishful thinking) then Le Pen's electorate has stabilized at a point slightly above ten percent, with significant strengths among younger voters and the unemployed (often the same), small shopkeepers, and artisans.[3]

The conservative leaderships have in the past tried to dodge the alliance question, refusing to admit that agreements with Le Pen were more than purely local arrangements. Seven regional governments now depend on National Front counselors' votes for their majorities, as do a scattering of city governments. After a "local" second round agreement in the Marseilles area for the 1988 legislative elections, Le Pen recommended that his followers give country-wide support to conservative candidates.

Two opinions exist in conservative ranks on future alliances with the National Front. The first was enunciated by former foreign trade minister Michel Noir: better to lose an election than lose your soul. The other was that of Charles Pasqua: there is no essential difference in "values" between the RPR and the National Front.

The practice of throwing support to the best-placed candidate in the second round of elections (or making formal alliances) is a traditional one between Socialists and Communists. The significant difference between this and support for the Front appears to be that Communists at the municipal level have not appeared particularly revolutionary. It is precisely at the municipal level, however, that the National Front is best able to spread and implement its racist ideas. Many UDF and RPR leaders are violently opposed to compromises with the Front and would much rather lick it than join it—but still worry about election results.

The conventional Right also suffers from the ambitions of too many leaders. Chirac would still like to rise from his ashes to lead the Right; Giscard hopes to reform a more powerful UDF and outmaneuver Chirac. Neither has lost the ambition to be a presidential candidate again. Léotard is momentarily taking a back-seat to Giscard, but still controls the PR. Barre too intends to remain in politics, or slightly above them, and become the godfather for centrist forces.

After the legislative elections Centre des Démocrates Sociaux leader Pierre Méhaignerie, proud of his party's fifty seats, announced the formation of a parliamentary group independent from the UDF called the Union du Centre (UDC). (The UDC nevertheless wants to keep its affiliation with the UDF, for the moment at least.) Giscard showed his displeasure; François Léotard, leader of the biggest party in the UDF, spoke of "treason," and possible expulsion. The UDC's ambition is to become a French version of the West German FDP. Success depends on the ability of its members to hold onto their voters and assure re-election to local and national bodies. Analysts have already noted that while German national and *Landtag* deputies can win under proportional representation with over five percent, in French winner-take-all elections a deputy needs 12.5 percent to avoid elimination in a second round. A new Center party may thus be difficult to form or sustain unless the election laws are again changed—which would also help the National Front.

The immediate effect of Mitterrand's precipitate dissolution of the National Assembly was to weld together a Right that was coming apart. But within this Right are forces desiring quite different policies. There are a few RPR leaders not averse to arrangements with the Socialists, left-Giscardians, and a regrouped Center still uncertain of its identity or its future. The vast bulk of the RPR and of Léotard's PR sees no virtue whatever in collaborating with Mitterrand. Add to this the clashing ambitions of the Right's leaders, and the hopes of Mitterrand and Rocard to move the more moderate part of the Right into a more lasting alliance with the PS, and there emerges an uncertain future.

THE COMMUNISTS

While the Communist party rallied in the legislative elections to win twenty-seven seats, these PCF deputies represent only eleven departments. To win these seats the leadership departed from its practice of preferring apparatchiks and put up a number of popular local mayors. The PCF did succeed in checking its slide toward total disappearance, but the test for the PCF, even more than for the other parties, will be the municipal elections of 1989. Communist mayors still govern fifty-one cities of more than 30,000 inhabitants, but the party risks losing some of these, as well as mayoralties in smaller towns.

The next few years will test the strategy which the PCF enunciated in 1978, abandoned in 1981, and resumed in 1984: that a tough-talking leftist party can regain votes from a Socialist party which is moving off to the right. The claim that the PS had moved to the right was untrue in 1977-1981 — but is not in 1988. How much political space remains on the left for the PCF? If sociological analyses of the causes of PCF problems are correct, the decline of the industrial working class means the inevitable decline of the party. The proletariat in France today is heavily North African, and the Communists have drawn *maghrebin* workers into the CGT, which though weakened remains the principal bulwark of Communist strength alongside the municipalities. The Communist party hesitates, however, to champion the right of resident foreigners to vote in local elections for fear of losing its current voters.[4] Many leaders of the PS (notably Pierre Mauroy, always sensitive to this question) nevertheless will continue to worry that an opening to the Center will re-open political opportunities for the PCF.

That said, the PCF in 1988 is far from united. Its relatively good results in the 1988 legislative elections represent a possibly momentary rallying of many openly dissident elements in a number of federations. The discrepancy between the PCF vote in the presidential and National Assembly elections underlines the fact that the party no longer controls its voters. They may or may not follow its lead, while its deputies-and-mayors in the parliamentary delegation will feel the pull of their constituencies. What these new factors will signify is as yet unclear.

The secretary generalship of Georges Marchais (born 1920) has been disastrous, but he and the central apparatus still control the party. The PCF is however further out of synchrony with French society than at any time since the 1920s, and unlikely to benefit from new industrial (or technological) growth, as it was able to do in the 1930s. The PCF suffers from a lack of imagination so stupefying that it has even been rebuked for this by the Soviets.[5] The French Communist party now seems unlikely to shrink to the proportions of a sect, but a large number of indicators suggest that it cannot again play a major role in French politics and society.

THE SOCIALISTS

The PS emerged from the double elections of 1988 as the party of a triumphantly re-elected president and that of the relative — and governing — majority. Its 37.52 percent in the legislative elections (counting the MRG and candidates running as "presidential majority") is, within one one-hundredth of a percent, the same score as in the miracle year 1981. The combined Right won a higher percentage of the 1988 vote — 40.52 percent but this compares poorly to its 44.88 percent in 1986. (These figures do not count the National Front, which won 9.65 percent of the vote in both 1986 and 1988.)

Thus the combined Right is stronger than the PS, but combined does not mean united. Mitterrand's political operations in the next years will undoubtedly devote much attention to encouraging and deepening existing divisions on the Right, in order to install the PS as the strongest and most durable party of government. Whether or not he succeeds in the long term, the PS with its allies and associates has another lease on government in France. Given the lack of a majority, however, this National Assembly may well not last out its five-year term.

The kind of government Mitterrand proposes and the policies the Rocard government expects to follow have been presented only in general terms. The ideologically tinted programs of 1981 are ancient history, and the declaration of general policy made by Rocard in early July 1988 was deliberately down to earth and modest.[6] What remains of PS ideology? The program agreed on in January 1988 was designed to be the party's own statement, concordant with but separate from the personal platform which Mitterrand would publish.[7] It attempted to retain a distinctively Socialist identity while taking account of what the Socialists learned in 1981-1986. Thus the utility of public ownership was affirmed and *libéralisme* decried, but the program did not call for re-nationalization of privatized industries. "The state neither can do everything nor should it," says the program. It emphasizes gradual change. "Transformations can work only at the rhythm by which citizens become aware of their necessity and legitimacy. . . . A parliamentary majority can translate options into law, but for them to become deeds, in a complex society, minorities must accept them."[8] The PS has come a long way from the *rupture* of 1980-1981.

Who are the leaders of this new PS? When Mitterrand named Rocard as prime minister gossip in Paris immediately supposed that the job was a poisoned gift, which would speedily destroy Rocard and make way for a more favored Mitterrand follower. Mitterrand, however, can scarcely want Rocard to fail—too much hangs on his success—although he might take a blow to Rocard's personal ambitions with complacency. Relations between the two men have never been close and are unlikely to be easy. Mitterrand has declared that he does not wish to interfere in the small details of government, and Rocard has often emphasized that he dislikes the clauses in the constitution permitting a government to impose its will on parliament. The upshot will show whether Mitterrand (and his friends and staff) can continue to abstain from fine tuning, and whether Rocard can manage both to govern without a majority and avoid frequent use of parliamentary gag rules like constitutional Article 49/3.

Although the Socialist deputies and party militants reacted badly in May and June 1988 to the offer of numerous ministerial portfolios to non-Socialists, the leadership backs Mitterrand's policy of *ouverture*. Yet the president is no longer all-powerful in his party. In the week after his re-election the now merged Mitterrand-Mauroy factions of the Socialist party met to choose a new first secretary to replace Lionel Jospin, who had announced several months earlier that he wished to leave the post. (The Rocard and Chevènement factions kept to the sidelines.) The declared candidate was former prime minister Laurent Fabius, who claimed to have the president's support.

Jospin and many other Socialists dislike this gifted but overly smooth young man who skated too easily and too fast from the left to the right wing of the party. They moved to block him by supporting Mitterrand's other former prime minister Pierre Mauroy. In the debate, Jospin denied that Mitterrand wanted Fabius in the job, declaring that the president intended "to cut the umbilical cord" with the party. Others who had talked with Mitterrand that day flatly contradicted Jospin. Mauroy spoke of the need for a first secretary who would not make the party the machine for his own (presidential) ambitions. Mauroy was the victor. A week after the president's triumphant re-election, the Socialist party had ignored Mitterrand's wishes.[9]

A reorganization of factions within the PS had been held in suspense only by the presidential campaign. Whether Mitterrand won or lost, the PS would have begun to look to the contests of the post-Mitterrand era. The Rocard faction will now thrive or decline to the degree the prime minister succeeds. Mauroy (an intermittent ally of Rocard and an old friend) will attempt to fashion a distinct Socialist identity in a period of quasi- coalition, which does not necessarily mean more than readjusting the party's rhetoric. Fabius, elected to the presidency of the National Assembly in a compromise gesture, will continue his quest for Mitterrand's succession. Rocard and Fabius occupy the same ideological ground (they are separated by differences of personality and identical ambitions). The Socialist left, as represented by Chevènement's *Socialisme et démocratie* faction (ex-CERES), may be somewhat hampered in its actions by its leader's acceptance of the defense portfolio (which he will administer as a French nationalist, not like a British Laborite). Jospin has his own presidential ambitions.

In PS internal affairs the Mitterrand era was marked by its leader's carefully calculated use of factions; only the future can tell whether the party will now be more than a cockpit for the ambitions of his successors. At circa 185,000 members the PS is organizationally rather weak, and many people have argued that it is unable to express the real voices in society. Because the PS has too many competing leaders, its father-figure, the president of the republic, may be obliged to exert his influence from on high to do something he has always neglected — to ensure a better PS anchorage in society and make his party more than a debating society and electoral device. The precise ideological bases for any such development are difficult to discern.

PROTEUS AS PRESIDENT:
THE AMAZING MR. MITTERRAND

At the end of a seven-year term rich in sudden changes in policy and fortune and at the beginning of a new one, one cannot pronounce any definitive historical judgment on the extraordinary life and career of François Mitterrand. It is equally impossible to abstain from all judgment. Mitterrand has occupied the political scene in France for forty-two years, and his reelection for seven years more provides an extraordinary spectacle of political variety and longevity. It finds no equal in length and levels of power attained in American history, not even Franklin Roosevelt (1913-1945) or Richard Nixon (1946-1974). In France only the forty-seven and fifty year political careers of Thiers and Clemenceau rival it, and their moments of power were interrupted and much shorter.

The inevitable comparison is of course with Charles de Gaulle, incomparably the greatest Frenchman of the twentieth century. Mitterrand, who says that de Gaulle is not the historical reference he applies to himself, has sought to avoid the comparison by describing de Gaulle as "the last of the great men of the nineteenth century."[10] Has Mitterrand adopted Gaullism by another name, in his domestic or foreign policy?[11] He adapted himself easily to the presidential institutions built by de Gaulle, while arrogantly remarking that they were dangerous before him and would be dangerous again after. Mitterrand wishes to believe that after what he concedes to be a slow start he moved, first with Mauroy, then with Fabius, to a concept of the presidency whereby "the president presides, the government governs, the parliament passes laws."[12] This judgment passes lightly over the first years when the Elysée interfered constantly in the details of government affairs, but also ignores his role in affairs like that of the private television channel *La Cinq*, his close attention to the lists for Socialist candidacies in 1988 and the parceling out of jobs in the cabinet.

In foreign affairs there are of course several versions of Gaullism — the exacerbated version of 1963-1969 and the constant version, which demands for France her due and fitting place among the great powers, firm in the belief that France is not really herself unless she is in the first rank. The most contentious Gaullism belongs to the period when the general could think that the Cold War was over and America had won, so that France not only could but must assert herself in order to be fully independent. A shift in French policy to take account of diminished American power and increased Soviet assertiveness in the 1970s would not have been foreign to the general's logic, and when this shift took place in the 1980s the neo-Gaullists did not shout treason, but followed suit. For his part, Mitterrand did not consider that he had broken with French policy traditions.

In fact, the presidency in the Fifth Republic is a Procrustes' bed — but one that no one lies in without a willingness to be shortened or stretched. The institutions govern the president, tempt him, shape him. Mitterrand has so far made no attempt to reshape them, and one wonders whether he ever will.

What is he like, this man of whom a biographer wrote in 1977: "François Mitterrand is an ambivalent man — sociable and misanthropic, naive and calculating, sincere and dissimulating. Like everyone? No, Mitterrand is more ambivalent than the average man."[13] One of his less admiring biographers has depicted him as a man of seven masks, and another, more admiring, has written of his "religions." (Note the plural.)[14] The abundant literature on him describes the mystery man without piercing the veil. Reserved and devious (even his friends call him "un Florentin" — a Machiavellian) he has always been able to manipulate men, alliances, and ideas. A moderate who became a Socialist, a Socialist who seems to have become a moderate, is Mitterrand a man without principles? Stanley Hoffmann remarks that his conversions appear both "genuine and limited." He has never reverted to his pre-Socialist positions (and said in a September 1987 television interview, "I was a Socialist, a Socialist I remain."). His deepest differences with the Right center on the question of justice, a term which recurs constantly in his writing and speeches. But, says Hoffmann, "his commitments have been as vague as they have been sweeping. Who can tell what his socialism means? A formal desire for justice, of course, but certainly no specific economic program."[15]

Mitterrand has moved from the nationalizer of 1981 to the Silicon Valley modernizer of 1984, from the moderate of the Fourth Republic to the vociferous Socialist of 1971-1983 to the Socialist/Left-republican of today. The man who opposed abuse of presidential powers interfered freely in all aspects of daily government. Curiously enough, several of the crucial economic decisions that shaped his *septennat* were imposed on him, not only by circumstances, but by associates and advisers who saw the necessity of austerity long before he was willing to recognize it. He then took the lead in deciding to make major and painful cuts in industrial support in late 1983 and 1984, but was again almost absent in the struggle that led to the debacle of the Savary bill in June 1984. Resourceful in misfortune as always, he disentangled himself using the tactics of a double referendum proposal and a change in governments.

In those years Mitterrand not only succumbed to the fascination for foreign affairs which afflicts all powerful presidents of ambitious countries, but also to the delights of constant travel. He made forty-four official visits to all continents (except Australia) just in his first four years in office, not counting some fifty-seven other stops — European and African summits and other trips. The pace slackened somewhat thereafter.[16]

How did Mitterrand recover from the deep unpopularity of 1983-1985? Aside from policy errors, he had offended many people by displaying in his first three years "from the [inaugural] rite in the Pantheon to the ridiculous Versailles summit to the pompous press conferences ... an unbelievable and almost obscene sensual pleasure in his own power."[17] Thereafter he began, with a variety of signals and informal television interviews (such as one showing him in informal clothes seated leaning against a tree) to emerge from his "Caesarean mask."

Polls showed a gradual improvement in the president's popularity by early 1986. But the manner in which Mitterrand accommodated himself to cohabitation won him more confidence. Accepting in quiet dignity a situation which deprived him of most of his power, contriving still to remain the supreme magistrate and guarantor of the constitution, Mitterrand appealed anew to many Frenchmen on the center and center-right. At the same time he retained the confidence of the Left by not disguising his opposition to Chirac's domestic policies. He thus won popularity by reigning but not ruling. He ceased to be Caesar and became the father (or rather, familiarly, "Tonton," the uncle) of his country. His opponents hoped his new popularity would not last beyond the declaration of a new candidacy. They turned out to be wrong.

What can Mitterrand claim as real achievements in his first term? He has reshaped the political landscape, diminished the PCF, established the PS, twice defeated the parties of the Right and driven them into division and confusion. The France of 1988, even with its persistent and heavy unemployment, is less divided and tense than the France of 1980. The Left has discarded most of a century-old wardrobe of threadbare doctrine and recognized the merits of profit and enterprise. The several economic policies of the *septennat* have, for all their insufficiencies and mistakes, strengthened French industry and left it better able to cope with the challenges of the 1990s. The electronic media have won the freedom given the press a century ago. The institutions of the Fifth Republic having been repeatedly tested by changes of government from Right to Left, and Right and Left again, appear stronger than ever.

The remarkable record of Mitterrand's first term nevertheless leaves large problems to address. Whatever his criticisms of de Gaulle's legacy may have been, he had never intended to dismantle the institutions of the Fifth Republic. He had wished to use them, both to modernize and reshape industrial society and improve the welfare state. In 1981, the Left's resentment at the style of the preceding conservative governments had clouded its appreciation of the extent of the welfare state it actually inherited, while its economic illusions and lack of understanding of the world economic crisis obscured the difficulty of enlarging welfare.

Socialist ideology and rhetoric, based on the idea of *rupture* and nationalization, broke down when "the magic wand didn't work." The PS fell back on the only available solution: good administration and technological modernization. The Right, abandoning its pseudo-social democracy as well as *dirigisme* (at least in rhetoric) then returned to power with the votes of those "disappointed by socialism," loudly trumpeting *libéralisme*. Socialism had turned out to be whatever a Socialist party does in office. *Libéralisme* failed to convince a people desiring a strong welfare state and still persuaded of the merits of an at least moderately important state role in the economy.[18] Communism had lost its old appeal for multiple historical reasons, which the idiocies of the Marchais period had only made worse. With few powerful mobilizing ideas current in the traditional parties, fear and resentment of immigrants allowed the National Front to move into the nearly empty role of the protest party.

By April 1988, all ideologies were in desuetude: on the Right the Gaullist social myth had been abandoned, and Pompidolian or Balladurian capitalism lacked compelling appeal. On the Left, the myth of the revolution was dead, the myth that only the Left could build the *real* welfare state had also collapsed — as well as the idea that France could become a socialist state different from other European nations. The PS no longer possessed a coherent body of doctrine or new ideas capable of mobilizing and rebuilding France in a time of crisis. The danger of too much ideology had been replaced by the danger of too few ideas.

The rise of a powerful and ugly racist party which draws votes from all camps is a sure sign that neither the conventional Right nor the Left has known how to speak to the fears and worries of at least a sixth of French voters. Numerous commentators voice their unease at a social situation where the political parties seem to have less and less relevance, less and less real ability to communicate with the people. When Mitterrand asked for re-election after seven years in office in which his reputation had plummeted and then been restored, he was gambling that a new term would win him a larger place in history than a graceful retirement to write his memoirs might achieve. He did not outline a clear program that went much beyond his electoral slogan of "France United," and perhaps does not even have one.[19] His proclaimed opening to the Center is unpopular with many Socialists. The Centrists are uncertain what it means and whether, if they ally themselves with the Socialists their voters will still love them. Mitterrand II thus begins with a triumphant re-election, a check but not a defeat in the National Assembly elections, and a future where open questions abound.

NOTES

1. Unattributed poll cited by Colette Lamys, "Le Mythe du grand parti conservateur," *Le Journal des élections*, no. 1 (May 1988), p. 20.

2. Annick Percheron et Pascal Perrineau, "22 régions au miroir de l'élection présidentielle," in *L'Election présidentielle 1988*, eds. Philippe Habert and Colette Ysmal (Paris: *Le Figaro*/Etudes politiques, 1988), p. 24.

3. Cf. André Gattolin, "FN: Stabilisation plus que reflux," *Journal des élections*, no. 3 (June 1988), p. 10.

4. On decline, see Stéphane Courtois, "Identité ouvrière, identité communiste: construction et déconstruction du communisme français," *Communisme*, no. 15/16 (1987), and Gérard Noiriel, *Les Ouvriers dans la société française* (Paris: Editions du Seuil, 1986). I am indebted to Professors Jean Ranger and François Platone for a long and illuminating discussion in March 1986 concerning the PCF dilemma of how to handle *magrebin* workers as potential voters.

5. *Le Monde*, May 4, 1988.

6. *Le Monde*, July 1, 1988.

7. "Lettre à tous les Français," *Le Monde*, April 8 and 9, 1988.

8. *Propositions pour la France*, supplement to *PS Info*, no. 351, (February 13, 1988), pp. 2-3.

9. *Nouvel Observateur*, May 20-26, 1988.

10. Interview with Jean Lacouture, *L'Express*, September 11, 1987.

11. Cf. Stanley Hoffmann, "Mitterrand's Foreign Policy, or Gaullism by any other Name," in *The Mitterrand Experiment*, eds. George Ross, Stanley Hoffmann, and Sylvia Malzacher, a revised version of an article in *Foreign Policy* 57 (Winter 1984-1985).

12. Lacouture interview, *L'Express*, September 11, 1987.

13. Franz-Olivier Giesbert, *François Mitterrand*, pp. 10.

14. Catherine Nay, *Les Sept Mitterrand* (Paris: Grasset, 1988), and Jean Daniel, *Les Réligions du Président* (Paris: Grasset, 1988).

15. Stanley Hoffmann, "Mitterrand, the Triple Mystery," *French Politics and Society* 6 April 1988, p. 5.

16. Cf. *Le Monde: Bilan du septennat*, pp. 44-45.

17. Paul Thibaud, "La France sous Mitterrand," *Esprit* 5 (May 1988), pp. 3-4.

18. The Louis Harris post-election poll of June 11, 1988 found thirty-two percent of respondents saying that the state should intervene a good deal in the economy; forty-two percent more thought it should intervene in moderation. Eighteen percent believed it should intervene a little, and only four percent said not at all. Four percent had no opinion. In the same poll, eighty-one percent of respondents affirmed their belief in state- backed old age and health insurance.

19. See Mitterrand's "Lettre à tous les Français," *Libération*, April 7, 1988, and *Le Monde*, April 8 and 9, 1988. *Le Monde* judged it "as much the exposition of a philosophy of power as a real program," and the general opinion of the press (including a newspaper favorable to Mitterrand like *Libération*) was that it was not only long but vague.

Bibliography

ADA (Association pour débattre autrement). *Bilan de la France 1986.* Paris: Editions de la Table Ronde, 1986.

Albert, Michel. *Le Pari français.* Paris: Editions du Seuil, 1982.

Ambler, John S., ed. *The French Socialist Experiment.* Philadelphia: ISHI, 1984.

Andrews, William G., and Hoffmann, Stanley, eds. *The Fifth Republic at Twenty.* Albany: State University of New York Press, 1981.

Ardagh, John. *France in the 1980's.* New York: Penguin, 1983.

Aron, Raymond. *Mémoires.* Paris: Julliard, 1983.

Bacot, Paul. *Les Dirigeants du PS.* Lyons: Presses Universitaires de Lyon, 1979.

Balassa, Bela. "Five Years of Socialist Economic Policy in France: a Balance Sheet." *The Tocqueville Review* 7 (1985-1986).

Barre, Raymond. *Réflexions pour demain.* Paris: Hachette, 1984.

Bauchard, Philippe. *La Guerre des deux roses.* Paris: Grasset, 1986.

_____. *La Crise sonne toujours deux fois.* Paris: Grasset, 1988.

Belorgey, Gérard. *La France décentralisée.* Paris: Editions Berger-Levrault, 1985.

Benoit, Francis Paul, et al., eds. *Collectivités locales.* Paris: Dalloz, 1984.

Berger, Suzanne. "Liberalism Reborn." In *Contemporary France; a Review of Interdisciplinary Studies,* edited by Jolyon Howorth and George Ross. London: Frances Pinter, 1987.

Birnbaum, Pierre. *Le Peuple et les "gros." Histoire d'un mythe.* Paris: Editions Pluriel, 1984.

Blackmer, Donald L. M. and Tarrow, Sidney, eds. *Communism in Italy and France.* Princeton: Princeton University Press, 1975.

Blanc, Jacques. *Les Nationalisations en 1982.* Paris: La Documentation française, 1983.

Bornstein, Stephen. "An End to French Exceptionalism? The Lessons of the Greenpeace Affair." *French Politics and Society* 5, September 1987.

Bothorel, Jean. *Le Pharaon.* Paris: Grasset, 1981.

Boublil, Alain. *Le Socialisme industriel.* Paris: Presses Universitaires de France, 1977.

Bourricaud, François. *Le Retour de la droite.* Paris: Calmann-Lévy, 1986.

Bréchon, Pierre; Derville, Jacques; and Lecomte, Patrick. "L'Univers idéologique des cadres RPR." *Revue française de science politique* 37, October, 1987.

Brown, Bernard E. *Socialism of a Different Kind.* Westport, Connecticut: Greenwood Press, 1982.

Cahiers français 220, March-April 1985. Special issue, *La décentralisation en marche.*

Cahm, Eric. "From Greenpeace to Cohabitation." In *Contemporary France, a Review of Interdisciplinary Studies,* edited by Jolyon Howorth and George Ross. London: Frances Pinter, 1987.

Casanova, Jean-Claude. "Après trois ans." *Commentaire* 7, Autumn 1984.

Cayrol, Roland. "L'Audiovisuel dans les années socialistes." *The Toqueville Review* 8 (1986-1987).

Cerny, Philip, and Schain, Martin, eds. *Socialism, the State, and Public Policy in France.* London: Frances Pinter, 1985.

CFDT-Aujourd'hui 86, September 1987. Special issue, *Syndicalisme et innovations.*

Cohen, Samy. *La Monarchie nucléaire.* Paris: Hachette, 1986.

Cohen, Samy, and Smouts, Marie-Claude. *La Politique extérieure de Valéry Giscard d'Estaing.* Paris: Presses de la Fondation Nationale des Sciences Politiques, 1985.

Colombani, Jean-Marie. *Portrait du Président.* Paris: Gallimard, 1985.

Colombani, Jean-Marie, and Lhomeau, Jean-Yves. *Le Mariage blanc.* Paris: Grasset, 1986.

Cotta, Michèle. *Les Miroirs de Jupiter.* Paris: Fayard, 1986.

Crozier, Michel. *On ne change pas la société par décrêt.* New edition. Paris: Grasset, 1983.

Dagnaud, Monique, and Mehl, Dominique. *L'Elite rose.* Paris: Ramsay, 1982.

De Closets, Francois. *Toujours plus.* Paris: Grasset, 1982.

Delion, André, and Durupty, Michel. *Les Nationalisations 1982.* Paris: Editions Economica, 1983.

Derogy, Jacques, and Pontaut, Jean-Marie. *Enquête sur trois secrets d'Etat.* Paris: Laffont, 1986.

Domenach, Jean-Marie. *Lettre àmes ennemis de classe.* Paris: Editions du Seuil, 1984.

Dupoirier, Elisabeth, and Grunberg, Gérard, eds. *Mars 1986. La drôle de défaite de la gauche.* Paris: Presses Universitaires de France, 1986.

Du Roy, Albert, and Schneider, Robert. *Le Roman de la rose.* Paris: Editions du Seuil, 1982.

Duverger, Maurice, *La République des citoyens.* Paris: Ramsay, 1982.

Ehrmann, Henry. *Politics in France.* 4th edition. Boston and Toronto: Little Brown and Co., 1983.

Estier, Claude, and Neiertz, Véronique. *Véridique histoire d'un septennat peu ordinaire.* Paris: Grasset, 1987.

Ferenczi, Thomas. *Le Prince au miroir.* Paris: Albin Michel, 1981.

Fiszbin, Henri. *Les Bouches s'ouvrent.* Paris: Grasset, 1980.

_____. *Appel à l'autosubversion.* Paris: Laffont, 1984.

Fonteneau, Alain, and Muet, Pierre-Alain. *La Gauche face à la crise.* Paris: Presses de la Fondation Nationale des Sciences Politiques, 1985.

Friend, Julius W. "A Rose In Any Other Fist Would Smell As Sweet." *French Politics and Society* 12, December 1985.

_____. "Soviet Behavior and National Responses: the Puzzling Case of the French Communist Party." In *Studies in Comparative Communism* 15 (1982).

Furet, François. *Penser la révolution française.* Paris: Gallimard, 1978.

Giesbert, Franz-Olivier. *François Mitterrand ou la tentation de l'histoire.* Paris: Editions du Seuil, 1977.

_____. *Jacques Chirac.* Paris: Editions du Seuil, 1987.

Gourevich, Peter Alexis. *Paris and the Provinces.* Berkeley: University of California Press, 1980.

Grémion, Pierre. *Paris/Prague, la gauche face au renouveau et à la régression tchécoslovaque, 1968-1978.* Paris: Julliard, 1985.

Hall, Peter. *Governing the Economy.* New York: Oxford University Press, 1986.

Hamon, Hervé, and Rotman, Patrick. *La Deuxième gauche.* New edition. Paris: Editions du Seuil, 1984.

Harrison, Michael. *The Reluctant Ally: France and Atlantic Security.* Baltimore: Johns Hopkins University Press, 1981.

Hoffmann, Stanley. *Decline or Renewal? France since the 1930s.* New York: Viking Press, 1974.

_____. "The Odd Couple," *New York Review of Books,* September 25, 1986.

Howorth, Jolyon, and Ross, George, eds. *Contemporary France; a Review of Interdisciplinary Studies.* London: Frances Pinter, 1987.

Intervention 5-6, August-September-October, 1983. Special issue, *Les Socialistes, croient-ils à leurs mythes?*.

Jaffré, Jérôme. "De Valéry Giscard d'Estaing à François Mitterrand: France de gauche, vote à gauche." *Pouvoirs* 20, 1982.

_____. "Front National: la relève protestataire." In *Mars 1986: la drôle de défaite de la gauche,* edited by Elisabeth Dupoirier and Gérard Grunberg. Paris: Presses Universitaires de France, 1986.

Jeambar, Denis. *Le P.C. dans la maison.* Paris: Calmann-Lévy, 1984.

Jelen, Christian, and Wolton, Thierry. *Le Petit Guide de la farce tranquille.* Paris: Albin Michel, 1982.

Jenson, Jane, and Ross, George. *The View from Inside.* Berkeley: University of California Press, 1984.

Joffrin, Laurent. *La Gauche en voie de disparition.* Paris: Editions du Seuil, 1984.

Johnson, Richard W. *The Long March of the French Left.* New York: St. Martin's Press, 1981.

July, Serge. *Les Années Mitterrand: Histoire baroque d'une normalisation inachevée.* Paris: Grasset, 1986.

Juppé, Alain. *La Double Rupture.* Paris. Editions Economica, 1982.

Kergoat, Jacques. *Le Parti socialiste.* Paris: Editions Sycomore, 1983.

Kesselman, Mark. "The Tranquil Revolution at Clochemerle: Socialist Decentralization in France." In *Socialism, the State, and Public Policy in France,* edited by Philip Cerny and Martin Schain. London: Frances Pinter, 1985.

_____. "Socialism without the Workers." *Kapitalistate* 10/11 (1983).

Kuisel, Richard F. *Capitalism and the State in Modern France.* Cambridge and New York: Cambridge University Press, 1981.

Lacorne, Denis. "Left-Wing Unity: Picardy and Languedoc." In *Communism in Italy and France,* edited by Donald L. M. Blackmer and Sidney Tarrow. Princeton: Princeton University Press, 1975.

Lacorne, Denis; Rupnik, Jacques; and Toinet, Marie-France, eds. *L'Amérique dans les têtes. Un siècle de fascinations et d'aversions.* Paris: Hachette, 1986.

Lancelot, Alain. "Le Brise-lame: les élections du 16 mars 1986." *Projet* 199, May-June 1986.

Lancelot, Alain, and Marie-Therèse. "The Evolution of the French Electorate 1981-1986." In *The Mitterrand Experiment,* edited by George Ross, Stanley Hoffmann, and Sylvia Malzacher. New York: Oxford University Press, 1987.

_____. *Annuaire de la France politique Mai 1981-Mai 1983.* Paris: Presses de la Fondation Nationale des Sciences Politiques, 1983.

Lauber, Volkmar. *The Political Economy of France: From Pompidou to Mitterrand.* New York: Praeger, 1983.

Lavau, Georges. *A quoi sert le PCF?* Paris: Fayard, 1981.

_____. "The Incomplete Victory of the Right," in *Contemporary France, a Review of Interdisciplinary Studies,* edited by Jolyon Howorth and George Ross. London: Frances Pinter, 1987.

_____. "The PCF, the State, and the Revolution." In *Communism in Italy and France,* edited by Donald Blackmer and Sidney Tarrow. Princeton: Princeton University Press, 1975.

Lavau, Georges, Grunberg, Gérard, and Mayer, Nonna, eds. *L'Univers politique des classes moyennes.* Paris: Presses de la Fondation Nationale des Sciences Politiques, 1983.

Lazitch, Branko. *L'Echec permanent.* Paris: Robert Laffont, 1978.

LeGall, Gérard. "Sondages, l'état de l'opinion." *Revue politique et parlementaire* 921, January-February 1986.

Lienemann, Marie-Noëlle, and Finel, Patrice, "Pour un libéralisme de gauche." *Nouvelle revue socialiste,* September-October 1984.

MacShane, Denis. *François Mitterrand.* New York: Universe Books, 1983.

Martinet, Gilles. *Cassandre et les tueurs.* Paris: Grasset, 1986.

Mauroy, Pierre. *C'est ici le chemin.* Paris: Flammarion, 1982.

_____. *A Gauche.* Paris: Albin Michel, 1985.

McCarthy, Patrick, ed. *The French Socialists in Power.* Westport, Connecticut: Greenwood Press, 1987.

Mény, Yves. "Le Cumul des mandats." *The Tocqueville Review* 8 (1986-87).

_____. "Decentralization in Socialist France: the Politics of Pragmatism." *Western European Politics* 7, no. 1 (January 1984).

Minc, Alain, and Nora, Simon. *L'Informatisation de la société.* Paris: La Documentation française, 1978.

Mitterrand, François. *Ma part de vérité.* Paris: Fayard, 1969.

_____. *Ici et Maintenant.* Paris: Fayard, 1980.

_____. *Politique. Textes et discours 1938-1981.* Edited by Georgette Elgey et al. Paris: Editions Marabout, 1984.

Le Monde, dossiers et documents. Supplement, *L'Election présidentielle, 26 avril-10 mai 1981,* May 1981.

_____. Supplement, *Les Elections législatives de juin 1981,* June 1981.

_____. Supplement, *Les Elections municipales de mars 1983,* March 1983.

_____. Supplement, *Les Elections législatives du 16 mars 1986,* March 1986.

_____. Supplement, *Les Elections législatives, 5 juin, 12 juin 1988,* June 1988.

_____. *Bilan du septennat, l'alternance dans l'alternance 1981-1988. Undated (1988).*

Nay, Catherine. *Le Noir et le rouge.* Paris: Grasset, 1984.

Nugent, Neill, and Lowe, David. *The Left in France.* New York: St. Martin's Press, 1982.

Parti socialiste. *Programme de gouvernement du Parti socialiste.* Paris: Flammarion, 1972.

_____. *Projet socialiste pour la France des années 80.* Paris: Club Socialiste du Livre, 1980.

Peyrefitte, Alain. *Le Mal français.* Paris: Plon, 1976.

Pfister, Thierry. *Dans les coulisses du pouvoir.* Paris: Albin Michel, 1986.

_____. *La Vie quotidienne à Matignon au temps de l'Union de la Gauche.* Paris: Hachette, 1985.

Plenel, Edwy and Rollat, Alain, eds. *L'Effet Le Pen.* Paris: Editions La Découverte/Le Monde, 1984.

Portelli, Hugues. *Le Socialisme français tel qu'il est.* Paris: Presses Universitaires de France, 1980.

Prigent, Michel, ed. *La Liberté à refaire.* Paris: Hachette, 1984.

Projet 185-186, May-June 1984. Special issue, *Décentraliser vraiment?*

Prost, Antoine. "The Educational Maelstrom." In *The Mitterrand Experiment,* edited by George Ross, Stanley Hoffmann, and Sylvia Malzacher. New York: Oxford University Press, 1987.

Quatrepoint, Jean-Michel. *Histoire secrète des dossiers noirs de la gauche.* Paris: Alain Moreau, 1986.

Quermonne, Jean-Louis. "La Présidence de la république et le système des partis." *Pouvoirs* 41 (1987).

Ranger, Jean. "Le Déclin du parti communiste français," *Revue Française de Science Politique* 36, no. 1 (February 1986).

Rémond, Réné. *Les Droites en France.* Paris: Aubier Montaigne 1982.

Revue Politique et Parlementaire 916-917, May-June 1985. Special issue, *Les Réformes de la gauche 1981-1984.*

Rosanvallon, Pierre. *La Crise de l'état-providence.* Paris: Editions du Seuil, 1981.

Rosanvallon, Pierre, and Viveret, Patrick. *Pour une nouvelle culture politique.* Paris: Editions du Seuil, 1977.

Ross, George. *Workers and Communists in France.* Berkeley: University of California Press, 1982.

_____. "Labor and the Left in Power." In *The French Socialists in Power,* edited by Patrick McCarthy. Westport, Connecticut: Greenwood Press, 1987.

_____. "The Perils of Politics: French Unions and the Crisis of the 1970s," in *Unions, Change, and Crisis: French and Italian Union Strategy and the Political Economy, 1945-1980,* edited by Peter Lange, George Ross, and Maurizio Vannicelli. London: George Allen & Unwin, 1982.

Ross, George, Hoffmann, Stanley, and Malzacher, Sylvia, eds. *The Mitterrand Experiment, Continuity and Change in Modern France.* New York: Oxford University Press, 1987.

Roucaute, Yves. *Le Parti socialiste.* Paris: Huisman, 1983.

Safran, William. "Rights and Liberties under the Mitterrand Presidency: Socialist Innovations and Post-Socialist Revisions." *Contemporary French Civilization* 12 (Winter-Spring 1988).

Salomon, André. *PS — la mise à nu.* Paris: Laffont, 1980.

Savary, Alain. *En toute liberté.* Paris: Hachette, 1985.

Schain, Martin. "The National Front and the Construction of Political Legitimacy." *West European Politics* 10, April 1987.

Schneider, Robert. *Michel Rocard.* Paris: Stock, 1987.

Serfaty, Simon, ed. *The Foreign Policies of the French Left.* Boulder, Colorado: Westview Press, 1979.

SOFRES. *Opinion publique 1984.* Edited by Olivier Duhamel, Elisabeth Dupoirier, and Jérôme Jaffré. Paris: Gallimard 1984.

_____. *Opinion publique 1985.* Edited by Olivier Duhamel, Elisabeth Dupoirier, and Jérôme Jaffré. Paris: Gallimard, 1985.

_____. *Opinion publique 1986.* Edited by Olivier Duhamel, Elisabeth Dupoirier, and Jérôme Jaffré. Paris: Gallimard, 1986.

_____. *L'Etat de l'opinion-Clés pour 1987.* Edited by Olivier Duhamel, Elisabeth Dupoirier, and Jérôme Jaffré. Paris: Editions du Seuil, 1987.

_____. *L'Etat de l'opinion-Clés pour 1988.* Edited by Olivier Duhamel, Elisabeth Dupoirier, and Jérôme Jaffré. Paris: Editions du Seuil, 1988.

Stoffaes, Christian. *La Politique industrielle.* Paris: Le Cours de Droit, 1984.

Tarrow, Sidney. *Between Center and Periphery: Grassroots Politicians in Italy and France.* New Haven: Yale University Press, 1977.

Tenzer, Nicolas. *La Région en quête d'avenir.* Paris: La Documentation française, 1986.

Tiersky, Ronald. *French Communism 1920-1972.* New York: Columbia University Press, 1974.

Touchard, Jean. *La Gauche en France depuis 1900.* Paris: Editions du Seuil, 1977.

Tristan, Anne. *Au Front.* Paris: Gallimard, 1987.

Vignon, Jérôme. "Le Delorisme en économie." Les Cahiers français 218, October-December 1984.

Vincent, K.S. *Socialism in France.* New York: St. Martin's Press, 1983.

Wilson, Frank Lee. "Socialism in France: A Failure of Politics, Not a Failure of Policy." *Parliamentary Affairs 38 (Spring 1985).*

Index

Popular Front, 9–10, 13; Soviet flirtation with in 1960s, 19; still PCF strategy in 1970s, 24
Portugal, crisis in, 76
Poujadiste movement, 121
Prague, Soviet invasion, 20, 196
Prefects, 60, 141–142
Prieur, Dominique, 130, 190
Priouret, Roger, 35
Private schools, 91–95. *See also* Education
Privatization, 162, 174, 182, 184–185
Profit, becomes acceptable term to Socialists, 105
Projet socialiste, 35, 141–142
Proportional representation, 109, 122, 128, 131–132, 170, 175, 217
PS, 9, 22–30, 32–36, 40–42, 46–47, 103, 169–170, 173; belief in power of legislation, 82; believes self upheld by forces of history, sociology, 57–58; candor in diagnosis, 1984, 108; congresses: Bagnolet, 26; Bourg-en-Bresse, 90; Epinay-sur-Seine, 22–23, 33; Lille, 188; Metz, 34, 43, 101, 108; Pau, 31; Suresnes, 24, 26; Toulouse, 2, 133, 187; Valence, 56–57; defense policies, and Hernu role in 1970s, 44, 195–196; dominates 1981 government, 46; economic ideas in 1981, 33–34; effects of ideological change on, 81; factions, 22, 26, 108–109; fails to win majority of 1988 legislatives, 192; fragile nature of majority, 58, 1981–1982, 85; foreign policy in 1970s, 195–196; growth in 1970s, 29–30; and Hersant law, 90; lacked clear defini-

tion socialism 1981, 83; leaders oppose Savary bill, 94; loses utopian spirit, 109–110; militants unhappy about *ouverture,* 190–191; and nationalization, 48–49, 184; need to reconcile rhetoric with policies, 101; and 1986 election, 169, 174; and PCF, 32, 35, 45, 74–75, 77; reconciled to "managing crisis," 104; reconciliation to social democracy, 110; relations with SPD, 199; retreat from ideology, 140; slow reaction to ideological change late 1970s, 79–80; thin skins of leaders, 62; view of Communist role in government, 47; weary, 1983, 82–83
PS government, agent, not architect of change, 139; effect of legislation on public opinion, 83; failures judged preeminently economic, 60; perceived softness on crime, 124; policy on New Caledonia, 128–129; policy on Third World, 205–207
PSU, 11–12, 30, 33

Questiaux, Nicole, 45
Quilès, Paul, 33, 56
Quotidien de Paris, Le, 62, 102

RACE, 202–203
Radical Socialists, 9
Radio broadcasting, 151
Radio France, 151
Radio Gazelle, 125
Radiodiffusion Télévision Française, 151
Radio Monte Carlo, 151
Radio-Télédiffusion Luxembourg (RTL), 151